# Information Age Economy

# Information Age Economy

K. Sandbiller
Dezentralität und Markt in Banken
1998. ISBN 3-7908-1101-7

M. Roemer
Direktvertrieb kundenindividueller
Finanzdienstleistungen
1998. ISBN 3-7908-1102-5

Frank Rose

# The Economics, Concept, and Design of Information Intermediaries

## A Theoretic Approach

With 59 Figures
and 11 Tables

Physica-Verlag

A Springer-Verlag Company

Dr. Frank Rose
Lilienstr. 12
D-34497 Korbach, Germany

ISBN 3-7908-1168-8 Physica-Verlag Heidelberg New York

Cataloging-in-Publication Data applied for
Die Deutsche Bibliothek – CIP-Einheitsaufnahme
Rose, Frank: The economics: concept and design of information intermediaries; a theoretic
approach; with 11 tables / Frank Rose. – Heidelberg; New York: Physica-Verl., 1999
　(Information age economy)
　ISBN 3-7908-1168-8

© Physica-Verlag Heidelberg 1999
Printed in Germany

The use of general descriptive names, registered names, trademarks, etc. in this publication does not imply, even in the absence of a specific statement, that such names are
exempt from the relevant protective laws and regulations and therefore free for general
use.

Coverdesign: Erich Kirchner, Heidelberg

SPIN 10695815　　　　88/2202-5 4 3 2 1 0 – Printed on acid-free paper

*To my parents and to Uta.*

# Foreword

The Internet provides an infrastructure that makes the steadily increasing amount of information accessible efficiently, quickly, and inexpensively. Closely connected with this opportunity is the danger that the available information will overcharge the individual information seeker's capability to process the information and to judge its quality. In this situation, *information intermediaries* can take upon the role of an expert and a guarantor of quality similar to intermediaries in markets for physical goods or finances. Thus, information intermediaries can be a trustworthy, information processing third party, mediating between information seekers and information sources.

The current technological development has created information technologies that are capable to efficiently process large amounts of information. However, the provision of intermediation services necessitates a thorough examination of the basic principles underlying the economics of information intermediaries as well as a sound foundation on information technologies. The present work by Frank Rose addresses the fundamental question concerning the economics of information intermediaries by means of an abstract model. The model focuses on services that concentrate on the search and mediation of information, and identifies the essential influencing factors of the intermediary's environment. The model is then employed to investigate the impact of environmental conditions on the information intermediary on the one hand, and the optimal strategy of the information intermediary as a reaction to environmental conditions on the other hand. From a scientific point of view this means a considerable step towards an integrated theory of information intermediaries. Besides the theory of information intermediaries, the author discusses the concept, design, and technology of real-life information intermediaries on the Internet. Hence, the practitioner can benefit from this work, because it provides deep insight in the basic principles of information intermediaries as well as their practical realization.

Wolfgang König

# Acknowledgements

The present thesis originated from the work on the concept and design of an Internet-based repository for reusable Java software components at the Institute for Information Systems of the department of economics at the Johann Wolfgang Goethe University Frankfurt. During the implementation of a prototype, questions about the basic principles of these *information intermediaries* arose. This was the starting point for the development of a theoretic model for information intermediaries, which deals with the economics, concept and design of this special type of intermediary from an abstract point of view.

Here I would like to take the opportunity to thank those people who have supported me in the different stages of the work. First of all, I would like to thank Professor Dr. Wolfgang König for giving me the chance to work on this thesis with much freedom as well as time and resources for my ideas. Thanks to Professor Dr. Dieter Ordelheide for his review and to Professor Dr. Malcom H. Dunn and Professor Dr. Heinz Isermann for their participation in the disputation.

I would like to direct special thanks to the following people: Dr. Peter Buxmann, Kurt Cotoaga, Stefan Markwitz, and Stephan Wolf for supporting the development of the Internet-based prototype of an information intermediary; Dr. Oliver Wendt, Falk von Westarp for helping with a lot of economic questions. Special thanks go to Thomas Rebel and Sascha Weber for many invaluable discussions; to Kerstin Jores for giving me excellent support in literature research; Oliver Christ, Andreas Meier, and Sven Burkard for writing their diploma thesis with me. Many thanks go to Katie Meyers for carefully reading the manuscript.

I am especially indebted to Uta Lagrèze for her continuous and affectionate aid during all stages of this work.

Finally, I am very grateful to my parents for their untiring and multifarious support during my education and during the work for this thesis.

Frank Rose

# Table of contents

# 1 Introduction

## 1.1 Information overload

'Entrepreneurial resourcefulness, driving the market process, is based on the realization and the exploitation of economically relevant information asymmetries.'[1] The necessity of 'being informed' and the promptness of becoming informed is thus undisputed and steadily gaining importance,[2] urged especially by the globalization[3] of nowadays economies. The term *information society*[4] is one possible description of this development.

However, the acquisition of information is subject to a variety of circumstances, one major problem is the amount of information available to an information seeker.[5] For a particular problem or question under consideration only a very small share of available information is relevant,[6] but the amount of available information is tremendously increasing because of two major effects: the steadily increasing production of information and the steadily improving access to information. Indicators for these statements are:

- Economically relevant information can be roughly distinguished as technological information and market information.[7] The domain of technological information can be roughly identified as the knowledge produced either in science or concerning technological innovations. An approximate measure for the knowledge and information created in this domain is the number of scientific publications that can be found in the different disciplines. During the 20th

---

[1]   Cf. [Wigand 97, p. 51].

[2]   Cf. [Hennes 95, p. 17], [Hoch 97], [Bode 97].

[3]   Besides the growth of international trade, cf. [Shigehara 97], this trend manifests itself in the global telecommunications market. International telephone calls, for example, have risen from under 4 billion minutes in 1975 to over 60 billion minutes in 1995, a growth rate of 15 % per year, cf. [ITU 96].

[4]   Cf. [Kuhlen 95, p. 45-52], [Ehrenberg 97].

[5]   This is a simple quantitative argument for difficulties occurring in the search for relevant information. See Section 5.1.1 for a detailed discussion.

[6]   Information is 'relevant for a particular task or decision problem,' if the decision or task is influenced by the information, see Sections 2.1.1.3 and 2.1.4.

[7]   Cf. [Hirshleifer 73, p. 33] and Section 2.1.1.3.

century the *amount of information* in science and technology shows an exponential growth, and has doubled every 5 to 15 years depending on the scientific discipline and the time of observation.[8]

- Besides the amount of information, the *opportunities for accessing* the information determine the amount of information that is available, for example, to a decision maker facing a particular decision problem. Electronic networks provide an ideal framework for information exchange, these allow the collection of information at any one point, and also the dissemination of information from that point.[9] The *Internet*[10] is the most prominent example of an open *Wide Area Network* (WAN).[11] The vision for its future development to a *Global Information Infrastructure* (GII) was expressed as follows: '... A planetary information network that transmits messages and images with the speed of light from the largest city to the smallest village on every continent....'[12] Logically, on the Internet every node in the network has the opportunity to be a more or less complex source of information accessible for the 'rest of the world.' As a simple measure for the amount of nodes in the network the number of Internet hosts can be seen,[13] each of these publishing various amounts of information with varying content, quality, and characteristics.

Nevertheless, it has to be pointed out that the amount of information cannot simply be put on a level with the amount of knowledge, because information can be subject to a considerable redundancy.[14] However, the figures stated above express the current situation and its prospective future development concerning the amount of information an information seeker is facing if being urged to locate information that is relevant for a particular problem.

Contrary to the growth of the amount of available information, the capacities of information processing have not developed in a manner that would enable the individual information seeker to cope with the complexity of the search for relevant information: Human information processing capacity is essentially determined by

---

[8]    Cf. [Kaminsky 77, p. 39-40], [Kreibich 86, p. 26-28], [Zelewski 87, p. 737], [Manecke 97b, p. 28-31].

[9]    Cf. [Macdonald 92, p. 55].

[10]   For the evolution of the Internet see [Zakon 97] and [Leiner 97]. For an overview of services constituting the Internet see [Kuhlen 95, p. 421-487].

[11]   See [Tanenbaum 96] for computer networks.

[12]   Excerpt from a speech of the United States Vice-President Al' Gore to the ITU World Telecommunications Development Conference, Buenos Aires, March 21, 1994 (cited from [ITU 95, http://www.itu.int/ti/wtdr95/ c2.html]).

[13]   The number of Internet hosts, i.e., computers connected to the Internet, is determined from a search of the *Domain Name System*, cf. [Internet 97]. This number has grown from a few hundred in the beginning of the 1980s to over 19.5 million computers in July 1997, see Figure 58 in Appendix A. The number of Internet users can only be estimated, a current number estimates about 100 million Internet users worldwide in January 1998, cf. [Internet 98].

[14]   See Section 2.1.2, especially Figure 2.

biological constants,[15] and therefore cannot be adapted to growing demands. Computer information processing capacities are growing with a significant pace,[16] but in the current stage of technological development human intelligence is superior to machine (or computer) intelligence as far as common sense and understanding of information is concerned.[17]

The consequence of these effects, i.e., the increasing amount of available information and the limitations of information processing capacities, is often referred to as *information overload*.[18] This can result in problems like increased expenses in the search for information, or the missing of relevant information resulting in missed business opportunities or, in the worst case, wrong decisions.

Besides finding the required information, the information seeker may encounter difficulties concerning the judgment of the quality of the information as well as the credibility of the information source. For example, the properties of information[19] entail that the true relevance of the information can only be determined if the information is completely revealed. Furthermore, the information seeker, being no expert in the particular domain under consideration, may not be able to accurately judge the quality of the information. In addition, the owner of the information source may have incentives to dishonestly reveal the information or to reduce effort after having received a payment for the information.

These (and other) incongruities between the supply and demand of information pose the demand for coordination of the players, i.e., information sources and information seekers, in the *market for information*.[20] In markets for physical goods or financial assets *intermediaries* or *middlemen*[21] operate as such coordinating economic agents that purchase from suppliers for resale to buyers or that help buyers

---

[15]  Cf. [Anderson 89, p. 27-45], [Kaminsky 77, p. 84].

[16]  The performance of microprocessors has increased at a rate of 35% per year in the late 1970s and over 50% per year since the mid 1980s, cf. [Patterson 96, p. 1-3]. The performance of a computer systems refers to the execution time for a particular task, [Patterson 96, p. 18-19].

[17]  Cf. [Alter 96, p. 28]. However, one question remaining is whether computers will ever reach the intelligence of human beings concerning understanding of information or analytical tasks.

[18]  Cf. [Knoblich 85, p. 559], [Zelewski 87], [Maes 94]. It should be pointed out that the problem of information overload does not only occur in electronic information networks, but there it has been intensified by the success and growth (especially of the Internet) that is currently observable. Information overload can also be described as follows: 'locating and processing the relevant information is difficult not because of the lack of such information but because of the very abundance of it,' cf. [Whinston 97, p. 278].

[19]  See Section 2.1.5.

[20]  For *markets for information* see [Hopf 83, p. 99-100] and Section 2.5.2.

[21]  Cf. [Rubinstein 87].

and sellers to meet and perform transactions.[22] In a similar way, *information inter-mediaries* can occupy the role of middlemen between the information seeker and the sources of information in the market for information, and provide services to overcome discrepancies between the demand and supply of information.[23] Information brokers are a typical form of *information intermediaries*. They perform search for information and other intellectual processing of information on behalf of their clients and aim to make profit with their activities.[24] The growth of information available via electronic networks has led to the emergence and expansion of further forms of information intermediaries offering services on the network. These are the topic of the present work.

## 1.2 The aim and procedure of the analysis

The aim of the present work is to perform a systematic analysis of information intermediaries with a focus on those operating in electronic networks.
The analysis can be subdivided into two major parts:
*   The first part of the analysis aims at a theoretical foundation of the economics of information intermediaries.
*   The second part of the analysis focuses the concepts and design of real-life information intermediaries as well as the technological realization of information intermediaries in electronic networks.
A major aim is the development and analysis of an economic model of an information intermediary that represents *search for information on behalf of clients* as the intermediary's central function. The model will be based on a microeconomic model of search; it abstracts from details of practical examples and makes a set of assumptions.[25] The assumptions of the basic theoretical model will be abandoned in the second part of the work, and the concepts and foundations of real-life information intermediaries will be analyzed.

## 1.3 The organization of this thesis

The structure of this thesis can be derived from the aims formulated above. Part one matches with Chapters 2-4, part two is presented in Chapter 5.
Chapter 2 reviews the basic conceptions and properties of information with focus on economic situations. The potential sources of information and the credibility of

---

[22]    Cf. [Spulber 96a, p. 135].
[23]    Cf. [Langhein 85], [Kaminsky 89].
[24]    Cf. [Lunin 76], [O'Leary 87].
[25]    For assumptions in economic theory see [Nagel 63].

information sources will be discussed, and the effects of information on markets as well as the basic principles of markets for information will be reviewed.

Chapter 3 examines the basic aspects and functions of intermediaries and their theoretical justification with a special focus on the theory of transactions and transaction cost reductions achieved through intermediation. Further, basic contract forms of intermediaries will be compared. Subsequently, the effects of intermediation on markets and the market microstructure will be analyzed.

In Chapter 4 the basic model of an information intermediary will be developed. The chapter starts with a basic characterization of information intermediaries and a review of related theoretic approaches to intermediaries. The economic theory of search will be discussed and a basic search model will be treated in greater detail. Subsequently, the *basic model of an information intermediary* based on the basic search model will be introduced and analyzed comprehensively. The influences of environmental conditions on the intermediary's strategy will then be derived by means of the model; and the effects of the information intermediary on social welfare as well as competition in a duopoly of information intermediaries will be analyzed. The chapter closes with a discussion of possible extensions to the basic model and a summary of the main results.

Chapter 5 provides an extended conception of information intermediaries. It starts with a basic characterization of an information seeker's information need and of basic forms of information mediation in markets for information. The information processing activities of information intermediaries will then be discussed and information brokers will be reviewed in greater detail. Subsequently, the concepts of intermediaries in electronic networks will be analyzed, especially the support of transaction phases in electronic markets. The following analysis of information intermediaries in electronic networks covers the environmental circumstances as well as technologies and architectures. The chapter closes with a discussion of economic aspects of information intermediaries that are closely related to the basic model of an information intermediary.

In Chapter 6 a summary of the basic results and a brief outlook to future developments concerning information intermediaries in electronic networks will be given.

# 2 Information

At the beginning of a scientific treatise a commitment about terms and notions used in the discussion has to be made.[26] The definition of information and its properties is one basis of this thesis, therefore, the present chapter treats the basic conceptions of information (Section 2.1) and deepens the properties and effects of information in economic situations. The different possibilities for information acquisition will be discussed (Section 2.2), and the credibility of information sources as well as measures to achieve trust in information sources will be examined from the perspective of principal-agent relationships (Section 2.3). Further, the effects of information on market efficiency will be reviewed briefly (Section 2.4) as well as the circumstances of information as an economic commodity (Section 2.5).

## 2.1 Basic aspects of information

### 2.1.1 Conceptions of information

The word *information* comes from the Latin word *informatio*, which means illumination, exposition, outline, unfolding.[27] Information, in the proper sense of the word, can only be defined indirectly by describing its properties.[28] Many scientific disciplines define some notion of information, and economic theory alone has a multitude of different conceptions and definitions of information.[29] From a *semiotics*[30] point of view, the characterization of information can follow three different conceptions.[31] The *syntactic conception* looks upon information as tokens

---

[26]  Cf. [Esser 77, p. 68 fp.].
[27]  Cf. [Kampis 92, p. 51].
[28]  Cf. [Haken 92, p. 155].
[29]  See [Hopf 83, p. 6 fp.] and [Bode 97] for a review of different conceptions of information in economics.
[30]  Semiotics is the *general theory of signs*, see [Oeser 92, p. 320], [Lyons 83, p. 25 fp.], [Eco 77].
[31]  Cf. [Hopf 83, p. 16], [von Weizsäcker 88, p. 168 fp.].

concatenated to form a message. This approach will be reviewed in the section about *information theory*, which conceives a gain of information as a loss of entropy. The *semantic conception*[32] of information refers to the contents of information and requires that information has a meaning. Approaches to a theoretical treatment of the content of information are found in cognitive science, artificial intelligence, and in the theory of complex systems. The third conception is the *pragmatic conception* of information favored in *economic theory*, because it conceives that information has an effect or consequence, usually identified as the reduction of uncertainty in economic situations.

### 2.1.1.1 Information theory: syntactic information

Information Science was established by a work of Shannon[33] called 'A mathematical theory of communication.' The theory is often referred to as *information theory*, but the approach only investigates the statistical structure of communication through noisy channels[34] rather than any linguistic or semantic properties of information. From a syntactical point of view, information is a *sequence of tokens*.[35] Hence, the value of a message containing information cannot be discussed in this approach. The value of information is always an individual measure depending on the recipient's environment (Section 2.1.4).

The syntactic definition of information conceives and measures a gain in information as a loss of entropy.[36] Entropy[37] is a synonym for the indefiniteness and uncertainty about the outcome of an experiment. An experiment $\mathcal{F}$ is a time-consuming operation with a particular result. It is described by a distribution with vector $p=(p_1, ..., p_n)$, in which each dimension gives the probability $p_i$ for the outcome of the experiment in a particular range or class[38] of outcomes. The entropy $H(\mathcal{F})$ is then defined by:[39]

---

32    Cf. [von Weizsäcker 88, p. 200 fp.]. Semantic information requires a receiver of the information, for whom the information has to be understandable. However, this results in the circumstance that semantic information is measurable only as pragmatic information, cf. [von Weizsäcker 88, p. 168 fp.].

33    Cf. [Shannon 48] and [Shannon 63], [van Lint 80, p. 24 fp.].

34    Cf. [Topsoe 74, p. 5 fp.], [Blahut 87, p. 2 fp.].

35    Cf. [Viterbi 79, p. 11 fp.], [Gallager 86, p. 5].

36    Cf. [Topsoe 74, p. 5], [Viterbi 79, p. 7 fp.].

37    In statistical physics entropy is defined as the logarithm of the number of accessible states of a macroscopic system for a certain energy times the Boltzmann factor $k_B$, cf. [Reif 85, p. 94 fp.]. The higher the entropy, the more states the system can access for a certain energy, and the more indefiniteness is in the system.

38    Cf. [Topsoe 74, p. 6].

39    This definition is referred to as the first *main proposition of information theory*, cf. [Topsoe 74, p. 25].

*(eq. 1)*     $$H(\mathcal{F}) = H(p_1,...,p_n) = -\sum_i p_i \cdot \log(p_i).$$

The units of entropy are identical to the information involved in an experiment with two outcomes having the same probability.[40] The unit is named *binary digit* or in short *bit*. What should be emphasized is that the uncertainty or entropy of an experiment before its realization is equal to the information gained through execution of the experiment. With this convention the interpretation of (eq. 1) is as follows: If the $i^{th}$ outcome is realized in the experiment, the information included herein is $-log(p_i)$ *[bit]*. The average information of one execution of the experiment is then given by the sum of the information results over all possible outcomes of the experiment times their probability. This notion of information (or of entropy) can be applied to determine the optimal length of a code-alphabet,[41] the trans-mission characteristics of a communication system,[42] consisting of a source, a noisy communication channel, and a recipient, and to study information processes at a molecular level[43] from a statistical point of view.

### 2.1.1.2 *The semantics of information*

From a semantics point of view, *'information is only what can be understood.'*[44] A syntactic understanding of information requires the recipient to be able to distinguish between the tokens used in the alphabet.[45] A semantic understanding in addition requires the understanding of the meaning of the particular information[46] described as a mapping between syntactic structures and objects of the task domain.[47]

One approach to formalize semantic effects of information, i.e., the attribution of meaning to a message, is by means of dynamic systems:[48] A system, physical,

---

[40]  In case of two possible outcomes the logarithm to the base 2 has to be taken, cf. [Topsoe 74, p. 26], [Viterbi 79, p. 8].

[41]  Cf. [Jürgensen 97].

[42]  Cf. [Topsoe 74, p. 67 fp.], [Viterbi 79, p. 3 fp.], [Gallager 86, p. 5 fp.], [Blahut 87, p. 8 fp.].

[43]  Cf. [Schneider 94].

[44]  Cf. [von Weizsäcker 88, p. 200].

[45]  Cf. [Viterbi 79, p. 12 fp.], [Gallager 86, p. 4 fp.].

[46]  Semantic understanding is usually connected with written or spoken human languages, cf. [Anderson 89, p. 322 fp.], but 'understanding' is not restricted to the exchange of information between humans. In biological systems we can find an extensive exchange of information, that requires semantic understanding, for example, in the reproduction process, cf. [Csányi 92].

[47]  Cf. [Rich 83, p. 304].

[48]  Haken interprets information as a property emergent in complex systems, and applies the theory of dynamic systems to formalize this conception, cf. [Haken 92, p. 153].

biological, or economic, can access particular states characterized by the state vector $q(t)=(q_1(t), q_2(t), ..., q_n(t))$. The dynamics of the system can be described by a differential equation:[49]

(eq. 2) $$\frac{dq}{dt} = N(q,\alpha) + F(t) \cdot$$

$N$ is the deterministic part, $F$ represents the fluctuating external forces affecting the system, and $\alpha$ represents the set of control parameters. The *theory of dynamic systems*[50] shows that such a dynamic system may possess *attractors*[51] dependent upon the properties of the deterministic part, and are described by the set $\alpha$ of control parameters. Ignoring the fluctuating forces $F$, the dynamic behavior of the system is fully determined by setting the set of control parameters $\alpha$ and the initial state $q_0=q(t=t_0)$ of the system. The receipt of a message by the system is interpreted as the setting of a new set of control parameters $\alpha$ and a new initial state $q$ of the system by the message. After a certain period of time the dynamic system will access one of its possible attractors. If the system remains in its initial state $q_0$, the information contained in the message is redundant and evidently meaningless for the system. Whereas, if the system possesses an attractor different from the initial state, the message brought new information to the system.[52]

In this formal approach the semantics of information were explained by the effect on a dynamic system, which itself has some ability to process the incoming message 'in the right way.'[53] The internal pre-existing information of the system necessary for this can be conceived as a kind of *knowledge* (Section 2.1.2).

### 2.1.1.3 Pragmatic information: information in decision problems and uncertainty

Pragmatic information results in an effect on the recipient.[54] This expresses that pragmatic information always has to have a consequence for the recipient or user, and that the pragmatic conception of information is closely connected to prior experiences.[55] This conception is different from the semantic interpretation, because it implicitly requires the active utilization of information by the recipient.

---

[49] Cf. [Haken 88, p. 16 fp.], [Haken 92, p. 162].
[50] Cf. [Scheck 90, p. 274 fp.].
[51] Cf. [Scheck 90, p. 292 fp.].
[52] On the basis of this model of a dynamic system Haken develops the concept of *relative importance* of messages to attribute a value to the messages received by the system, cf. [Haken 88, p. 16 fp.], [Haken 92].
[53] For a discussion of the activities and preconditions of information processing within systems see Section 2.1.6 and [Haefner 92b, p. 7 fp.].
[54] Cf. [von Weizsäcker 88, p. 201].
[55] Cf. [von Weizsäcker 72] according to [von Weizsäcker 88, p. 201].

The exploitation of information to improve decisions under uncertainty is a domain of economic theory: Uncertainty about a decision-maker's environment is involved in almost any economic situation. This gives rise to the *theory of uncertainty*.[56] Uncertainty can be described as the 'dispersion of individual's subjective probability (or belief) distributions over possible states of the world.'[57] In these situations, information about the environment can change the probability distribution that is underlying the decision and therefore the decision-maker's uncertainty. Information aids the decision-maker to come to a better decision and has, in this context of decision problems, a common property with information in information theory: it reduces uncertainty.[58] Hirshleifer claims the activities of 'gathering more evidence prior to terminal action' as the domain of the *economics of information*.[59]

A formal description of decision problems is given by the *basic model of decision theory*.[60] The decision-maker has the choice between alternative actions $A_a$, and is exposed to an environment with several alternative states $S_s$ each with a probability $w(S_s)$. The decision-maker's return $e_{as}$ for a particular choice of action $A_a$ depends on the state of the environment $S_s$. The decision-maker's aim is to choose an action in order to maximize the expected return.[61]

The formulation of this basic model of a decision problem reveals three domains of information:[62]

- Information about the probability $w(S_s)$ for the states of the environment, about
- the returns $e_{as}$ of the particular action-state combinations, and about
- additional actions $A_a$ the decision-maker can perform.

Hirshleifer makes a slightly different distinction of the contents or domain of information in decision problems under uncertainty.[63] In case of *technological uncertainty*, decision-makers are interested in information concerning their resource endowments and/or productive opportunities.[64] In case of *market uncertainty* decision-makers are fully certain about their own endowments and productive opportunities and uncertain about the supply and demand of other market

---

[56] Cf. [Lippman 79, p. 1 fp.].
[57] Cf. [Hirshleifer 73, p. 31].
[58] See the meaning of uncertainty (or entropy) in the definition of information in Section 2.1.1.1.
[59] Cf. [Hirshleifer 73, p. 31-32].
[60] Cf. [Schneeweiß 66], [Laux 91, p. 32 fp.].
[61] Various decision rules, depending on the decision-maker's risk assessment, can be applied to the choice of an appropriate action, cf. [Laux 91], [Eisenführ 94].
[62] Cf. [Laux 91, p. 281].
[63] Cf. [Hirshleifer 73, p. 33]
[64] Technological information is usually produced by means of research and development (R&D), which is the basis for an increase in knowledge and a precondition for economic progress, cf. [Hopf 83, p. 74].

participants. This conception is not completely congruent with the one given in the basic model of decision theory, because technological as well as market uncertainty can influence the returns $e_{as}$ of the particular action-state combinations. Market information can be further differentiated in information about *prices* and information about *quality*.[65] This distinction is significant, because uncertainty about prices or about quality has different consequences on market efficiency[66] and requires different formal descriptions.[67] Prices are measurable and authentic so that price information can be easily treated in decision problems and in mathematical models. On the other hand, quality may be multidimensional, and unquantifiable, and it may contain an irreducible subjective element. The authenticity of quality information given by sellers is in most cases questionable.[68] As a consequence, uncertainty about quality opens a much larger variety of economic effects in the real world as well as in economic models.[69]

### 2.1.1.4 *Concluding definition of information*

The three conceptions of information (syntactic, semantic, and pragmatic) reviewed above pose growing demands on the impact of information. In economic situations the reduction of uncertainty through information is focused, and it is distinguished between technological and market information. This corresponds with Wittmann's conception of pragmatic information in economic systems and situations as 'knowledge dedicated to a certain purpose.'[70]

The following statement can be seen as a *concluding definition of information* for the further analysis, however, is not claiming to describe the notion of information in every possible context:[71]

*Definition 1:*    *Information is to be understood as a message that has significance for a recipient system.*

---

[65]    Cf. [Hirshleifer 73, p. 36 fp.].

[66]    Cf. Section 2.4.

[67]    Commodities are valuable because they possess attributes which consumers desire. The quality of a product can therefore be specified by describing the amount of a desirable attribute it possesses. And a product with multiple attributes determining the quality can be described by a *vector* of the different *product attributes* having particular values, cf. [Kihlstrom 74a, p. 415 fp.].

[68]    Cf. [Hirshleifer 73, p. 35].

[69]    See Sections 2.3.2 and 2.4.

[70]    Cf. [Wittmann 59] according to [Bode 97, p. 454 fp.].

[71]    Significance of information for the recipient system means that 'information enables the system to initiate meaningful systematic activities that would not be possible without the information', cf. [Haefner 92b, p. 5]. Hence, the definition is closely related to the pragmatic conception of information.

## 2.1.2 Knowledge

Information science makes a clear distinction between information and know‑ledge.[72] Contrary to information which can be easily transferred, knowledge is closely connected with a system or individual. A clear conception of the term *knowledge* is not undisputed, nevertheless, the following working definition of the conception of knowledge can be given: Knowledge is to be understood as a set of models about objects, domains of objects, or facts, which is at a certain time freely disposable.[73] Another conception of knowledge is based on the conception of information, it characterizes knowledge as the *purposive interconnection of information,*[74] or stated in other terms 'synthesized information constitutes knowledge.'[75] In a conceptual hierarchy knowledge is on the highest level (Figure 1). Single *tokens* are on the lowest level, tokens put together represent *data, information* requires a context, and *knowledge* requires an interconnection of information.[76]

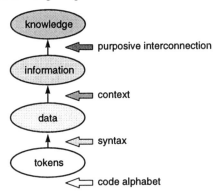

*Figure 1:*    *Conceptual hierarchy of tokens, data, information, and knowledge, according to [Rehäuser 96, p. 6].*

At a certain point of time, knowledge is the sum of hitherto substantiated individual or collective experiences, understanding, and realization.[77] Thus, knowledge is not restricted to one individual, but can also be represented by a group of people, an organization,[78] or all mankind, i.e., knowledge can be *individual* or *collective* knowledge.[79]

---

[72]    Cf. [Kuhlen 95, p. 38].

[73]    Translation of [Kuhlen 95, p. 38].

[74]    Cf. [Steinmüller 93, p. 263], [Rehäuser 96, p. 5].

[75]    *Synthesized information* refers to internally processed information, cf. [Tuthill 90, p. 5]. For a comprehensive treatment of the concepts of knowledge see [Tuthill 90] as well.

[76]    Cf. [Rehäuser 96, p. 2 fp].

[77]    Translation of [Kuhlen 95, p. 38].

[78]    Cf. [Sydow 96], [Willke 96], [Kuhlen 95, p. 38].

[79]    Cf. [Rehäuser 96, p. 7].

Knowledge can only be exchanged or communicated if it can be transformed into information;[80] this kind of knowledge, which can be processed by means of information technology, is labeled as *disembodied knowledge*.[81] The second form of knowledge, which only exists in peoples' heads, is labeled *embodied knowledge*.[82] The transformation of knowledge into information is not unequivocal, i.e., the same knowledge can be represented in several forms of information.[83] On the one hand, this enables producers of information to focus the needs of the recipient and provide personalized information products. On the other hand, this leads to a discrepancy between the evolution of new knowledge and of new information over time (Figure 2).

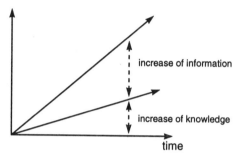

increase of information

increase of knowledge

time

*Figure 2:*    *Discrepancy between the increase of knowledge and the increase of information, according to [Kuhlen 95, p. 43].*

Formal methods for the representation of knowledge[84] are developed in cognitive science[85] and artificial intelligence.[86] Knowledge itself is at least the product (or result) of experience,[87] for example, of past activities or behavior. Therefore, the representation of knowledge is closely connected to the system in which the knowledge is represented.[88] One example of a formal representation of knowledge

---

[80]    Cf. [Kuhlen 95, p. 38].

[81]    Cf. [Rehäuser 96, p. 7].

[82]    Cf. [Rehäuser 96, p. 6].

[83]    Cf. Section 2.1.6 and [Kuhlen 95, p. 42-43]. Kuhlen speaks about different *information products*.

[84]    For an overview about methods of knowledge representation see [Tuthill 90, p. 226-245] and [Reimer 97], a comprehensive treatment can be found in [Reichgelt 91].

[85]    Cf. [Anderson 89, p. 79 fp., 103 fp., 206 fp.].

[86]    Cf. [Luger 89, p. 28 fp.].

[87]    Cf. [Kolodner 86, p. 1].

[88]    Kreutzer and McKenzie describe knowledge representations as a set of syntactic and semantic conventions 'to describe things,' where 'things' may be objects, relations, actions, events or processes. This stresses the fact that representation and interpretation are closely intertwined, cf. [Kreutzer 91, p. 198].

is semantic networks, able to represent the semantics of natural languages and can be implemented in computer systems.[89]

### 2.1.3 The organization of knowledge and information

Since the quantity of knowledge and information is steadily expanding (Figure 2) the organization[90] and retrieval[91] of information has become a major task. Roughly, two main directions to organize information can be distinguished: The *classification* of information (e.g., a document or more generally objects), usually done manually, e.g., by librarians, arranges every object of information in one or more classes.[92] The classes are usually arranged in a hierarchy[93] comparable to those in object-oriented programming. The other group of methods, referred to as *indexing*, focuses the retrieval of the contents;[94] these methods are usually performed automatically. A number of different methods to extract the index information out of the original information exists.[95] As a result, an *information retrieval* (IR) system is built to support efficient access to the indexed information, it is usually applied to unstructured information such as texts.

The quality of information retrieval systems can be expressed by the values of *recall* and *precision*:[96]

*(eq. 3)*

$$recall = \frac{number\ of\ relevant\ documents\ retrieved}{total\ number\ of\ relevant\ documents\ in\ the\ system} .$$

$$precision = \frac{number\ of\ relevant\ documents\ retrieved}{total\ number\ of\ documents\ retrieved}$$

The value of recall is inversely proportional to the precision of a system, therefore the system (and especially the index) has to be designed to obtain an appropriate

---

[89]  For a comprehensive review of semantic networks see [Sowa 90, p. 1011 fp.] and [Mac Randal 88], for their application to language understanding see [Rich 83, p. 295 fp.]. An overview about linguistics from a cognitive science point of view is given in [Anderson 89, p. 281 fp.].

[90]  For a comprehensive treatment of the organization of knowledge and information see [Rowley 92].

[91]  See [Salton 83] for information retrieval (IR).

[92]  Cf. [Manecke 97a].

[93]  Cf. [Manecke 97a, p. 142-143].

[94]  See [Knorz 97] for an overview.

[95]  Examples are: manual methods, full-text methods, linguistic methods, retrieval-oriented methods (weighted term schemes, vector models, probabilistic retrieval methods), see [Knorz 97] for details.

[96]  Cf. [Rowley 91, p. 170-173].

combination of the two values for each particular application.[97] In general, the organization of information is always adjusted to a particular aim,[98] so a particular form of index or classification can only be valued according to the particular purpose of the system. Hence, a general judgment about the quality of a particular form or method of organization of information is not possible.[99]

In all these methods *meta-information*,[100] i.e., information about information, is produced, for example, abstracts, information about the author, or the reference to the original information.[101]

### 2.1.4 The value of information in economic situations

Concluding from decision theory[102] the acquisition of information has the aim to overcome the uncertainty about decision problems and to improve the expected return compared to the original situation. Hence, information can be assigned a value in the context of a particular decision problem under the given environmental conditions.[103] In general, the value of information is always dependent on a particular context or situation,[104] i.e., the particular decision problem a decision-maker is facing. The value of information can be determined as the difference of the return from a decision with and without information.[105]

In the *basic model of decision theory* the value of information $V_I$ can be easily determined in a formal treatment of information about the probability $w(S_s)$ of alternative environmental states $S_s$.[106]

For a risk neutral decision-maker the expected return $D$ of a decision without information is given by:

(eq. 4)
$$D = \max_a \sum_{s=1}^{\bar{s}} w(S_s) \cdot e_{as}.$$

---

[97] Cf. [Rowley 91, p. 171], [Knorz 97, p. 138]. A more differentiated method to describe and measure the quality of results obtained from an information retrieval system is described in [Wand 96], see [Jeusfeld 97, p. 493] as well.

[98] Cf. [Rowley 92, p. 3].

[99] Cf. [Knorz 97, p. 122-123].

[100] See, for example, [Alter 96, p. 164], [Reichgelt 91, p. 14].

[101] For *references* see [Rowley 92, p. 14-15], for *abstracting* see [Kuhlen 97].

[102] Cf. [Allen 90] and Section 2.1.1.3.

[103] Examples are given by [Kihlstrom 74a] and [Kihlstrom 74b] who implicitly derive the value of information in markets with uncertain product quality, [MacMinn 80] who examines the value of information in the context of a search model, and [Milgrom 82] who investigates the value of information in a sealed-bid auction.

[104] Cf. [Milgrom 82], [Gilboa 91, p. 444, 456], [Nink 91, p. 62-63].

[105] Cf. [Bamberg 76], [Laux 91, p. 299], [Saliger 93, p. 141].

[106] Cf. [Laux 91, p. 297 fp.], [Saliger 93, p. 141].

The expected return $D_I$ of a decision after the acquisition of information is given by:

(eq. 5)
$$D_I = \sum_i w(I_i) \cdot \max_a \left( \sum_{s=1}^{\bar{S}} w(S_s | I_i) \cdot e_{as} \right).$$

Here $w(S_s | I_i)$ is the conditional probability[107] that the environmental state $S_s$ will be realized if the result of the acquisition of information is $I_i$. Therefore, the value of information is determined by $V_I = D_I - D$.

The result reveals some general properties and dependencies of the value of information in decision problems.

- The magnitude of $V_I$ :[108]
  - The value of information $V_I$ is never negative ($V_I \geq 0$).
  - The value of information is zero if information procurement does not result in the choice of a different action $A_a$.
  - It is strictly positive ($V_I > 0$) if the optimal action $A_a$ is dependent on the result of information procurement.
  - It reaches a maximum if the future environmental state is known with certainty.
- Dependency of the value of information on the environment:
  - The value of information is dependent on the probability $w(I_i)$ for a particular result of information procurement.
  - It is dependent on the conditional probability $w(S_s | I_i)$, which can be interpreted as the 'quality of the information.'

These results reflect properties of the value of information under idealized conditions. However, in the context of economic problems with asymmetric information[109] and overt information acquisition these results can be attenuated, as Akerlof's 'market of lemons'[110] shows. Information can have a negative value in the following sense: if one agent is known to have extra information, the others alter their behavior in a way unfavorable to him/her.[111]

---

[107] The conditional probability is determined by application of Bayes' theorem, cf. [Hartung 89, p. 102], [Laux 91, p. 285 fp.]:

$$w(S_s | I_i) = \left( w(I_i | S_s) \cdot w(S_s) \right) \Big/ \sum_{s=1}^{\bar{S}} \left( w(I_i | S_s) \cdot w(S_s) \right) .$$

[108] Cf. [Laux 91, p. 305 fp.].

[109] Cf. Sections 2.3.2 and 2.4.

[110] Cf. [Akerlof 70].

[111] In Akerlof's model the seller of a used car is assumed to have private information about the quality of his/her car, and the buyer knows that the seller is so informed. Consequently, the buyer worries that the car is offered because it is a 'lemon.' If the buyer can be sure that the seller has no private information, the car would be sold for the

Detached from the basic model of decision theory, the value of information is dependent on a series of economically significant *information attributes*:[112]

- The *certainty* of information describes the correlation of the result of information procurement with the actually realized state of the environment. In the basic model of decision theory the conditional probability $w(S_s|I_i)$ can be interpreted as a measure for the certainty of the information.

- The *diffusion* of information refers to its value depending on its scarcity. In an economic situation with strategic interdependence[113] of agents in a market, an agent's valuation of information depends on the information possessed by others.[114]

- The *applicability* of information refers to the decision-maker's ability to apply the information and make inferences from it. This depends on the individual's capacity of information processing,[115] and the knowledge already accumulated.[116] If, for example, more information is available than the decision-maker can process in given time the problem of information overload can occur (Section 1.1).

- The *content* of information describes the domain of the decision problem for which information can resolve uncertainty. One classification of the content of information is, for example, information about tastes, endowments (resources), technology (the production functions), and information about market characteristics like prices or quality.[117] In the formal treatment of the basic model of decision theory information only covers environmental states belonging to the domain of market characteristics.

- The aspect of *decision-relevance* of information distinguishes between economically relevant and irrelevant information. As can be seen from the basic model of decision theory, information only has a positive value if the optimal action is dependent on the result of information procurement, thus differentiating between relevant and irrelevant information.

It should be pointed out here that in real-life situations the measurement of the value of information acquisition in terms of monetary units is usually limited. The major problems concern the registration of effects and their accountability to informational activities.[118]

---

expected value. But the seller's private information lowers the selling price, and therefore is of negative value for the owner. Cf. [Milgrom 82].

[112] Cf. [Hirshleifer 73, p. 32-33].

[113] For strategic interdependence see [Rasmusen 89, p. 21] and Section 3.4.

[114] Kamien and Tauman, for example, analyze the dependence of the value of technological information, i.e., cost-reducing innovations, on the number of possessors of the information, cf. [Kamien 86].

[115] Cf. [Salop 77].

[116] Cf. [McKelvey 90].

[117] Cf. Section 2.1.1.3 and [Hirshleifer 73, p. 33].

[118] Cf. [Schwuchow 97, p. 753 fp.], [Reichwald 87].

### 2.1.5  Properties of information

The value of information is heavily dependent on the context of its use, as the previous section has shown. Hence, information can be defined indirectly by a description of its properties. Detached from any domain of application the common properties of information are the following:[119] information can be stored, it can be transferred, it can be multiplied, it can be read off reliably, it can be processed, and it shall be able to cause specific actions in a receiver.

Information, however, has further properties which are significant for comprehensive treatment and understanding of effects resulting from information acquisition or possession, especially in a market context.[120] These general properties of information are listed in the following:

- Information itself is an *immaterial good* that does not wear out by use.[121]
- *Distribution* of information can either be done by the transfer on a material storage medium or by transmission over communication networks.[122] Compared to physical products information can be *duplicated and circulated easily.*[123]
- The production of information usually causes *high fixed costs* for the first 'copy' of the information and small or even vanishing marginal costs for every additional copy over a wide range of outputs.[124] However, information is not a 'free' good, but a *scarce resource*, only unselected data and messages exist in excess.[125]
- Information is *indivisible* and useful only in integer amounts.[126]
- Information has features of a *public good*:[127]
  - Information *requires no exclusivity of use*. Information can be used by several agents without altering the information for any of the agents. However, the value of the information can in some cases depend on the spreading of the information.
  - The *disclosure problem*: The use of information by one agent may reveal the information to others. For example, under rational expectations agents will be unwilling to invest in their own production of information, especially of market information, if the same information is revealed by prices and thus available gratuitously.[128] As an effect, the market may suffer from an under-

---

[119]  Cf. [Haken 92, p. 155].

[120]  Cf. Section 2.4.

[121]  Cf. [Bode 93, p. 37], [Herget 97, p. 782].

[122]  Cf. [Bode 97, p. 452].

[123]  Cf. [Bode 93, p. 38 fp.].

[124]  Cf. [Allen 90, p. 271], for the production of information and different sources of information see Section 2.2.

[125]  Cf. [Herget 97, p. 782].

[126]  Cf. [Allen 90, p. 270].

[127]  For commodity aspects of information see Section 2.5.1.

[128]  Hayek argues that in a decentralized economy all relevant information is effectively disseminated via the price system, cf. [Hayek 45]. See Section 2.4.1 as well.

production of information if too many agents behave this way.[129]

- Information can be traded and exchanged as an economic *commodity*,[130] which states that information has some *private good features* as well.[131] Traders of information can benefit from sale and dissemination of information and therefore undertake the costly process of information acquisition and production.

- Information is *not exclusively transferable*: If the property rights on information are transferred between producer and user, usually only a copy of the information is sold, and the actual information can still kept at the producer.

- Information *cannot be inspected without being revealed*. The inspection of information, for example, before purchasing the information, must completely reveal the information in order to fully judge its quality. In case of a partial disclosure of the information the true value can only be estimated with uncertainty. Therefore, the true value of information cannot be predicted ex ante, which is usually referred to as the *fundamental paradox of information*.[132]

- The *value* of information is closely connected to the user of the information and the particular utilization of the information. Information only is of value for the user if it enables him/her to improve decisions[133] or productive activities. The individual agent's valuation of the information depends on two further properties of information: the *novelty* and the *truthfulness* of the information.[134] An information already possessed is valueless as well as a wrong information, which can even be of negative value if assumed true.[135]

- Information has a *life cycle* from production over dissemination to its terminal use.[136] The *decay* and *lifetime* of information are highly dependent on the type of information. Market information can be expected to have a shorter lifetime than technological information.

### 2.1.6 Information processing systems

The previous sections have shown that information is usually applied within a system, that the purposive application of information always needs some internal information available,[137] and that the value of information is dependent on the context and the situation it is used in. The activities of (a) 'decoding' the syntax of

---

[129] Cf. [Hirshleifer 73, p. 34], [Hopf 83, p. 44 fp.], [Allen 90, p. 270 fp.].
[130] Cf. Section 2.5 and [Herget 97, p. 782].
[131] Cf. Section 2.5.1 and [Allen 90, p. 271].
[132] Cf. [Arrow 62], [Williamson 86, p. 161], [Picot 96, p. 109].
[133] This refers to the pragmatic conception of information (Section 2.1.1.3) and the basic model of decision theory (Section 2.1.4).
[134] Cf. [Bode 97, p. 453].
[135] In the conception of the basic model of decision theory, however, information can only have a positive value, cf. Section 2.1.4.
[136] See Section 2.5.
[137] Cf. [Haefner 92b, p. 7].

messages, (b) 'understanding' semantic information and (c) 'acting' as a consequence of dealing with the pragmatic aspect of information involved herein can be summarized as *information processing*.[138] The internal,[139] pre-existing information of the system, i.e., knowledge, is continuously undergoing changes during information processing, which can be conceived as *learning* behavior of the system.

Generally speaking, *information processing systems* are matter/energy structures[140] that enable the following functions:[141]

- receiving and decoding 'relevant' information,
- storing internal information,
- manipulating information: producing 'new' information from 'old' information,[142]
- altering the internal structure of the (information processing) system,
- sending information outside the system in a given code.

These information processing systems require three *main components*:[143]

- A processor to perform operations based on particular rules,
- a memory to store rules and data,
- input- and output-devices to exchange messages with the outside world.

*Information economics* formally describes information processing systems by means of a projection $\eta$ from a set of states of the environment $Z$ to signals (or messages) $\omega \in \Omega$.

These messages are elements of a set of signals $\Omega$ :[144]

*(eq. 6)*      $\eta : Z \to \Omega, \quad z \mapsto \eta(z) = \omega.$

The projection assigns each environmental state $z \in Z$ exactly one signal (or message) $\omega$. In this context, an information processing system is characterized by the set $\Omega$ of possible signals and the conditional probability $w(\omega \mid z)$ for receiving the signal $\omega$ if $z$ is the true state of the environment. In case of a *deterministic*

---

[138] Cf. [Haefner 92b, p. 7].

[139] For a discussion of 'internal information' in matter/energy systems see [Lazlo 92].

[140] A very general conception conceives all matter/energy structures that perform the quoted functions as information processing systems. These information processing system come along as physical, biological, social, and technical systems, cf. [Haefner 92b].

[141] Cf. [Haefner 92b, p. 8] and [Alter 96, p. 365]. For the application of this conception to information production in economics see [Müller 87].

[142] New information can be produced out of existing information, for example, by rearranging the information or by producing an abstract, cf. [Kuhlen 95, p. 86]. Other forms of manipulating information are: sorting, reformatting, or various types of calculations, cf. [Alter 96, p. 365]. This process, however, does not primarily affect the knowledge represented by the information, the new information is mainly a different representation of the same knowledge, cf. Section 2.1.2.

[143] Cf. [Müller 87, p. 128], [Seng 89, p. 48 fp.], [Corsten 90, p. 159].

[144] The surjective projection $\eta$ is called an *information function*, cf. [Kiener 90, p. 10].

information processing system, the projection η allows to conclude the realized state of the environment from the signal ω.[145] The processing of information in this formal model is examined by means of a *Bayes-analysis*.[146] The embodiment of economic information processing systems is manifold: these can simply gather information about the environment or can undertake observations, process, and transfer the information.[147]

*Computer science* gives an abstract system-theoretic definition of information systems.[148] In *systems theory* a system $S^G$ is defined as a relation over sets $V_i \in V=\{V_i : i \in I\}$ as the components of the system:

(eq. 7)        $S^G \subseteq \underset{i \in I}{\times} V_i.$

The set of tupels $\left\{ (V_i, V_j) : i, j \in I \wedge i \neq j \right\}$ defines the system's behavior, and each component of the system can itself be a system built up of components.[149] One specialization of such a system that processes some input and generates an output is a functional *input-output system*:[150]

(eq. 8)        $S^{IO}: IN \rightarrow OUT \; with$

$$IN = \underset{i \in I_{IN}}{\times} V_i, \quad OUT = \underset{i \in I_{OUT}}{\times} V, \quad I = I_{IN} \cup I_{OUT}, \quad I_{IN} \cap I_{OUT} = \varnothing.$$

*Business information systems* are special instances of information processing systems. These can be discriminated according to their business application as *administrative information systems* that rationalize mass data processing, *decision support systems* that support or take decisions for structured decision problems, *planning and controlling information systems* that support and control unstructured decision problems on a wider time scale.[151] A second characterization of business information systems focuses the issues of design and implementation of informa- tion systems.[152] This characterization distinguishes four views on information systems: An *organizational, functional,* and *data view,* and a fourth *control view.*

---

[145]  If this condition does not hold, the information processing system is denoted *stochastic,* cf. [Kiener 90, p. 10].

[146]  Cf. [Ehemann 83] according to [Kiener 90, p. 12], see Section 2.1.4.

[147]  Cf. [Marschak 75].

[148]  Cf. [Ferstl 93, p. 11 fp.], see [Guntram 85] for a review of the *general theory of systems.*

[149]  Cf. [Ferstl 93, p. 12].

[150]  Cf. [Ferstl 93, p. 14], [Guntram 85, p. 302].

[151]  Cf. [Mertens 91, p. 10 fp.].

[152]  Cf. [Scheer 95].

## 2.2 Sources of information

The role of information for an individual decision-maker has become obvious from Section 2.1.4, but the decision-maker is confronted with a multitude of possible sources of information having different costs and qualities. Mainly two distinctions about the process of information acquisition can be made: From the information seeker's point of view, we can distinguish between *active* and *passive* acquisition of information. Regarding the type of information, we can distinguish between *technological* information and *market* information.[153] Market information implies price information and information about product quality, which can be further sub-divided in search and experience characteristics.[154] *Search characteristics* of products can be revealed through observation during a simple search process,[155] whereas *experience characteristics* of products will only be revealed after completion of the consumption experience.

The purpose of the present section is to characterize the different sources and activities of information procurement from the information seeker's point of view and to discuss their pros and cons.

### 2.2.1 Active acquisition of information

Information seekers can *actively* acquire new, economically valuable information by either producing the information themselves or buying the information from the producer.[156] *Technological information* is mainly produced by a firm's privately conducted research and development (R&D) activities,[157] usually intended for private use, and rarely disseminated to the public without charge.[158] But techno-logical information can be purchased from the producer, for example, by licensing a product, a technology, or a production process.

*Market information*, on the other hand, has at first sight no productive value of its own, but is demanded and produced because it helps decision-makers to improve the outcome of their decision-problems.[159] The active acquisition of market infor-mation is mainly done by search for products or services, or more generally speaking, objects with particular characteristics requested by the decision-maker.

---

[153]    Cf. Section 2.1.1.3.
[154]    Cf. [Nelson 70].
[155]    Cf. Section 4.2.1.
[156]    Cf. [Hirshleifer 73, p. 32].
[157]    For an economic treatment of R&D activities see, for example, [Kamien 70], [Weitzman 79], [Dasgupta 89].
[158]    Cf. [Hirshleifer 73, p. 33 fp.].
[159]    Cf. [Kihlstrom 74a, p. 414] and Section 2.1.4.

The search process itself is an economic problem[160] because the object's characteristics are randomly distributed in the market under investigation. Search is
usually costly, i.e., each observation conducted in the search process is a time- and
money-consuming activity for the information seeker. The economic principle of
information acquisition and search activities is illustrated in Figure 3. For an
increasing intensity of search the return from information acquisition is increasing
with a decreasing slope, whereas the search costs are increasing with an increasing
slope. The *optimal amount of search* or information acquisition is then given by
the maximum difference of the two curves. In terms of marginal quantities it is
given by the equality of the slopes of the two curves, i.e., the marginal costs and
the marginal return respectively (dashed lines in Figure 3).[161]

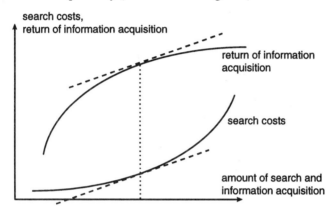

Figure 3:     The economic principle of search for information, according to [Hopf 83, p.
              56].

Therefore, search costs and the return from information acquisition determine the
optimal amount of search. The optimal search behavior in a situation with
uncertainty about the distribution of objects' characteristics and with costly communication is a *sequential search process* with a stopping rule given by a
reservation value[162] determined from the characteristics of the market and the costs
for a single observation. For an introduction to the *economic theory of search* and a
review of the basic literature see Section 4.2. Besides search, a second possibility
of active information procurement is the purchase of market information from a
third party that actively performs information gathering about product markets.
The value and quality of the information actively produced or gathered, i.e., the
certainty and truthfulness, the applicability, and the decision relevance,[163] depend

---

[160]    Stigler introduced the *economics of information*, pointing attention to the economics of
         search processes, see [Stigler 61] and [Gastwirth 76] for an overview.
[161]    Cf. [Hopf 83, p. 56].
[162]    Cf. [McAfee 88] and Section 4.2.2.1.
[163]    Cf. Section 2.1.4 and 2.1.5.

on two main factors: First, the information seeker's personal *ability and capacity of information processing*,[164] for example, R&D on a particular topic requires special academic skills, and the search for information in a product market requires knowledge about products and suppliers in the market. Second, the *intensity* of R&D or of search determines the outcome of information acquisition: The investment in R&D effort is directly correlated with the result,[165] for search processes the intensity of search determines the expected outcome of information gathering.[166]

### 2.2.2  Passive acquisition of information

In situations with imperfect information the passive acquisition of information disseminated by suppliers and third parties is an alternative source for consumers and decision-makers to acquire market information. For example, in product markets suppliers disseminate information about their products and particularly about the quality of their products[167] to create a competitive advantage over their competitors. Information about prices can be circulated unproblematically, either directly on the product or by way of messages sent to the consumer,[168] because prices are measurable and for price information authenticity is manifest.[169] In contrast to that, firms have two major possibilities to disseminate information about product quality, which can be subject to selfish and therefore dishonest behavior: advertising and signaling.[170]

*Advertising* can be seen as an instrument applied by suppliers to help consumers with heterogeneous tastes to locate their preferred price-quality combinations.[171] Firms can choose the intensity of their advertising, for example, the number of messages sent to consumers,[172] to vary the number of potential consumers reached by the information. These firms may have an incentive to misrepresent the quality of their products in advertising quality information to attract a larger number of consumers as would be substantiated by their actual price-quality combination.[173] Empirical results show that advertising has only a weak correlation with quality so

---

[164]  In general, the outcome of a decision problem is dependent on the mental resources and the effort spent, cf. [Johnson 85].

[165]  Cf. [Dasgupta 89, p. 131].

[166]  Cf. [Kihlstrom 74a, p. 421], [Yoon 81].

[167]  The dissemination of information about products offered is one important entrepreneurial task, cf. [Kaas 90].

[168]  Cf. [Butters 77].

[169]  Cf. [Hirshleifer 73, p. 36] and Section 2.1.1.3.

[170]  Cf. [Kaas 90, p. 541].

[171]  Cf. [Bagwell 93, p. 200, 225].

[172]  Cf. [Butters 77], [Sass 84, p. 37 fp.], [Guimaraes 95].

[173]  Cf. [Bagwell 93, p. 224 fp.].

that advertising cannot be used as a definite criterion to distinguish high from low quality.[174]

*Signaling* of product quality is done through the terms of the contract. A common contract attribute used to signal quality is the product price, high prices are usually interpreted as a signal for high product quality.[175] Other special terms of contract that can signal product quality are refund promises and free trial periods.[176]

A third and independent source for passive acquisition of market information is newspapers, magazines, consumer information organizations, retail firms or brokers,[177] publishing or disseminating market information, acquired by search and evaluation activities. And, of course, information can be acquired by word of mouth from friends or relatives.

Consumers passively absorb all this information disseminated by suppliers or third parties and have to decide whether or not to trust the information source because suppliers of goods or services may have an incentive to present their products as having higher quality than is actually justified.[178]

### 2.2.3 The costs of information production

The production of information by individuals is either done actively or passively, in both cases, costs for the information arise. Individuals perform *active production* of either market information or technological information because it is valuable for their allocation of resources, for example, in decision problems (Section 2.1.4), or the information can be sold profitably (Section 2.5). The *production costs* for *market information* are (variable) costs for search, which are

---

[174]  Tellis and Fornell conclude: 'For consumers, advertising cannot be used as a guide to either high or low quality. Though a more heavily advertised brand may be of better quality, the relationship between advertising and quality, albeit positive, is not large enough for advertising to be a good indicator of quality.' Cf. [Tellis 88, p. 70], [Bagwell 93, p. 203].

[175]  Introductory prices above the full-information profit-maximizing price that decline over time as information about the product diffuses are assumed to be a signal of high product quality, cf. [Bagwell 91], [Macho-Stadler 97, p. 212 fp.]. A precondition for prices to signal product quality is a minimum amount of private information a consumer has about the supplier and the products offered prior to the acquisition of price information, cf. [Judd 94]. For a discussion of the concept of *signaling* in job markets see [Spence 73].

[176]  Cf. [Doyle 89].

[177]  Cf. [Kihlstrom 74b, p. 99], [Sass 84], [Hänchen 85], [Bagwell 94].

[178]  Cf. [Bagwell 93, p. 225]. Akerlof argues in a slightly different way, in his 'market for lemons' informed sellers offer cars with a quality below the average quality offered on the market, and thus introduces a negative difference between the true quality level and the one expected by consumers, cf. [Akerlof 70].

mainly opportunity costs of time,[179] and fixed costs for an investment in productive capital, i.e., human capital, for example, in form of the searcher's ability to perform search, and the technology that supports search. In case of *technological information* active production of information is usually performed by R&D divisions within a firm.[180] The costs involved in R&D are mainly fixed costs in form of costs for personal, the education and training of the personal, and for scientific equipment.[181] The costs for an active acquisition of information are therefore determined by a large portion of fixed costs and only a small amount of costs depending on the amount of information actually produced. This argument especially holds for the acquisition of technological information, but the acquisition of market information can be subject to fixed costs as well, for instance, if the search for information requires knowledge about the market or about the characteristics of the products.

The *passive absorption of information* is the second form of information acquisition. In this case the receiver of the information only pays indirectly for the information in form of opportunity costs. These opportunity costs[182] are the difference between the utility arising from the information received and the utility that would be achievable through the best alternative which can be realized in an active acquisition of information minus the search costs that would be caused.

## 2.3  The credibility of information and trust in the information source

Economic situations are usually characterized by *asymmetric information*[183] and *uncertainty*. In *agency relationships* under these circumstances, i.e., one individual depends on the actions of another, trust and credibility play an important role. The relationship between consumers and producers of information is one particular example of a *principal-agent relationship* that is subject to problems of inducement and enforcement.

---

179    Cf. [Stigler 61, p. 216].
180    Cf. [Kamien 70], [Weitzman 79], [Dasgupta 80].
181    Cf. [Hopf 83, p. 192].
182    Cf. [Varian 93, p. 316 fp.].
183    In an economic relationship one participant has some private information that the other does not have, cf. [Arrow 85, p. 37 fp.], [Rasmusen 89, p. 133 fp.].

### 2.3.1 Excursion: principal-agent theory

The aim of *principal-agent theory*[184] is the design of efficient organizational and contractual structures or forms of cooperation that can overcome the problems arising in principal-agent relationships. The main sources of these problems are the asymmetric distribution of information between principal and agent, and uncertainty about the future states of the environment and the actions taken by the agent.

#### 2.3.1.1 The principal-agent relationship

In *principal-agent relationships*[185] the agent (e.g., the provider of a service) acts on behalf of the principal (e.g., a user of the service). The outcome of the action performed affects the welfare of both the agent and the principal.[186] The principal expects the agent to serve him/her in the best possible manner, but the higher the agent's effort the higher will be the costs, inducing incentives for the agent for carelessness or fraud. As a result, the principal will devote resources to monitoring the agent or to the design of an appropriate incentive scheme.[187] Since the agent is usually closer to the subject than the principal is, control is costly and in most cases not perfect. Two main cases of uncertainty in principal-agent relationships are distinguished in economics literature:[188]

- the agent's action is not directly observable by the principal, and
- the outcome is affected but not completely determined by the agent's action.

Thus the principal-agent relationship mainly results from the principal's inability to perfectly and inexpensively monitor the agent's actions and private information.

#### 2.3.1.2 Agency costs

As a matter of fact, principal-agent relationships under uncertainty do not function as well as they would if all relevant information were freely shared or the incentives of principals and agents were perfectly aligned. The losses (or opportunity costs) resulting from this imperfection, i.e., the difference between the situation with symmetric and complete information and a situation with asymmetric information, are referred to as *agency costs*.[189]

---

[184] For an overview of principal-agent theory see [Ross 73], [Jensen 76], [Pratt 85], [Spremann 87], [Spremann 90], [Kiener 90, p. 19 fp.], [Ordelheide 93, p. 1844], [Picot 96, p. 47 fp.].

[185] Cf. [Pratt 85, p. 1 fp.].

[186] Cf. [Arrow 85, p. 37].

[187] Cf. [Pratt 85, p. 17].

[188] Cf. [Arrow 85, p. 37].

[189] Cf. [Pratt 85, p. 3], [Spremann 88, p. 617].

Agency costs are determined as the sum of:[190]
- monitoring expenditures by the principal,
- bonding expenditures by the agent, and
- the residual loss from shirking that remains.

### 2.3.1.3  Types of information asymmetries

Uncertainty in principal-agent relationships can result from different reasons, mainly three types of asymmetric information are distinguished:[191]
- *Uncertainty about quality*: The principal is imperfectly informed about the quality of the agent or the product or service provided by the agent.
- *Holdup*: Undesired dependencies can occur in principal-agent relationships if the principal has already incurred relationship-dependent sunk costs before the agent has fulfilled his/her part of the transaction or contract. In these cases the principal is implicitly dependent on the agent's part of the transaction, and the agent's actions can be subject to truthful or egoistic behavior, without an opportunity for the principal's intervention.
- *Moral hazard*: The principal is unable to monitor the agent's actions. This disability to become perfectly informed, even ex post, can be caused by the principal's lack of specialized knowledge about the agent and the agent's business. As a result, the agent can take advantage of the full scope of opportunities and maximize the return by selfish behavior.

In the terminology of principal-agent theory these sources of information asymmetry are designated *hidden characteristics*, *hidden intention*, and *hidden action* respectively.[192]

### 2.3.1.4  Cooperation design: efficient agency structures

Since in most cases a symmetric distribution of information between principal and agent cannot be achieved, agency theory aims to design *agency structures* to overcome the imperfections; these are only *second-best designs*.[193] The *principal's problem* is to reap the greatest advantage from the relationship through incentives which influence the agents' behavior without making them quit. The assumptions to this are (a) that the principal is in a position to design the monitoring and incentive mechanism, and (b) that all the benefits from improvements in performance go to the principal.[194] The aim of cooperation design is to find the optimal trade-off between the three main contributions to the agency costs and thus mini-

---

[190]  Cf. [Jensen 76, p. 308].
[191]  Cf. [Spremann 90, p. 562 fp.], [Arrow 85, p. 38 fp.].
[192]  Cf. [Picot 96, p. 49].
[193]  Cf. [Spremann 88, p. 617], [Spremann 90, p. 575].
[194]  Cf. [Pratt 85, p. 17].

mize agency costs or maximize the principal's utility.[195] For practical cases a multitude of efficient[196] cooperation designs exists. Hard and smooth forms of cooperation design can be distinguished:[197] A *hard design* is highly formalized, precisely regulated, attached to objectively observable facts, and is always enforced. On the contrary, a *smooth design* is less formal and is not strictly enforced. Examples are:

- *Hard forms* of cooperation design:
  - *Reward of the agent*: The profit is shared among principal and agent, i.e., the agent receives a share of the total return achieved in the relationship. Losses are completely borne by the principal.[198]
  - *Punishment of the agent*: In case of losses the agent is punished, including the possibility of the absence of a reward.[199]
  - *Guarantees*:[200] The agent guarantees to provide the principal repair, conversion or compensation in case of failure or loss. Guarantees also imply securities and contracts of suretyship.
- *Smooth forms* of cooperation design:
  - *Reputation*:[201] An agent's reputation is a valuable asset in repeated transactions to make a distinction to other market participants. This is an incentive for the agent not to risk a good reputation and spend the required effort in the relationship. Principals contracting with a reputable agent can expect to receive the desired result.
  - *Information policy*:[202] Informational activities either performed by the principal or by the agent can reduce the information asymmetry. Examples for these informational activities are:[203]
    - *Screening*: The principal ex ante gathers additional information about the agent and about the services offered.
    - *Signaling*: The agent ex ante signals the characteristics of distinctive attributes of products or services by advertising or reporting.
    - *Monitoring*: The principal ex post gathers information about the outcome and the characteristics of the agent's behavior.
  - *Self-selection*:[204] The principal designs a situation in which agents have to take a decision that reveals their main characteristics.

---

[195] Cf. [Spremann 88, p. 617], [Picot 96, p. 48].
[196] The term 'efficient' refers to informational efficiency, see, for example, Section 2.4.1.
[197] Cf. [Spremann 90, p. 577].
[198] Cf. [Spremann 88, p. 618].
[199] Cf. [Eccles 85, p. 152 fp.].
[200] Cf. [Spremann 88, p. 620].
[201] Cf. [Spremann 88, p. 618 fp.].
[202] Cf. [Spremann 88, p. 621 fp.].
[203] Cf. [Picot 96, p. 49-50].
[204] Cf. [Picot 96, p. 50].

## 2.3.2  The credibility of information

The contact between consumers and suppliers of products, services, or information is a particular form of a *principal-agent relationship*. The principal (in this particular case the consumer) hires an agent (the supplier) to perform a task, i.e., the revelation of information about the quality of products offered. Asymmetrically distributed information and the divergent incentives of principal and agent lead to uncertainty about the credibility and reliability of the information exchanged between the two.[205] This general statement applies to the acquisition of information as well, either for technological or market information - the quality of information is always subject to uncertainty. The information seeker, i.e., the principal, can never be certain, whether the information received from the agent, e.g., a supplier or a third party information provider, is complete or whether it is true or not, unless a thorough investigation of the product, service, or information is undertaken. The examination of the true quality of the information can be rather costly for the information seeker. These monitoring costs depend on the principal's ability and capacity[206] to investigate the object and on the characteristics of the product itself. In most cases the principal's monitoring cannot completely reduce the uncertainty so that residual losses from the agent's shirking will remain.

Nelson has introduced the distinction between search and experience characteristics[207] that have different properties as far as the revelation of information about quality is concerned. The quality of *search goods* can be simply inspected before purchase, because the quality of these goods mainly depends on external characteristics, for example, color, shape, and material. The costs of inspection are thus only costs for transport and opportunity costs of time.[208] In case of *experience goods* the quality can be examined best by purchase and subsequent consumption. The costs of an investigation of the good's quality prior to purchase would be a multiple of the costs that arise from experiencing the good, being the opportunity costs that arise from a reduction of utility offered by the good compared to the best known alternative.[209]

For a third type of products with *credence qualities*,[210] the information seeker is not able to investigate the true quality of the product or service at all, even after purchase, because the characteristics that determine quality are not observable or the costs for an examination would be prohibitively high.[211]

---

[205]  Cf. [Arrow 85, p. 46 fp.].
[206]  Cf. Section 2.2.1 and [Johnson 85].
[207]  Cf. [Nelson 70].
[208]  Cf. [Kaas 90, p. 543].
[209]  These characteristics hold, for example, for services that require a high degree of experience, knowledge and education, cf. [Kaas 90, p. 543].
[210]  Cf. [Darby 73, p. 68 fp.].
[211]  Cf. [Darby 73, p. 69], [Kaas 90, p. 543].

Hence, the quality and credibility of information is always subject to uncertainty. However, different types of information will result in different tradeoffs between the principal's monitoring costs, the agent's bonding expenditures, and the residual loss caused by the agent's shirking, i.e., the three main contributions to the agency costs.

### 2.3.3 Achieving trust in the information source

Basic forms of cooperation design to overcome principal-agent problems were mentioned in Section 2.3.1.4. The supplier of information can actively apply several instruments to establish trust in the relationship with consumers. A firm's *reputation* is one main instrument to reduce uncertainty about the trustworthi̇ness.[212] Reputation is built up on basis of a supplier's past effort and performance and is especially valuable for firms that aim at repeated relations with consu̇mers,[213] whereby in later periods firms can profit from truthful and honest behavior in earlier periods. A further instrument to reduce the negative effects that consumers may bear from low quality offers can be *warranties of quality*, which assure repair or conversion for products, or securities for services.[214] A further possibility to achieve trust between consumers and suppliers is the introduction of a *third party*[215] who licenses, certifies or monitors the supplier. *Licensing*[216] can be done by demanding potential market participants to engage in a minimum level of investment in human capital and to pass an examination before entering the market. *Certification*[217] of a supplier means that the third party periodically gathers some private information about the supplier and 'marks suppliers as certified' if they fulfill a specified quality standard. *Monitoring*[218] is the third party's continuous, costly acquisition of information about the supplier which implicitly exercises pressure on the supplier to offer high quality and true quality information.

---

[212] Cf. [Hopf 83, p. 54], [Spremann 88], [Rasmusen 89, p. 169].

[213] The role of reputation has been extensively studied in game theory, cf. [Kreps 82], [Sabourian 89], [Holler 93, p. 173 fp.].

[214] Cf. [Spremann 88].

[215] Third parties have the opportunity to efficiently perform monitoring and quality assuring tasks because they can concentrate in a special thematic area, become experts in determining the quality of products and services, and spread the costs for information acquisition among a large number of clients. See Section 3.2.3.2.

[216] Licensing is a form of input market regulation that is usually found in the public sector, for example, for physicians or lawyers, cf. [Leland 79], [Shapiro 86].

[217] Cf. [Lizzeri 96].

[218] Examples of third parties that perform monitoring can be found in the literature of financial intermediation, see, for example, [Diamond 84]. See Section 3.2.3.2 as well.

## 2.4 Information and market efficiency

Information is usually not dispersed homogeneously among all market parti‐
cipants,[219] i.e., a situation in which not all the agents possess all relevant information. We thus face market uncertainty,[220] either caused by *incomplete* or *missing*
*information*,[221] i.e., market participants do not have all information that is poten-
tially available on the market,[222] or by *asymmetric information*[223] about the quality
of the product or service offered by the traders.

### 2.4.1 The price system

Hayek argued that in an economic system with prices an agent need not have
perfect information about all the other agents and their demand and supply,
because the *price system* efficiently communicates such information: 'in a system
in which the knowledge of the relevant facts is dispersed among many people.'[224]
Thus the price system can be considered as a distributed, economic information
processing system[225] having the agents' individual supply and demand as input and
a vector of prices as output.

If prices reflect all relevant information available in the market,[226] the market is
*informationally efficient*.[227] A more detailed conception distinguishes between
three levels of market efficiency:[228]

- *Weak form of market efficiency*: prices only reflect historical information.
- *Semi-strong form of market efficiency*: prices incorporate historical information and all present information publicly available on the market.

---

[219] Cf. [McAfee 87, p. 699].

[220] Cf. Section 2.1.1.3.

[221] Cf. [Rothschild 73], [McAfee 87].

[222] Information available on the market is, for example, buyers' demand and sellers'
supply, cf. [McAfee 87, p. 700]. Under costly information acquisition this information
is not acquired by all market participants. A result may be, for example, that agents do
not know when and at what prices they can sell or buy, cf. [Ioannides 75, p. 248].

[223] Cf. [Spremann 90] and Section 2.3.2.

[224] Cf. [Hayek 45, p. 525].

[225] Cf. Section 2.1.6. The formation of prices in auctions and bidding is studied in
[McAfee 87].

[226] Cf. [Spremann 90, p. 574]. Here, private information of single agents is completely
redundant, cf. [Bray 89, p. 263].

[227] In an informationally efficient market there would be no alternative price vector that
leaves everyone at least as well off and makes some strictly better off. This can be
derived from the definition of Pareto-efficiency, cf. [Varian 93, p. 15, 299 fp.], [Hopf
83, p. 61].

[228] Cf. [Fama 70, p. 383].

- *Strong form of market efficiency*: prices reflect historical information, present information publicly available on the market, and insider information, i.e., information not publicly available.

An illustration of price-quality combinations for three goods with different quality levels (A < B < C) on an informationally inefficient market is given in Figure 4. A market with price-quality combinations only lying on the curve indicated in the figure would be informationally efficient, because no better price-quality combination can be achieved.

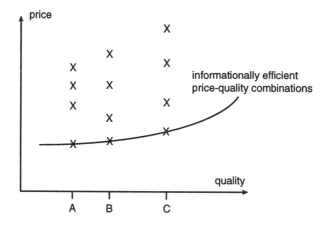

*Figure 4:*    Price-quality combinations on a market for three goods with quality levels A < B < C and the line of informationally efficient combinations, according to [Hopf 83, p. 61].

Economic systems that perfectly embody relevant information in the price system are (stock) exchanges. In these systems the auctioneer or the tatônnement process perfectly procures and disseminates all relevant information.[229] In markets that have no central auctioneer, economic agents have to acquire information themselves.[230] They also have to decide how many resources, no longer utilized for production or consumption, to dedicate to information procurement.[231] Under the condition of costly information acquisition markets cannot be informationally efficient.[232] The argument usually applied is that the price system is more infor-

[229]  Cf. [Hopf 83, p. 52]. For a comprehensive treatment of auctions and a review of the related literature see [Stark 79], [Engelbrecht-Wiggans 80], [McAfee 87]. Especially capital markets are assumed to be informationally efficient: 'at any time prices fully reflect all available information,' cf. [Fama 70, p. 383].

[230]  Cf. Section 2.2.

[231]  The optimal amount of information acquisition is given by the condition that the marginal costs of information acquisition equal the marginal returns from the information, see Section 2.2.1, [Hopf 83, p. 56], and Section 4.2.

[232]  Cf. [Grossmann 80].

mative the more agents become informed,[233] but agents attempt to avoid costly information acquisition, which is of no disadvantage for them because prices fully reflect all relevant information. As a consequence, the market will suffer from an underproduction of information if all market participants behave this way. In case of an underproduction of information, it will be profitable for some agents to become informed[234] and exploit the competitive advantage of *private information*. For most economic situations the value of private information is enormously greater to an individual than the value of the same information publicly dispersed.[235] An example is given by Stigler, who examined information gathering in labor markets: The information an individual 'possesses on the labor market is capital: it was produced at the costs of search, and it yields a higher wage rate than on the average would be received in its absence.'[236]

## 2.4.2  Effects of asymmetric information

The effects of asymmetric information on market equilibrium have been studied in a multitude of economic situations and models,[237] the models can be differentiated as *search models* and *bargaining models*.[238] The presence of information gathering agents in markets with asymmetric information has positive external effects on the other agents. For example, in product markets the active search of some individuals keeps prices in the market low. As a consequence, price-quality combinations will be close to or on the line of informationally efficient combinations (Figure 4). Agents who do not search will profit from this.[239] Moreover, active search for the lowest price can influence firms' entry and exit decisions in a market with different production costs.[240] As soon as search costs decrease, the most inefficient firms drop out of the market, because with decreasing search costs the reservation value[241] of acceptable prices in the search process decreases as well. In a set of firms with different production costs only firms with the ability to offer sufficiently low prices will have enough clients and will be profitable. In

---

[233]  Cf. [Grossmann 80, p. 394], [Hopf 83, p. 42].

[234]  Cf. [Grossmann 80, p. 395], [Milgrom 82].

[235]  Cf. [Hirshleifer 71, p. 567]. Hirshleifer argues in terms of *foreknowledge*, which he defines as the ability to successfully predict future states of the environment, cf. [Hirshleifer 71, p. 562].

[236]  Cf. [Stigler 62, p. 103].

[237]  A review of different models is given in [Rothschild 73].

[238]  Roughly speaking, search models usually investigate the aspect of missing information in markets, see for example [Ioannides 75]. Whereas, bargaining models mainly focus the effects of asymmetrically informed market participants, cf. [Chatterjee 83].

[239]  Cf. [Salop 77].

[240]  The argument was derived by means of a sequential search model, cf. [MacMinn 80].

[241]  For a definition of reservation values in sequential search processes see Section 4.2.2.1.

bargaining models sellers and buyers, who have different valuations for the good expressed by bid and ask prices respectively, seek to find trading partners to exchange goods. The resulting transaction price on the market then conveys all the relevant information available on the market.[242] In bargaining situations the value of an agent's private information, such as information other agents do not have, is usually positive and rises with additional information gathering.[243] The existence of private information, however, can result in disequilibrium, so that the 'market does not clear' and no unique equilibrium price prevails, or it can result in total market failure as in *Akerlof's market of lemons.*[244]

What we can conclude from the above discussion is:

- Economic markets are information processing systems with limited reliability, in the sense that the price system in real markets embodies some but not all information available in the market.[245]
- The informational content of the price system depends on the portion of market participants who are informed.[246]
- The information available and dispersed in a market situation has effects on the performance of the market as a whole.
- The outcome of an individual agent's market activities depends on the amount of information available and whether the information is private or public information.
- Information acquisition is resource and time consuming and therefore costly, restricting the activities of information procurement.[247]

Several theoretical and applicational directions in economic theory discuss and develop approaches to solve the problems of incomplete and asymmetric information in market situations. *Agency theory* examines the optimal incentives and contracts in market and other relationships between principals and agents.[248] *Organization theory* examines the optimal design of organizations to reduce transaction costs and implement particular contract forms.[249] Another source for a reduction of the costs of information acquisition is *information technology*[250] reducing communication costs and thus reducing the total costs of information procurement. *Intermediaries* involved in market transactions or in the process of

---

[242] Cf. [McAfee 87, p. 711 fp.].

[243] Cf. [Milgrom 82], [Engelbrecht-Wiggans 83], [Glosten 85].

[244] Cf. [Akerlof 70].

[245] Cf. [McAfee 87, p. 733]. 'Information available on the market' here encloses publicly available information as well as private information.

[246] Cf. [Grossmann 80, p. 394].

[247] Cf. [Hopf 83, p. 56]. Costs for information acquisition are part of the transaction costs, cf. Section 3.2.2.2.

[248] Cf. [Pratt 85], [Spremann 87], [Laux 90], and Section 2.3.1.4.

[249] Cf. [Williamson 86], [Simon 91].

[250] Cf. [Malone 87].

information acquisition can be a further opportunity to overcome the effects of asymmetric information.[251]

## 2.5 Information as an economic commodity

Information possessed by an agent in a market can either be used privately or disseminated for a price or without pull of compensation.[252] The basic life cycle phases and different utilization modes of information are depicted in Figure 5. The arrows indicate the possible stages information can pass through in its life cycle.

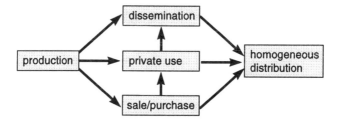

*Figure 5:*    *The utilization of information and the different stages information can pass through, cf. [Hirshleifer 73].*

The common properties of information, i.e., information can be stored, transferred, multiplied, and processed (Section 2.1.5), very generally describe information, however, the particular instances of information are multifarious. Information (information goods) can come along in form of stock market quotes, books, computer software, news messages, pictures and many other forms, having in common an easy *digitization*. To be (profitably) sold in a market, information must possess some requirements common to all economic commodities:[253]

- Commodities have to directly or indirectly satisfy a human need. More-over, economic commodities are limited and their production compete for scarce resources with other commodities.
- Economic agents have to be aware of the correlation of satisfaction of their needs and the properties of the good.
- The economic agents must have property rights on the commodities and the commodities must possess an exchange value.

The fact that information satisfies a human need has become obvious from the discussion of the value of information in Section 2.1.4. The demand for market information is a derived demand in the sense that economically acting agents

---

[251]  See Section 3.4.

[252]  Cf. [Hirshleifer 73, p. 32].

[253]  Cf. [Hopf 83, p. 69].

demand information for it makes better purchases or better decisions possible,[254] thus the economic agent is (privately) aware of the satisfaction of his/her needs through information. The acquisition of information and the costs of information production were discussed in Section 2.3.2. Hence, the property-rights aspects of information as an economic commodity remain to be discussed; this will be done in the following. The remainder of the section reviews markets for information, enterprises in the market for information, and strategies for the sale of information and the pricing of information goods.

## 2.5.1 Property rights and commodity-characteristics of information

The *property rights* on a good or resource allow the possessor to use the resource, to retain the returns, to alter the resource, and to alienate the resource.[255] Property rights on a good or resource are characteristics of *private goods*, and are the precondition for the good to be exchanged for a monetary compensation and to possess an exchange value. Goods or resources that do not possess the characteristics of *public goods* are described by two main attributes:[256]

- *Non-exclusivity*: no one can be excluded from utilization,
- *Non-rivalry*: the marginal costs for an additional user are zero.

Information can possess characteristics of public and of private goods,[257] depending on the type of information[258] and the stage of information processing.[259] Privately produced information, for example, technological information about a new material or production process, possesses the characteristics of private goods and thus can be traded on a market in exchange for a monetary compensation. On the other hand, market information can have characteristics of public goods, for example, the price system[260] which embodies market information to a certain extent can be used freely by any market participant, and an additional market par-

---

[254] Cf. Section 2.1.4, [Kihlstrom 74b, p. 100], and [Laux 91, p. 185 fp.] respectively. Menger [Menger 68, p. 7-31] distinguishes between *first-order commodities*, i.e., commodities that directly satisfy consumer needs and *higher-order commodities*, i.e., commodities that substitute or improve the consumption of first-order commodities, cf. [Hopf 83, p. 71-72]. Market information can be characterized as a *third-order commodity*, for it improves the satisfaction of consumers' needs, cf. [Hopf 83, p. 74].

[255] Cf. [Tietzel 81, p. 210]. Alchian describes property rights as 'socially recognized rights of action,' cf. [Alchian 72]. See [Ordelheide 93, p. 1842] for a brief overview about property rights approaches, and [Whinston 97, p. 175-212] for aspects of copyright protection for electronic products.

[256] Cf. [Andel 92, p. 383], [Musgrave 73, p. 52 fp.]. Musgrave characterizes these goods as *social goods*, cf. [Musgrave 73, p. 51 fp.].

[257] Cf. [Hopf 83, p. 80 fp.].

[258] Cf. Section 2.1.1.3 and Section 2.3.2.

[259] Cf. Figure 5.

[260] Cf. Section 2.4.1.

ticipant who uses the price system to make a purchase decision does not cause any further costs for the market.

Under particular circumstances, even public goods can attain characteristics of exclusive use, for example, if the amount of information is so large that the information processing capacity of the individual is exceeded extensively[261] or the costs for the dissemination of information are so high that a homogeneous distribution of information is impossible.[262] There exists a third class of so called *mixed goods* that possess only one of the two attributes of public goods.[263] For example, either the exclusion of unauthorized users causes prohibitively high costs or an additional user causes no considerable wear or negative effects on other users and therefore the marginal costs of utilization are zero.[264]

Information can possess the characteristics of all three types of goods, depending on the stages the information is in (Figure 5). Information tends to attain properties of private goods in production and sale, in the stage of dissemination information attains characteristics of *mixed goods*, and homogeneously distributed information can be characterized as a public good.[265] Only in case of private goods the possessor can exert full property rights on the good, i.e., the owner can use the good and retain the returns. However, this is not true in some cases, especially for information used in a market context.[266] For example, market participants who have acquired private information about the market reveal this information to other market participants through their behavior in the market,[267] or the use of technological information in the production of a new product induces competitors to imitate the product.[268] The conclusion is that for private and mixed goods the property rights are attenuated,[269] in the way that transaction costs for an entire enforcement of the property rights are prohibitively high. In this case these goods are subject to *externalities*,[270] i.e., the private production and use of the good by one agent has a bearing on other agents. In case of private production and public use of information the result may be an underproduction of the good because of

---

[261]  Cf. [Musgrave 73, p. 58 fp.].

[262]  Cf. [Hopf 83, p. 85].

[263]  Cf. [Andel 92, p. 385 fp.], [Musgrave 94, p. 63 fp.].

[264]  Cf. [Andel 92, p. 385-386].

[265]  Cf. [Hopf 83, p. 87].

[266]  Cf. [Hopf 83, p. 93].

[267]  Market participants following the decisions of other market participants can utilize the information inherent in the decisions of those agents. In capital markets these effects are known as *herd behavior*, cf. [Pfister 98, p. 1, 28], [Banerjee 92].

[268]  However, in case of technological information the utilization of the information by competitors is to a large extent restricted to the producer through patents, cf. [Hirshleifer 73, p. 33].

[269]  Cf. [Tietzel 81, p. 211 fp.].

[270]  Cf. [Hopf 83, p. 86], [Musgrave 94, p. 77 fp.].

free-rider problems.[271] Hence, the question about the optimal form of the provision of information arises. The conditions and consequences of a provision of information in markets will be discussed in the following section.

## 2.5.2 Markets for information

If the *exclusion principle* can be applied, goods can be exchanged between suppliers and consumers by utilization of the market mechanism.[272] Thus, information can be exchanged via markets whenever it is in the 'stage' of private information, i.e., technological or market information that is produced privately and hidden. The return from the production of information can be retained and internalized if it can be protected against unhindered disclosure by secrecy and if homogeneous dissemination is delayed. But, as was seen in the discussion of the credibility of information sources in Section 2.3.2, not all market participants have an incentive to honestly reveal or transmit their true information. Additionally, information cannot be inspected prior to purchase, because this would reveal the information at once. As a consequence, the quality of information received or purchased from other market participants is always subject to uncertainty.[273] This inherent uncertainty about the quality of information as an economic commodity gives rise to the question whether markets are able to provide the necessary amount and quality of information and can assure a homogeneous distribution.[274] Goods possessing these undesirable characteristics are designated as *merit goods*.[275] These are goods that in principle can be provided via markets, but a pure market provision would lead to a suboptimal allocation.[276]

On *markets for information* knowledge and information is produced, processed, distributed, mediated, and utilized.[277] Kuhlen distinguishes mainly between two markets for information: one is mainly driven by economic or commercial interests, the other is driven by scientific interests.[278] The properties described above and in the previous section indicate a need for *institutional regulations* if markets for information should accomplish the aims stated so far. Hopf distinguishes between market and non-market institutional regulations both aiming to ensure an efficient provision of information.[279] A non-market institution would be,

[271] Cf. [Bagnoli 89].
[272] Cf. [Musgrave 73, p. 52].
[273] Hopf puts it: 'information is a typical lemon good,' cf. [Hopf 83, p. 76, 92], which indicates a tendency to market failures in markets for information.
[274] Cf. [Hopf 83, p. 88].
[275] Cf. [Musgrave 73, p. 80 fp.], [Andel 92, p. 386 fp.].
[276] Cf. [Hopf 83, p. 89].
[277] Cf. [Kuhlen 95, p. xxiii].
[278] Cf. [Kuhlen 95, p. 3-23].
[279] Cf. [Hopf 83, p. 97].

for example, the governmental acquisition and dissemination of information. An institutional regulation connected to the market, on the other hand, has to ensure that the provision of information on the market suffices the requirements concerning the amount and the quality of information. This can, for example, be done by introducing additional, independent market participants, whose sole purpose and sole source of income is the production and dissemination of information. One main aspect and precondition for an efficient information provision by an independent provider of information and a working market for information is the consumer's trust in the information source. According to Section 2.3.3 several instruments can be applied to implement trust and credibility in the relationship of a third party information provider with information seekers; reputation is one instrument, warranties are another. These third party information providers, referred to as *information intermediaries*, will be examined comprehensively in Chapters 4 and 5.

The *market structure* of markets for information is not that of a perfectly competitive market,[280] it will be that of monopolistic competition among suppliers[281] or another form of imperfect competition.[282] The argument is based in two basic characteristics of information: the high amount of *fixed costs* in the production of information and the *inherent uncertainty* about the quality of information:[283] The processing of information and the production of new information requires some existing knowledge.[284] This ability to produce new information is the result of previous investments in human or other productive capital. The fixed costs involved herein implicitly build up a barrier to entry for potential competitors in the market. The possessor of this knowledge can exploit the knowledge to realize economies of scale with decreasing average costs through repeated utilization.[285] The result of the high fixed costs is a tendency towards monopolistic market structure in markets for information. The *reputation* of an information provider is an instrument that can be applied to overcome the problems resulting from the inherent uncertainty of information: To efficiently act in a market for information, the information provider has to invest in his/her credibility and reputation. These are usually the result of efficient past performance, and therefore can exclude new entrants from market participation as well, and can be a further reason for a tendency towards monopolization.

However, a perfect exclusion of competitors from the market for information seems unrealistic. For example, a new technology might provide new and more efficient possibilities for the production of information and may allow an innova-

---

[280] On perfectly competitive markets prices have to be taken as externally given by every market participant, cf. [Varian 93, p. 282].

[281] Cf. [Allen 90, p. 271].

[282] A monopoly or an oligopoly, cf. [Hopf 83, p. 179, 208].

[283] Cf. Section 2.2.3 and Section 2.3.2 respectively.

[284] Cf. Section 2.1.1.2 and 2.1.6.

[285] Cf. [Hopf 83, p. 191 fp.].

tive agent to enter the market. Therefore, the market structure will not be that of a pure monopoly. Markets for information can be anything between a pure monopoly and a fully competitive market.[286] For example, information markets can be monopolistically competitive with the reputation of an information provider as one form of product differentiation or an oligopoly with only a small number of information providers.

### 2.5.3 Enterprises in markets for information

A characterization of enterprises operating in markets for information is useful in order to cope with the many different kinds of real-life examples. In general, three types of enterprises operating in *markets for information* can be distinguished.[287] All of these have in common the aim to cover an outside need[288] for information. This distinction is based on the utilization of information by the particular enterprises:[289]

- *Information producers* use information as raw material.
- *Information middlemen* conceive information as a commodity.
- *Information service providers* perform information processing on behalf of their clients.

The aim of all these enterprises is to make profit by providing the information demanded by other economic agents, i.e., information seekers.[290] The main fields of activities of these businesses are the acquisition, the processing, and the dissemination of information.[291] The basic activities can be further characterized in order to describe the different enterprises operating in markets for information:[292]

- **Acquisition of information**:
  - *Type of information*: e.g., information about an industry, markets, firms, persons, products.
  - The *source of information*.
  - *Comprehensiveness of the information*: e.g., full text, abstracts, references.
  - *Topicality* of the information and the *dynamics* of the information.
  - *Intimacy of the information*.
  - *Necessity for explanation* of the information.

---

[286] Cf. [Hopf 83, p. 208 fp.].

[287] Cf. [Knoblich 85, p. 561], [Bessler 85, p. 18-27].

[288] The primary need for information occurs in a different enterprise, which is not the enterprise under consideration here, cf. [Knoblich 85, p. 562].

[289] Cf. [Bessler 85, p. 18-27].

[290] The principle functions: combination of production factors, independence, and making profit are according to Gutenberg the basic aspects that characterize enterprises, cf. [Gutenberg 83, p. 2 fp.].

[291] Cf. [Höring 80, p. 914].

[292] Cf. [Knoblich 85, p. 564-565].

- *Origin of the information*: either primary or secondary information sources. (Primary information sources are producers of information, secondary sources only provide derived information.)
- *Availability of the information source*: once, irregularly, or permanently.
- *Principles of information acquisition*: the activities of information acquisition can be induced by demand, or can be performed independent from demand.
- *Costs of information acquisition*: free of charge, for a non-monetary compensation, for a payment.
- **Information processing**:
  - *Quality*: the information can be processed analytically, i.e., larger amounts of information are disintegrated, or it can be processed synthetically, i.e., smaller amounts of information are bundled to a new information product.
  - *Quantity*: the information can be collected from many sources, or submitted to many recipients, or both.
  - *Spatial aspect*: the activities of information processing can have several different aspects concerning the acquisition and the distribution of information, i.e., no, low, medium, or high spatial compensation between supply and demand of information.
  - *Temporal aspect*: the emergence of new information and the demand for information differ in time, hence information processing activities are either induced by the demand market side or by the supply market side.
  - *Preparation of the information*: e.g., technical, in substance, graphical.
- **Dissemination of information**:
  - The *degree of personification* of the information.
  - *Target market of clients*: private or commercial.
  - The *mode of publication*: regularly or irregularly.
  - *Charging for dissemination*: duty-free, or dutiable.
  - *Restriction of dissemination*: the information is either freely available to anyone, restricted to authorized recipients or delivered to a private party of users.
  - *Form of information transmission*: online or off-line.
  - Type of the *carrier of information*.

According to this catalog the major characteristics of enterprises operating in the market for information can be described. An *Information broker*,[293] for example, searches in multiple secondary, mostly dutiable information sources for client-specific information, which is then bundled in order to offer a personalized information product with low dynamics and a high need for explanation. Information brokers restrict the dissemination of the information to their customers whom they charge for the information.[294]

---

[293]    For a detailed discussion of *information brokers* see Section 5.1.4.
[294]    Cf. [Bessler 85, p. 173].

### 2.5.4  Strategies for pricing and selling information goods

A pricing scheme based on marginal costs is not applicable for information, because the production of information causes high fixed costs, and an additional copy of one piece of information causes only vanishing costs compared to the first copy.[295] Pricing based on the valuation of the information by the consumer is more appropriate.[296] Different consumers have different valuations for one particular piece of information indicating a different *willingness to pay* for that information. This gives importance to techniques of *differential pricing* for information goods.

If the valuation of a particular information, i.e., the willingness to pay, is correlated with *observable characteristics* of consumers, such as membership in certain social or demographic groups, prices can be keyed to these observable characteristics.[297] Student discounts and senior citizen discounts are examples for this *third-degree price discrimination*.[298] Members of those groups with a lower willingness to pay can purchase the good, which is the same as the one sold to the rest of the market, for a reduced price.

In contrast, if the consumers' willingness to pay is not correlated with any observable characteristic, price discrimination tends to get the consumers to *self-select* the appropriate price-quality combination of the good. In a situation with different but unobservable willingness to pay among consumers there are three cases to distinguish.[299] The seller's optimal strategy would be a *perfect price discrimination*, in which the seller charges every single consumer the actual price he/she is willing to pay for the product offered.[300] The seller would then be able to collect the complete consumers' surplus. This first strategy is usually not applicable because of its potential for arbitrage and high costs for control and enforcement. A second strategy might be a *flat price*, which is either that low to encourage all consumers to purchase the good or that high that only consumers with a high willingness to pay will buy the good.[301] The third strategy for price discrimination is a *versioning* of the goods offered. In this case a seller offers at least two versions of the good,[302] i.e., *price-quality combinations (p, x)* where 'quality' refers to some

[295]  Cf. [Hopf 83, p. 202 fp.].
[296]  Cf. [Hopf 83, p. 206], [Varian 95], [Varian 97a], [Varian 97b].
[297]  Cf. [Varian 95], [Varian 97b].
[298]  *Third-degree price discrimination* means that different purchasers are charged different prices, but each purchaser pays a constant amount for each unit of the good bought, cf. [Varian 89, p. 600 fp.].
[299]  Cf. [Varian 89, p. 599], [Varian 97b].
[300]  *Perfect price discrimination* occurs in a situation in which the seller makes a single take-it-or-leave-it offer to each consumer, cf. [Varian 89, p. 601].
[301]  Here, we simply assumed that there are only two groups of consumers, one with a high and another with a low willingness to pay. In real-life settings, however, there is usually a continuum of the willingness to pay, cf. Section 4.3.1.2.
[302]  Cf. [Varian 97b].

attribute or property of the good valued by consumers. One version $(p^h, x^h)$ is dedicated to consumers with a high willingness to pay and one $(p^l, x^l)$ is for those with a low willingness to pay.[303] The relative advantage of a particular strategy and therefore the choice of a strategy for a certain market depends on the distribution of willingness to pay in the population of consumers, the costs of enforcement, and the seller's potential return of a certain strategy.[304] Social surplus is always increased by versioning, if only consumers with a high willingness to pay were served under flat pricing and the low end of the market was not served at all.[305]

For information goods the *novelty* or *delay* and the *resolution* are candidates for quality attributes[306] that can be the basis of different versions of a good. For stock market quotes, as one example of an information good, professional users like stock brokers are willing to pay more for real-time stock market quotes than for the same information slightly delayed. The delayed information, however, is still appropriate for private investors and can be given away at a discount or even free of charge. The *resolution* of information, for example, the noise inherent in signals containing the information[307] or the functionality and the computational precision or speed of a software[308] can be used as another source of product differentiation.

*Bundling* of goods can be further strategy to sell goods to a market with heterogeneous willingness to pay.[309] The bundling of several pieces of information to new information goods can reduce the heterogeneity of the consumers' willingness to pay, because a low willingness to pay for one piece of the bundled good might coincide with a high willingness to pay for another piece, resulting in an increased willingness to pay for the new, bundled product.

The quality of information sold by an information provider is also of importance if the utilization of the information is subject to *external effects*,[310] for example, for market information purchased by competing traders in securities markets. If information is sold as is, the information would be revealed through informed traders' behavior in the market. One way to sell information under these circumstances is a slight differentiation of the good by addition of some noise to the information.[311]

Another way might be the *indirect selling* of the information through a service offered by the provider of the information, for example, a provider of information

---

[303]  It is $p^l < p^h$ and $x^l < x^h$.
[304]  Cf. [Varian 97b, p. 8].
[305]  Cf. [Varian 97b, p. 9].
[306]  Cf. Section 2.1.5.
[307]  Cf. [Admati 86].
[308]  Cf. [Varian 97b, p. 7].
[309]  Cf. [Varian 89, p. 626 fp.], [Varian 95], [Bakos 96], [Bakos 97a].
[310]  Cf. [Admati 86].
[311]  Cf. [Crawford 82], [Admati 86].

in a securities market can provide the service of portfolio management to his/her clients instead of selling the information directly.[312]

## 2.5.5 The carrier of information

Since information itself is an immaterial good[313] the choice of a strategy to sell information always includes the choice of the *carrier of information* for transfer between producer and consumer.[314] In case of time-dependent information the transfer will be done through channels like telecommunication networks, whereas, if the amount of information to be transferred is very high and time dependence is not that important, physical media as CD-ROMs will be utilized. These media derive most of their value from the information they contain.[315] However, with further development of high-bandwidth communication networks this distinction of the amount and the time-dependence of information becomes less relevant, because as communication costs decline the transfer of information is further shifted to telecommunication networks.[316]

---

[312] Cf. [Admati 90].

[313] Cf. [Bode 97, p. 452] and Section 2.1.5.

[314] Cf. [Schwuchow 97, p. 776].

[315] Cf. [Alter 96, p. 294-295].

[316] Cf. [Zahedi 96, p. 2088], for telecommunication and computer networks see [Alter 96, p. 470-485], [Tanenbaum 96].

# 3 Intermediation

In economic systems we can find institutions that mediate between buyers and sellers. Different fields of economic theory, especially trade and finance, are focusing slightly different aspects of these *intermediaries*, but a common characteristic of intermediation is buying and selling in a market with the aim of making profit, first defined by Stewart in 1770.[317] Intermediation introduces a further step of transactions in the value chain and therewith causes additional transaction costs. So intermediation can only be advantageous if the increase of value added through intermediation overcompensates the transaction costs additionally incurred.[318]

However, the aspect of intermediation is not limited to the activity of buying and selling in the same market - intermediaries provide matching services and, in addition, a multitude of value-adding services closely connected to their basic activities. Intermediaries therewith fulfill functions that can overcome market imperfections and increase market efficiency; these are the subject of the present chapter. In Section 3.1 the basic functions and roles of intermediaries especially in trade and in financial markets will be introduced. Section 3.2 reviews theoretic concepts of intermediation and approaches to a justification for the existence of intermediaries, the focus is on the reduction of transaction costs. Questions of contract forms and the income of intermediaries are discussed in Section 3.3. The effects of intermediation on markets and the market microstructure of markets for intermediary services are reviewed in Sections 3.4 and 3.5 respectively.

## 3.1 Basic concepts and functions of intermediaries

'In an economy based on the division of labor, trade has the task to compensate spatial, temporal, quantitative, and qualitative tensions between processes of production and consumption.'[319] This very broad definition of the tasks of trade given by Barth [Barth 96] includes any exchange of goods and services, and also covers firms selling their goods directly to consumers. In a more differentiated view there exist two theoretic conceptions of intermediation.[320] Intermediaries can either be

---

[317] Cf. [Stewart 1770], citation according to [Yanelle 89b, p. 1].

[318] Cf. [Hellwig 88].

[319] Citation translated from [Barth 96, p. 1].

[320] Cf. [Winkler 89].

treated as ordinary producing firms, located somewhere in the production chain and using a good together with other inputs to produce a 'similar but different good.'[321]

In the second basic view of intermediation intermediaries are pure *middlemen*[322] buying and selling the *same good*. Besides trade, intermediary services play an important role in financial markets.[323] Financial intermediaries are mainly concerned with the exchange of capital instead of physical goods. Nevertheless, from an abstract point of view the basic concepts of intermediation are applicable to intermediaries either in capital markets or in markets for physical goods. A third domain of intermediaries is the mediation and processing of information;[324] information intermediaries will be analyzed separately (Chapters 4 and 5).

### 3.1.1 Intermediaries in trade

In general, there are two possibilities of defining an intermediary: the first is a definition focusing the functions performed by the intermediary, the second focuses the roles undertaken by the intermediary. Oberparleitner[325] stated six functions of intermediaries in trade listed in Table 1.

*Table 1:*      *Functions performed by an intermediary in trade, [Oberparleitner 30] according to [Gümbel 85, p. 96].*

| intermediary function | intermediary activity |
|---|---|
| spatial function | Location of partners for the exchange of goods |
| temporal function | Compensation of temporal differences between demand and supply of goods |
| quantitative function | Augmentation or reduction of the quantities in contracts |
| qualitative function | • Classification of goods<br>• Arranging an assortment of goods |
| credit function | Compensation of temporal differences between delivery and payment by arranging credits |
| contact and advertising function | • Increase of the intermediary's economic power<br>• Acquisition of trading partners for multiple activities |

---

[321] The intermediary's inputs are transformed so that consumers' preferences are fulfilled, cf. [Gurley 60].

[322] Cf. [Rubinstein 87].

[323] Cf. [Spulber 96a].

[324] Cf. [Spulber 96a, p. 136 fp.].

[325] Citation of [Oberparleitner 30] taken from [Gümbel 85, p. 96].

Common to all these functions is the *bridging of incompatibilities* between the two market sides exchanging goods. Rubinstein[326] describes these incompatibilities as *'trade frictions that give rise to the function of intermediation'*. For example, a retailer bridges spatial, temporal, quantitative, and qualitative incompatibilities between the two market sides.[327] These functions are the basis of the scientific approach in the functional theory of trade.[328]

*Table 2:    Roles of an intermediary in trade, according to [Gümbel 85, p. 72-76].*

| intermediary role | intermediary activity | description |
|---|---|---|
| **assortment builder** | Selection of goods and combination to an assortment | The intermediary weighs out the interests of producers, who only want their products in the intermediary's assortment, and consumers, who want an assortment as broad as possible. |
| **organizer** | Coordination of the different domains of the assortment and assignment of resources to these domains | The intermediary assigns personal, capital, and room for the exhibition to the parts of the assortment. |
| **transformer of quanta** | Transformation of quantities in supply and demand | The transformation of quantities is fundamental for the existence of intermediaries, cf. Section 3.2.3.1. |
| **contractor** | Contracting with suppliers and consumers | Independent intermediaries contract with sellers, acquire proprietary rights on the goods traded, and sell the goods to buyers. |

The second possibility to characterize intermediaries is by means of the intermediary's roles in the economy or in the value chain. Gümbel[329] states four roles an intermediary can have in trade (Table 2). One important aspect of intermediation indicated by the roles of intermediaries in Table 2 is their (economic and legal) independence. Gümbel[330] states the *intermediary's independence* as the *foundation of efficiency increasing effects from intermediation*. The intermediary's independence implies that intermediaries perform their activities with the aim of making

---

[326]    Cf. [Rubinstein 87, p. 581].
[327]    Cf. [Meyer 63], [Falk 92, p. 45].
[328]    Cf. [Gümbel 85, p. 96].
[329]    Cf. [Gümbel 85, p. 72-76].
[330]    Cf. [Gümbel 85, p. 50, 124 fp., 143, 245].

profit. The profit maximizing aim is the main incentive for intermediaries to enter the market and to perform the functions stated above.[331]

### 3.1.2 Intermediaries in financial markets

Intermediaries in financial markets can balance the divergence of incoming and outgoing payments of market participants by providing services of *investment* and *financing*.[332] Functions performed by financial intermediaries refer to the characteristics of capital assets, but have the aim of *bridging the incompatibilities* between the two sides of the market as well.

In perfect markets investors and borrowers would be able to contract directly, i.e., without an intermediary. However, real-life markets are subject to imperfections like informational asymmetries[333] giving rise to existence of financial intermediaries.[334] Under these circumstances, gathering, processing, and dissemination of information about borrowers in capital markets is a central function of financial intermediaries.[335] Hence, the financial intermediary is an information processing system[336] who indirectly[337] sells information by providing (transformational) services in capital markets to both market sides. The *transformational functions* (Table 3) performed by a financial intermediary alter the attributes of the financial asset through contracts made with borrowers and lenders (*qualitative asset transformation: QAT*[338]).

Besides qualitative asset transformation, financial intermediaries can provide *brokerage services*, i.e., matching of lenders and borrowers of capital.[339] A comparison of the main types of financial intermediaries and the functions performed is given in Table 4.

---

[331] Cf. [Baligh 67, p. 128], [Yanelle 89b, p. 1], [Gümbel 85, p. 13-15, 25 fp.].
[332] Cf. [Gerke 95].
[333] Cf. Section 2.3.1.3.
[334] Cf. [Leland 77].
[335] Cf. [Bhattacharya/Thakor 93, p. 38 fp.]. Diamond, for example, analyses monitoring of borrowers as an informational function of financial intermediaries, cf. [Diamond 84], [Diamond 91].
[336] Cf. Section 2.1.6.
[337] Cf. Section 2.5.4.
[338] Cf. [Bhattacharya/Thakor 93].
[339] Cf. [Bhattacharya/Thakor 93, p. 3], [Coym 95].

*Table 3:      Transformational services of financial intermediaries, according to [Gerke 95, p. 732-733].*

| transformation of ... | intermediary activity |
|---|---|
| **lot size** | Aggregation of small size investment contracts to large size credit contracts |
| **risk** | Balance of diverging attitudes towards risk by means of:<br>• rating of credit risks and credit rationing<br>• diversification of risk<br>• allocation of risk through direct financing and securities<br>• liability of own capital resources |
| **term** | Transformation of short term invested capital into long term credits |
| **information** | Monitoring and control of borrowers |

*Table 4:      Functions performed by financial intermediaries, according to [Bhatta-charya/ Thakor 93].*

| intermediary function | intermediary activity |
|---|---|
| **Brokerage** | |
| **matching** | Bringing together providers and users of capital without changing the nature of the asset |
| **transacting** | Managing the transaction |
| **QAT: qualitative asset transformation** | |
| **credit allocation** | Screening creditworthiness of borrowers |
| **liquidity transformation** | Funding of illiquid assets with liquid liabilities |
| **maturity transformation** | Financing assets with liabilities of shorter maturity |

### 3.1.3  Concluding definition of intermediation

Viewed in detail, intermediation in trade and in financial markets are very different businesses, but from an abstract point of view the basic concepts of intermediation resemble strongly for intermediaries in both types of markets. Common to conceptions of intermediation is the *existence of market imperfections*[340] and the *bridging the incompatibilities* between the two market sides involved in the exchange of objects, i.e., goods or capital, the *independence*, and the *profit maximizing aim*. Intermediaries can be introduced whenever transactions have to be coordinated between a large number of independent economic agents, cf. Section 3.2.2.3, hence, intermediation is not restricted to a market environment. The transformation

---

[340]   Cf. [Winkler 89, p. 300].

of attributes of the products or services exchanged is the intermediary's activity to add value to a pure mediation of contacts.[341] The following concluding definition of intermediaries and intermediation summarizes the basic aspects stated so far:

*Definition 2:*     *An intermediary is an independent, profit-maximizing economic agent mediating between two market sides in presence of market imperfections.*

*Intermediation is the bridging the incompatibilities between the two (market) sides involved in a transaction by transformation of output attributes of the supply market side to appropriate input attributes of the demand market side.*

Inputs and outputs mentioned in the definition can be physical goods, capital, services, messages or information. The definition leaves open whether the intermediary buys and sells objects at his/her own risk or acts as a pure coordinator in the market.[342] These different forms of intermediary contracts will be discussed in Section 3.2.4.

## 3.2 Justification of intermediaries

The present section briefly introduces the main theoretic approaches to intermediation. Two basic approaches given by Ricardo and Edgeworth, that can be extended to a justification of intermediaries, are described in Section 3.2.1. Section 3.2.2 reviews the basics of the theory of transactions and Section 3.2.3 discusses the reduction of transaction costs through intermediation.

### 3.2.1 Comparative advantages from the exchange of goods and services

A very basic theoretic approach to intermediation explains and justifies the existence of trade and therewith the existence and income of intermediaries in trade by savings of resources on a level of the whole national economy.[343] One argument is given by *Ricardo*, who introduced the *comparative advantages in costs*, the other by Edgeworth, concerning advantages in utility.

Ricardo[344] analyzed two countries (A and B) specialized on the production of two different goods ($\alpha$ and $\beta$ respectively). The countries can barter the goods at a

---

[341]  Cf. [Spulber 96a, p. 136].

[342]  Cf. [Baligh 67, p. 118 fp., 123 fp.].

[343]  Cf. [Gümbel 85, p. 77].

[344]  Cf. [Ricardo 1817] according to [Gümbel 85, p. 77 fp.]

certain rate of exchange. The production of the good $\alpha$ causes lower costs for country A than for country B, which is in turn specialized on the production of good ß. If both countries aim to consume both goods, it is advantageous for the two countries to specialize on the production of one good and exchange an excess in production of the good for the other good not produced. In a more detailed analysis several aspects of the exchange process, like the amount of the good exchanged or the costs of the transaction, were taken into account.[345] These refinements of the model do not alter the qualitative results of the simplified argumentation stated so far, as long as the costs of the exchange process do not use up the cost advantages. Hence, the tendency to a greater specialization is limited by the accompanying increase in coordination costs.[346] One result is that it can be advantageous to introduce an intermediary, i.e., a third party specialized to exploit economies of scale in the process of exchange, if the costs of direct transactions between the trading partners are significantly high.[347]

The second justification is based on an argument given by *Edgeworth*,[348] who showed that without an increase in the total stock of goods the pure exchange of goods between two agents (A and B) can achieve an increase in the utility of at least one of the agents without making the other worse off. This argument is simply that of *Pareto efficiency*[349] of the situation after the exchange. In an isolated exchange with only two trading partners an opposite valuation of the good to be exchanged must exist, i.e., the problem of the *double coincidence of wants*.[350] Whereas in a market with multiple agents the probability of an exchange is increased because the probability for the existence of opposite valuations is higher. However, finding a trading partner causes (search) costs, that can be reduced by the introduction of an intermediary coordinating the process of exchange between the traders in the market.

In general, the introduction of intermediaries in the exchange process would be inefficient in markets without imperfections like information asymmetries or search costs.[351] So one main justification for the existence of intermediaries in the process of exchange is the existence of market imperfections that can be overcome by these third-party agents.[352] A further reason for the efficiency of intermediaries in the exchange process is the reduction of transaction costs and the necessity of asset specific investments as a precondition for the execution of transactions (cf. Section 3.2.3).

---

[345]  Cf. [Gümbel 85, p. 79 fp.].
[346]  Cf. [Picot 96, p. 24].
[347]  Cf. Section 3.2.3.
[348]  Cf. [Edgeworth 1881] according to [Gümbel 85, p. 87 fp.].
[349]  Cf. [Varian 93, p. 15 fp.].
[350]  Cf. [Spulber 96a, p. 143].
[351]  Cf. Section 2.4.
[352]  Cf. [Gümbel 85, p. 90, 92].

### 3.2.2 Excursion: the theory of transactions

The theory of intermediation is strongly influenced by the *theory of transactions* and by *transaction cost theory*.[353] Intermediaries are specialists in performing transactions, and the source of their efficiency is a reduction in the costs of these transactions compared to transactions without an intermediary.[354] The present section briefly summarizes basic elements of the theory of transactions and transaction cost theory.

#### 3.2.2.1 Transactions

The term *transaction* appears in many different circumstances: Computer science defines a transaction as a composition of non-empty, atomic steps to an indivisible entirety.[355] In information systems transactions are business events that generate or modify data stored in an information system.[356] Finance describes transactions as larger financial business events, for example, borrowing or the increase of capital;[357] in stock markets transactions are an exchange of ownership titles.[358] In an economic context, transactions occur *when a good or service is transferred across a technologically-separable interface, and one stage of processing or assembly activity terminates and another begins.*[359] Examples for commercial or bargaining transactions[360] are the exchange of goods, factors of production, debt claims, payments or other economically relevant factors between two economic agents.[361] A transaction fulfills two main functions:[362]

- *Exchange function*: The redistribution of goods or services.
- *Coordination function*: The coordination of the activities of economic agents.

The major aim of transactions is the coordination and execution of exchange processes, therefore, transactions implicitly involve information transfer and information processing. Dimensions that can be used to describe transactions are uncertainty, the frequency with which transactions recur, and the degree to which invest-

---

[353] Cf. [Coase 37], [Picot 82], [Picot 86], [Williamson 86], [Picot 90a], [Ordelheide 93, p. 1843].

[354] The statement was mainly based on intermediaries in trade, cf. [Gümbel 85, p. 145].

[355] Cf. [Kratzer 97, p. 412].

[356] Cf. [Alter 96, p. 221].

[357] Cf. [Gebauer 96, p. 4].

[358] Cf. [Demsetz 68, p. 35].

[359] Cf. [Williamson 86, p. 139].

[360] Commons distinguishes three types of transactions: *bargaining* transactions, *managerial* transactions, and *rationing* transactions, cf. [Commons 34/90, p. 58 fp.]. In the context of the present discussion only bargaining transactions are of importance.

[361] Cf. [Hübl 92, p. 53], [Gebauer 96, p. 4].

[362] Cf. [Gebauer 96, p. 9].

ments are idiosyncratic, i.e., the specificity of the transaction.[363] Disregarding the dimension of uncertainty, commercial transactions can be characterized according to Table 5; additionally, the table states typical examples for the particular cases.

*Table 5:*     *Characterization of commercial transactions according to frequency and investment characteristics, according to [Williamson 86, p. 112].*

| | | investment characteristics of the transaction | | |
|---|---|---|---|---|
| | | non-specific | mixed | idiosyncratic |
| frequency of the transaction | occasional | purchasing standard equipment | purchasing customized equipment | constructing a plant |
| | recurrent | purchasing standard material | purchasing customized material | site-specific transfer of intermediate product across successive stages |

### 3.2.2.2  Transaction phases and transaction cost theory

According to Coase the *transaction costs* involved in transactions on markets are the price to be paid for using the *price mechanism* in a market system.[364] Arrow[365] characterized transaction costs as the '*costs of running the economic system.*' A further study of transaction costs differentiates between *internal transaction costs*, arising from planning and control within companies or more generally in hierarchies, and *external transaction costs*, incurred in transactions on markets with other independent economic agents.[366] In a general conception of transactions, not restricted to transactions on markets, several successive phases are distinguished:[367]

- *Information phase*: Economic agents gather information about potential partners for the transaction, the prices and quality offered, and the particular terms of the transaction.
- *Negotiation phase*: The conditions of the transaction and terms of the contract are negotiated between the two (or more) potential partners of the transaction found in the information phase. Transaction partners have to agree about the objects exchanged, the amount, the compensation, and the terms of the contract.[368]

---

[363]  Cf. [Williamson 86, p. 111].
[364]  Cf. [Coase 37] cited according to [Bössmann 81, p. 668].
[365]  Cf. [Arrow 69, p. 48] cited in [Williamson 86, p. 176].
[366]  Cf. [Wegehenkel 81] according to [Gümbel 85, p. 149, 151 fp.].
[367]  Cf. [Williamson 85, p. 20 fp.].
[368]  Cf. [Meyer 90, p. 151 fp.].

- *Execution and controlling phase*: The exchange of the objects (goods or services and payments) is performed physically and legally binding according to the terms of the transaction that resulted from the negotiation phase. The execution of the transaction is controlled whether it is in accordance with the terms of the contract.

The *costs of a transaction*[369] include all costs occurring in the three phases of the transaction, i.e., costs for the acquisition of information (*information* or *search costs* and costs for *contacts* between buyers and sellers[370]), costs for negotiations between buyers and sellers (*negotiation costs*[371]), costs for the execution of the transaction (*costs of execution*[372]), and the costs for monitoring and controlling the transaction (*controlling costs*[373]).

The amount of the transaction costs is dependent on several influences. The major determinants of the transaction costs are:[374]

- *specificity of the transaction,*
- *frequency of the transaction,*
- *uncertainty of the environment,*
- *technological limitations,*
- *legal framework.*

Transaction costs are further dependent on asset specific investments which are a precondition for the execution of the transaction by an economic agent.[375] These specific investments can be characterized in the following way:

- *Site specificity*: Investments in geographical sites.
- *Physical specificity*: Investments in machines, manufacturing plants, technologies.
- *Human asset specificity*: Investments in human capital like education, know-how, experiences.
- *Dedicated asset specificity*: Investments necessary for a transaction with a particular customer.
- *Brand name capital*: Investments in brand name as a source of product differentiation.

---

[369] Economics literature gives a multitude of distinctions of transaction costs, which name the different types of costs differently.

[370] Cf. Section 2.2.3, Section 4.2, and [Wigand 97, p. 269].

[371] These include the costs of the time required for the negotiation, cf. [Williamson 86. p. 96]. A detailed discussion of the theoretic approach to negotiations is given by [Schöpe 85].

[372] The costs of the execution include the costs of transport and the costs for the assurance of the exchange process.

[373] Cf. [Kiener 90, p. 2].

[374] Cf. [Picot 82, p. 271].

[375] Cf. [Williamson 84, p. 202 fp.], [Williamson 89, p. 143], [Gebauer 96, p. 74 fp.].

In most cases these investments only pay off if the transaction is performed repeatedly. One consequence can be a barrier to entry for new market participants.[376] The need for asset specific investments in situations that allow only a low volume of the transaction (or only small numbers of transactions) for the single economic agent can be one reason for the existence of intermediaries specialized on the execution of these transactions. Intermediaries can incur the risk of the asset specific investment and divide the costs among all market participants who perform transactions through the intermediary.

### 3.2.2.3 The coordination function of transactions

Coordination is a target-oriented reconciliation of interdependent parts of a larger system,[377] a very broad conception defines coordination as 'managing dependencies between activities.'[378] Transactions are in two ways connected with coordination processes:[379] (a) Transactions that reconcile the activities of the elements of a larger system are in itself a form of coordination of the system, and (b) the preparation, execution, and completion of transactions involve coordination processes. The main problem in coordination processes is an asymmetric distribution of information between economic agents who participate a transaction. A major source of transaction costs is therefore expenditures necessary for information acquisition.[380]

Coordination processes are dependent on the environment of the system and the elements of the system to be coordinated. The selection of a particular coordination mechanism can be based on Williamson's *organizational failure framework*.[381] The concept includes human and environmental factors, and the transaction atmosphere as essential determinants for the choice of an optimal coordination mechanism. Price mechanisms become too transaction costs intense in situations that are characterized by opportunism and bounded rationality of the transaction partners, relations with a high degree of uncertainty, and information asymmetries. In such cases organizational forms guaranteeing a more intense integration of transaction partners, i.e., hierarchical coordination forms, have to be implemented in order to limit transaction costs.[382] In general, the optimal form of coordination is determined by a number of factors:[383]

---

[376] Cf. [Williamson 86, p. 210].
[377] Cf. [Gebauer 96, p. 21].
[378] Cf. [Malone 94, p. 90].
[379] Cf. [Gebauer 96, p. 29].
[380] Cf. Section 2.4.2 and [Hayek 45].
[381] Cf. [Williamson 91], [Picot 96, p. 42 fp.], [Wigand 97, p. 37 fp.].
[382] Cf. [Wigand 97, p. 37-38].
[383] Cf. [Coase 93], [Hayek 45, p. 519 fp.], and [Williamson 85, p. 8] according to [Gebauer 96, p. 70-71].

- *Uncertainty* about the environment.
- Because of incomplete information about the future only *incomplete contracts* between transaction partners can be signed.
- *Opportunistic behavior* of transaction partners.
- *Technologies* to support or execute transactions.
- Individuals' *bounded rationality*, i.e., the limited capacity for information processing.
- *Idiosyncratic knowledge* and abilities of individuals.

In principle, three different types of coordination and thus of transactions can be distinguished: The coordination of agents over *markets*, *hierarchical coordination* within companies or organizations, and hybrid forms of the former two forms called *networks*.[384] Two major characteristics of transactions can be selected to describe the most efficient form of coordination for a particular task: the specificity of the task and the complexity of the description or the variability of the task itself.[385] Typical forms of coordination depending on these two parameters are displayed in Figure 6.

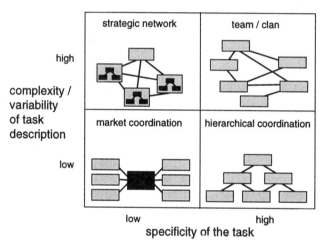

Figure 6:     Typical forms of coordination for different characteristics of the task, according to [Picot 96, p. 167].

The resources necessary for coordination in these different settings depend to a large extent on the *number of agents* involved in the system. In case of decentralized coordination, i.e., every agent contacts every other agent in the system, the resources[386] necessary for coordination increase with the number of agents. In such

---

[384] Cf. [Malone 87a, p. 485], [Gebauer 96, p. 34 fp.].
[385] Cf. [Malone 87, p. 487], [Picot 91, p. 292], [Picot 94b, p. 109-111], [Picot 94a, p. 552].
[386] The resources involved in coordination cannot be employed for the actual productive task.

cases the investment in information systems or in additional system elements, for example, intermediaries specialized on the coordination of these systems, can reduce the total expenses for coordination. The standardization[387] of the process interfaces of all partners involved in the transaction is a necessary precondition for the efficiency of the whole system.[388] An example of a coordination form with a high demand for a coordinating intermediary is the model of a *dynamic network*.[389] In this model independent agents, for example, engineers, producers, suppliers, and distributors, each specialized on particular tasks like R&D, production, financing, and marketing, are coordinated by a third party[390] (Figure 7).

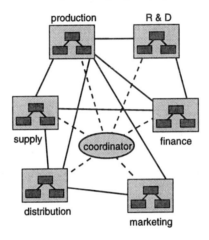

*Figure 7:*     *Example of a dynamic network, imitation of [Szyperski 93, p. 194].*

### 3.2.3  Reduction of transaction costs through intermediation

Intermediaries in trade are *specialists in the reduction of transaction costs*[391] occurring in the exchange of physical goods. The occurrence of high transaction costs is a main prerequisite for the existence and the justification of intermediaries.[392] Therefore, the gains of intermediaries have to be interpreted as *savings of economic resources* resulting from the coordination of economic agents.[393] The

---

[387]  Standardization is the unification of system elements aiming at a simplification of the interaction of at least two elements of the system, cf. [Buxmann 96, p. 10].
[388]  Cf. [Picot 96, p. 169].
[389]  Cf. [Miles 86]. In the terms of Figure 6 a *dynamic network* is strategic network.
[390]  Cf. [Miles 86, p. 64 fp.], [Szyperski 93].
[391]  Cf. [Gümbel 85, p. 168], [Wigand 97, p. 270].
[392]  Cf. [Gümbel 85, p. 145, 147-148].
[393]  Cf. [Gümbel 85, p. 149]. See Section 3.1 for examples.

basic discussion[394] of intermediary efficiency is twofold: a first justification focuses the exploitation of *structural or institutional circumstances* of transactions by intermediaries, the second elaborates the active execution of intermediary functions to bridge market incompatibilities as a *behavioral* or *functional source* of intermediary efficiency.[395]

### 3.2.3.1 Structural sources of intermediary efficiency

Gümbel[396] categorizes three effects that isolate and formalize structural principles of transactions; these can be exploited by intermediaries to realize cost reductions. The first effect is based upon the *volume of a transaction*. If the marginal costs per quantity are decreasing with an increase of the volume of the transaction, it is advantageous to combine several smaller transactions or activities to a single larger one. In the theory of trade the warehouse-location approach argues that the existence of transit stores is advantageous because of decreasing marginal-transport costs for increasing load volumes.[397] Intermediaries are introduced in this scenario to coordinate the participating agents, to operate the transit stores, and perform the transport, thus reducing the *costs for the execution* of the transaction.

A second effect focusing *the frequency of transactions* is taken from a discussion of inventory management.[398] The main issue of this approach is the relation between the total volume $Q$ of the transaction, the frequency $f$, and the lot size $q$ of the transaction: $Q = f \cdot q$. If frequency dependent costs $c_f$ and volume dependent costs $c_q$ of the transaction exist, the total costs of the transaction are $C_{total} = (c_f f + c_q q)$ with $Q = f \cdot q = constant$. The minimization of these total transaction costs implies a trade-off between the two types of costs. This can be a source of coordination problems in the relationship between opposite market sides or different stages of a value chain. The coordination of these relationships can be performed more efficiently by a mediating third party if the costs for the installation and operation

---

[394] Descriptive oriented approaches to intermediation in trade discuss decision oriented aspects of intermediation, e.g., the evaluation of alternatives or allocation problems, cf. [Gümbel 85, p. 93]. The main approaches are the following (cf. [Gümbel 85, p. 93-103]): the activity-analytical approach [Oberparleitner 1918], the theory of regrouping of goods [Schäfer 43], the theory of chains in trade [Seyffert 51], the gatekeeper-theory [Hansen 76], theory of expansion threshold [Kotler 67].

[395] Gümbel distinguishes between advantages in efficiency that arise from logical or scientific principles, which are independent from the existence of intermediaries [Gümbel 85, p. 144], and advantages that can only arise from the activities performed by intermediaries, i.e., the execution of intermediary functions and the resulting reduction of coordination and transaction costs [Gümbel 85, p. 145 fp., 168 fp.].

[396] Cf. [Gümbel 85, p. 104 fp.]

[397] Cf. [Bartels 78, p. 70] and [Gümbel 85, p. 106-108].

[398] Cf. [Gümbel 82, p. 258-274] and [Gümbel 85, p. 108-110]. For a further discussion of *inventory management* see [Lambert 82, p. 274 fp.].

of this intermediary service are smaller than would be the sum of costs for all trading partners to install a mechanism for coordination without the intermediary.[399]

The third source of cost reductions from intermediation, known as the *Baligh-Richartz effect*,[400] examines the *number of contacts* necessary between potential trading partners.[401] The argument is that the existence of an intermediary reduces the number of contacts necessary between all suppliers and all consumers in a market if the intermediary holds relationships to all market participants. The situation is best illustrated by a very simple picture (Figure 8). In case of direct contacts between the $m$ suppliers and the $n$ consumers $(nm)$ contacts are necessary in the whole system. If an intermediary is introduced in the system, the number of contacts necessary is reduced to $(n+m)$. Assuming that the costs $C_c$ of a single contact between suppliers and consumers equal the costs for contacts between suppliers and the intermediary, and the intermediary and consumers, one can conclude that the introduction of an intermediary into the system reduces the sum of all contact costs if $(n\,m)>(n+m)$. This is the case for $n,m>2$, i.e., whenever more than two agents participate on each side of the market.

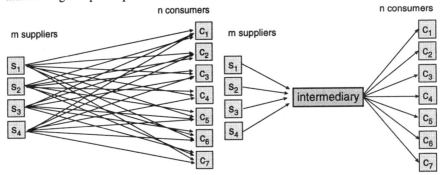

*Figure 8:*    *The reduction of necessary contacts through intermediation (Baligh-Richartz effect), cf. [Gümbel 85, p. 112].*

With a growing number of market participants ($n$ and $m$)[402] a system with multiple levels of intermediaries, i.e., a vertical hierarchy of intermediaries, can become advantageous.[403] The optimal number of intermediary levels and the optimal number of intermediaries on each level is determined by the number of suppliers and consumers, and by the distribution of gains from intermediation among

---

[399]    Cf. [Gümbel 85, p. 110].

[400]    Cf. [Maas 80, p. 207], [Gümbel 85, p. 111].

[401]    Cf. [Baligh 67, p. 19 fp., 93 fp., 113].

[402]    Equal contact costs for direct contacts as well as for mediated contacts between suppliers and consumers are assumed.

[403]    Cf. [Gümbel 85, p. 99, 115 fp.].

preceding and following market sides.[404] As a result of this structural effect, several types of distribution channels can occur[405] (Figure 9).

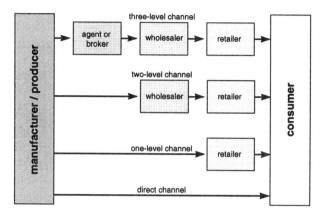

*Figure 9:*    *Typical structures of distribution channels, cf. [Lambert 82, p. 6].*

The exploitation of these structural principles by intermediaries requires *asset specific investments* (cf. Section 3.2.2.2), for example, investments in special competencies, facilities, equipment, and reputation. One example is the installation of *supplier and client networks*, as it is assumed in the Baligh-Richartz effect. The arrangement of these networks is a costly investment and a precondition for intermediary activities and efficiency.[406] The possession and control of an installed network, however, is a competitive advantage making the intermediary a specialized information center.[407] The larger the networks are the higher is the probability for successful matches through the intermediary; the probability for successful matches can be interpreted as the *intermediary's service quality.*[408]

In general, if a transaction is either performed only rarely or the transaction is not a core competency of the business, the specific investment represents an unde‐sirable[409] factor of fixed costs that can be avoided by outsourcing the execution of the transaction.[410] Intermediaries make use of this opportunity, specialize in the execution of these transactions, and offer their services to a large number of clients. The investments can be divided among a multitude of agents, which

---

[404]    Cf. [Gümbel 85, p. 118 fp.].

[405]    Cf. [Lambert 82, p. 5 fp.], [Gümbel 85, p. 98 fp.], [Kotler 88, p. 532 fp.], [Nieschlag 91, p. 378 fp.].

[406]    Cf. [Balderston 58], [Gehrig 96, p.101, 103].

[407]    Cf. [Gümbel 85, p. 169].

[408]    Cf. [Gehrig 96, p. 103].

[409]    An investment is desirable as a barrier to entry for potential competitors if it affects the core processes and competencies of the corporation, cf. [Prahalad 90, p. 84].

[410]    Cf. [Ramser 79], [Bretzke 94], [Witt 91, p. 205 fp.].

reduces the share of the costs for every single agent. Hence, intermediaries exploit *economies of scale*[411] due to specialization effects, learning-curve effects, and application of special technologies[412].

### 3.2.3.2 Functional sources of transaction cost reductions

Functions performed by intermediaries that give rise to reductions of transaction costs are subject of the present section; an emphasis of these *intermediary services* is on the information phase of the transaction.

**Searching and matching**
In search for potential transaction partners suppliers and consumers incur search and contact costs, i.e. the costs resulting from information acquisition about the opposite market side.[413] Intermediaries offer the opportunity of a centralized exchange of information avoiding decentralized search and communication acts, and the transaction costs incurred therein.[414] The intermediary actively gathers all relevant information about the market (more generally: about the environment of the transaction) and about potential transaction partners, and then sells the information either directly or indirectly.[415] The sale of information by the intermediary can be of three different modes:[416]

- *Direct sale of information* to the market participants.[417]
- Indirect sale of information by mediating contacts between both market sides[418] (*matchmaking*), examples are real estate brokers and employment agencies.
- Indirect sale of information by actively buying and selling in the market and setting bid and ask prices[419] (*market-making*), examples are used-car dealers, specialists in stock markets, and banks managing portfolios and allocating credits.

Therefore, from an abstract point of view, an intermediary can be conceived as an *information processing system* (Section 2.1.6).

---

[411] Economies of scale are characterized by a reduction of the costs per single unit of the transaction for an increase of the total volume of the activity, cf. [Bohr 96, p. 377].
[412] Cf. [Gould 80, p. 185].
[413] Cf. Section 2.2. For the theory of search see Section 4.2.
[414] See [Demsetz 68], [Townsend 78], [Rubinstein 87], [Yavas 92], [Gehrig 93], [Cosimano 96], [Yavas 96] for economic models that deal with intermediaries involved in the matching of opposite market sides.
[415] The different strategies for selling information were discussed in Section 2.5.4.
[416] See Section 3.2.4 for different contract forms for intermediaries.
[417] See Chapters 4 and 5.
[418] Cf. [Rubinstein 87], [Yavas 92].
[419] See [Demsetz 68], [Garman 76], [Amihud 80] for market-making models, and [Gehrig 93], [Yavas 96] for intermediaries in bilateral search markets.

Closely connected with the reduction of search and information costs, that implicitly include the *opportunity costs of time*,[420] is the *reduction of buyer's and seller's waiting time* for a transaction through transaction with an intermediary instead of transacting directly on the market.[421] The intermediary holding an *inventory*[422] can immediately transact with suppliers and consumers and therefore offers *availability of products* and *immediacy*.[423] Another argument is that intermediaries offer an increased probability for successful matches,[424] because an intermediary provides a multitude of possible trading opportunities (see the Baligh-Richartz effect in Section 3.2.3.1) and of bargaining possibilities since intermediaries can effectively tax or subsidize transactions.[425]

### Monitoring and guaranteeing

Due to informational asymmetries and strategic behavior of independent economic agents, participants in a transaction will always be uncertain about the true characteristics of the other market side, for example, buyers are uncertain about product features and product quality.[426] The uncertainty can only be overcome by information acquisition about the potential transaction partner. In most cases the products or services exchanged in a transaction are highly specialized, requiring expertise for the investigation of the true characteristics of the products or services and for monitoring the behavior of the transaction partners. The necessity of investments in expertise for the evaluation of quality results in high monitoring costs: Therefore, monitoring can be performed centrally and offered as an intermediary service to the market participants. *Delegated monitoring*, i.e., the delegation of information acquisition to specialized intermediaries,[427] is an opportunity for reductions of transaction costs in the information and control phase. Two main effects foster the advantage of centralized monitoring performed by an intermediary. First, the intermediary can acquire *special skills* in the determination of product quality and

---

[420] The opportunity costs of time are one part of the transaction costs, cf. [Spulber 96b, p. 560].

[421] Cf. [Rubinstein 87].

[422] An inventory can be either an inventory of physical goods [Spulber 96a, p. 142 fp.] or simply a base of possible transaction partners, e.g., a supplier- and client-network [Gehrig 96].

[423] Cf. [Clower 75], [Yavas 96], [Spulber 96a, p. 145]. In financial markets intermediaries holding inventories to offer liquidity fulfill a stabilizing and price smoothing role for the market, cf. [Demsetz 68, p. 35 fp.], [Peck 90].

[424] Cf. [Gehrig 93, p. 101].

[425] Cf. [Spulber 96a, p. 146].

[426] Cf. Section 2.3.

[427] Delegated monitoring and the resulting reduction of transaction costs is an effect discussed in the theory of financial intermediation, cf. [Diamond 84].

become an *expert* in a certain market.[428] Second, intermediaries can exploit *cross-sectional and temporal reusability* of information once acquired about the market or about market participants.[429]

Besides monitoring, a second possibility to reduce information costs in transactions between independent economic agents are *guarantees* for product or service quality given by the intermediary. The intermediary can become a *guarantor of quality*,[430] who has the reputation of selling (or certifying, cf. Section 2.3.3) only products of high quality.[431]

**Negotiation and contracting**

Once transaction partners have found each other the *terms of the contract*, i.e., prices, amount, quality, delivery time, and so forth, have to be negotiated.[432] The outcome of the negotiation phase is to a great extent dependent on the distribution of information and bargaining positions between the participants in the trans‾action.[433] An intermediary providing *standardized contracts* for transactions can lead to a shortened or even skipped negotiation phase for his/her clients, hence reducing negotiation costs and the opportunity costs of time. The sources of intermediary efficiency in contracting[434] are again twofold: First, the intermediary has a higher frequency of transactions, so that investments in *negotiation skills* and *bargaining position* pay-off earlier than for ordinary participants in transactions. Second, because of larger transaction volumes (cf. Section 3.2.3.1) the intermediary can achieve more favorable terms of the contract, for example, quantity discounts or longer contract terms.

The intermediary's *reputation* is the main precondition for an efficient execution of all services mentioned so far, because the intermediary service itself is subject to uncertainty. The investment in reputation[435] is valuable for the intermediary acting repeatedly, because consumers usually prefer to buy high quality products and thus will consult the intermediary who is known to offer these products.

---

[428] Cf. [Marvel 84], [Biglaiser 93]. Intermediaries usually buy larger amounts of products and stay in the market for a longer period of time than individual consumers do, so that the investment in special skills to determine product and service quality is valuable for the intermediary in repeated transactions.

[429] Cf. [Chan 86] according to [Bhattacharya/Thakor 93, p. 8].

[430] Cf. [Biglaiser 94].

[431] High quality should be interpreted as a preferable quality-price combination.

[432] For a review about the theory of contracts see [Williamson 86, p. 101 fp.], [Picot 96, p. 51 fp.], and [Wigand 97, p. 45 fp.].

[433] Cf. [Gebauer 96, p. 17].

[434] One argument for the efficiency of intermediaries is the *exploitation of different contract structures* in supply and demand, cf. Section 3.3.1.

[435] Cf. Sections 2.3.3 and 3.2.2.2. The value of reputation is higher for intermediaries, because in contrast to ordinary suppliers they usually stay in the market for a longer time, cf. [Chemmanur 94], and contract with a larger number of consumers.

### 3.2.3.3  Summary

The main intermediary services and the resulting reductions of transaction costs are summarized in Table 6.

*Table 6:*    *Sources of transaction cost reductions from intermediation.*

| | intermediary service | cost reduction |
|---|---|---|
| **structural sources of transaction cost reductions** | | |
| volume of the transaction | • exploitation of economies of scale concerning the transaction volume <br> • transformation of contract volumes <br> • operation of transit stores and transport | • coordination costs <br> • costs for the execution of the transaction |
| frequency of the transaction | • transformation of transaction frequencies <br> • managing the trade-off between volume and frequency dependent transaction costs <br> • inventory management | • coordination costs <br> • costs for the execution of the transaction |
| Baligh-Richartz effect | • installing and managing a consumer/supplier network | • joint contact costs |
| **functional sources of transaction cost reductions** | | |
| searching and matching | • direct sale of information <br> • matchmaking <br> • market-making | • search costs <br> • opportunity costs of time |
| availability of products and immediacy | • inventory management <br> • compensation of variances in demand and supply | • opportunity costs of time |
| monitoring and guaranteeing | • expertise in determining product and service quality <br> • cross-sectional and temporal reuse of information <br> • guaranteeing high product quality | • information costs <br> • monitoring and control costs <br> • costs resulting form uncertainty <br> • investments in expertise |
| contracting | • strong bargaining position <br> • exploitation of differences in contract terms between supply and demand market side <br> • standardized contracts | • negotiation costs |

### 3.2.4  Social welfare and distribution of resource savings

The hitherto discussion of intermediation has revealed two main justifications of intermediaries and of intermediary efficiency: One is the exploitation of comparative advantages concerning production costs and utility through enabling the exchange of goods and services (Section 3.2.1). The other is based on savings of resources involved in market transactions (Section 3.2.3). From a macroeconomics point of view these sources of intermediary efficiency contribute to an increase of the *social welfare*[436] of the economy as a whole. On a microeconomic level the resource savings generated through intermediation have to be distributed among the participants of the transaction. A theoretic treatment of this question applies a game-theoretic approach to formalize the interplay of the economic agents involved in the transaction.[437] The coordination and agreement of transaction partners about the distribution of resource savings causes (transaction) costs. The introduction of an *economically independent intermediary* can save these expenditures.[438] The intermediary's income can therefore be conceived as a share of the resource savings achieved through the activities performed.[439]

## 3.3  Intermediary contracts and sources of income

Transactions between independent economic agents require agreements concerning the exchange of goods and services. *Contracts* are the explicit or implicit binding agreement between agents, who agree on the arrangement because they expect an improvement of their situation.[440] The design of efficient contracts is a central issue in *contract theory* (Section 3.3.1). Intermediary contracts with clients have two basic forms, resulting in the distinction between merchant and broker intermediaries (Section 3.3.2).

### 3.3.1  Contract theory and intermediation

Common to all intermediaries is that they mediate between suppliers (or sellers) and consumers (or buyers) of goods or services. Thus, intermediaries have to find agreements and make arrangements with both market sides. Usually the contract terms of the supply market side are different from those desired by consumers on the demand side. So the intermediary's service is the *transformation of contract*

---

[436]  Social welfare in the sense of *different economic agents' added utility*, cf. [Varian 93, p. 535 fp.].

[437]  Cf. [Gümbel 85, p. 139 fp.] and [Griebel 82].

[438]  Cf. [Gümbel 85, p. 143].

[439]  Cf. [Gümbel 85, p. 45 fp.].

[440]  Cf. [Wolff 95, p. 38], [Wigand 97, p. 45-46].

*attributes* between the two market sides.[441] Contract theory provides several typologies of contract types.[442] One classification distinguishes between classical, neoclassical, and relational contracts:[443]

- *Classical contracts* are usually related to standardized goods and are closed for the purpose of short-term services exchange between anonymous contract partners.
- *Neoclassical Contracts* are related to a fixed period of time and remain partially incomplete at the time of the contract's closure.
- *Relational, long-term contracts* are mainly subject to implicit agreements based on mutual trust, evolving over time in the relationship.

Although the appropriate contract type to be chosen is dependent on the task to be completed, and therefore dependent on the goods or services exchanged, a general distinction of *intermediary contracts* can be made: (a) The intermediary contracts in long-term relationships with the supply market side and transforms the long-term contract attributes into well defined, standardized contract terms for the demand market side. Here, the intermediary is engaged in neoclassical contracts on the supply market side and classical contracts on the demand market side. (b) The intermediary only matches and mediates the contracting parties in a bilateral exchange process. Contracts concerning the good or service being exchanged are closed directly between supplier and consumer. The intermediary is involved in contracts, either with the supply market side or with the demand market, concerning the matching with the opposite market side. These types of intermediary contracts lead to the distinction of merchant and broker intermediaries (Section 3.3.2). Relational long-term contracts are based on the identity of the contract partners and the quality of the relation developed in the past. Therefore, these contracts cannot be mediated by third parties. However, relational, long-term contracts based on the intermediary's reputation are essential for intermediaries and their relations to both market sides.

### 3.3.2 Sources of income: merchant vs. broker intermediaries

According to the characterization of the previous section, intermediaries can be characterized either as *merchant intermediaries* or as *broker intermediaries.*[444] Merchant intermediaries buy and sell goods in a market, i.e., they acquire property rights on the goods traded, take over risks, and therefore realize their profit from

---

[441] Cf. Definition 2 in Section 3.1.3.

[442] Cf. [Picot 96, p. 51], [Wigand 97, p. 46].

[443] Cf. [MacNeil 78]. This typology of contracts and other typologies are described in [Picot 96, p. 51 fp.], [Wigand 97, p. 46 fp.].

[444] Cf. [Hackett 92]. Baligh distinguishes between intermediaries as *order-fillers* [Baligh 67, p. 118], similar to merchant intermediaries, and intermediaries as *pure coordinators* [Baligh 67, p. 123], similar to broker intermediaries.

the spread in buying and selling prices.[445] Broker intermediaries, in contrast, facilitate the exchange of goods or services by matching buyers and sellers without taking ownership on the goods traded. Broker intermediaries are compensated for their activities by a revenue-sharing commission either paid by the seller, by the buyer or split up between the two.[446]

The design of intermediary contracts has to take into account *principal-agent problems*[447] inherent in a relationship between the intermediary, i.e., the agent, and the principal, i.e., the user or client of the intermediary. In general, most of the instruments of cooperation design (Section 2.3.1.4) can be applied to intermediary contracts, depending on the type of intermediary and the services provided.[448] The choice of a particular contract form has consequences on the *profitability* of the intermediary and on the intermediary's *incentives to invest in effort.*[449]

Merchant intermediaries buy goods at a time when their demand is uncertain. This will usually result in an inventory either too high or too low, which will lower the intermediary's expected profit. Conversely, under broker-intermediation goods are not exchanged until after the exact demand is realized and the broker intermediary does not have to take over any inventory risk. Thus, an increase in the demand variance will increase the relative profitability of broker intermediaries compared to merchant intermediaries.

An intermediary's investment in effort to increase the efficiency of the activities performed generates purely private costs, but an increased efficiency of the intermediary will also increase the welfare of the intermediary's trading partners by better matching supply and demand. Merchant intermediaries are able to fully internalize these increases of joint surplus from exchanges through their price spreads. Whereas, broker intermediaries are only compensated for their effort by a commission and therefore cannot fully participate the increases in joint surplus. Concluding from this argument, merchant intermediaries have incentives to choose the expected-joint-surplus maximizing level of their investments in effort.[450]

Yavas[451] gives examples for the two different types of intermediary contract forms. He distinguishes between *market-makers* (similar to merchant intermediaries), for

---

[445] The optimal buying and selling prices under uncertain demand and supply, often labeled bid- and ask-prices, are examined in detail in [Amihud 80] and [Ho 81].

[446] Cf. [Sass 84, p. 109 fp.].

[447] Cf. Section 2.3.1.

[448] The application of the smooth instruments of coordination design, for example, reputation or information policy, to intermediaries is not different from the application to information sources presented in Section 2.3.3. Hence, only hard forms of cooperation design will be discussed in this section.

[449] Cf. [Hackett 92, p. 301].

[450] Cf. [Hackett 92, p. 301].

[451] Cf. [Yavas 92].

example, specialists in stock markets[452] and used-car dealers, and *matchmakers* (comparable to broker intermediaries), for example, real estate brokers, travel agencies, and employment agencies. Yavas discusses the relative advantage of these two types of intermediary contracts in a bilateral search framework[453] and finds the following:[454] If search is efficient and inexpensive, market-making is preferable to matchmaking. In contrast, if search is relatively inefficient and sufficiently costly, matchmaking is preferable to market-making. In a further study of *intermediary contracts* based on the theory of contractual choices[455] Sass examines conditions for the choice of a special contract form:[456] If measuring the real market value of a good mediated by a broker intermediary is costly, the commission is optimally determined after the transaction has taken place, and then is based on the actual sale price so that the commission will reflect the true gains from trade for the seller. The determination of the actual sale price before the transaction takes place would be too expensive for relatively heterogeneous goods, like in the real estate market. Whereas, if the good mediated by a merchant intermediary is of relatively high standardization, the intermediary will buy the good outright and sell it for an easily determinable selling price. The basic aspects of merchant and broker intermediary contract forms are summarized in Table 7.

*Table 7:*     *Comparison of merchant and broker intermediation.*

|  | merchant intermediary (market-maker) | broker intermediary (matchmaker) |
|---|---|---|
| *activity* | • buying and selling goods<br>• acquiring proprietary rights on goods | • matching of supply and demand<br>• coordinating buyers and sellers |
| *source of income* | • price spread between buying and selling prices | • fixed or percentage commission paid either by buyer or seller, or split up between the two |
| *risk of activity* | • risk from buying goods when demand and selling prices are uncertain | • risk from investment in matching technology and effort |
| *optimal contract form if ...* | • demand variance is relatively low<br>• search is relatively efficient and inexpensive<br>• products are homogeneous | • demand variance is relatively high<br>• search is relatively inefficient and costly<br>• products are heterogeneous |

---

[452]  Some special examples for the two types of intermediaries in the New York Stock Exchange (NYSE) are given by [Demsetz 68].

[453]  For a further review of different intermediary models see Section 4.1.2.

[454]  Cf. [Yavas 92, p. 55].

[455]  For the theory of contractual choice see, for example, [Cheung 83].

[456]  Cf. [Sass 84, p. 84 fp., 108 fp.].

## 3.4 Effects of intermediation on markets

The existence of intermediaries is largely due to the existence of market imperfections that cannot be resolved by other market mechanisms:[457] Intermediation also has consequences on the market equilibrium[458] and market efficiency[459] of the economy. Besides the reduction of transaction costs (Section 3.2.3), this is the second major role of independent intermediaries in an economy. Markets show two major characteristics that might lead to inefficiencies: asymmetric information[460] and strategic interdependence of agents:[461] *Asymmetric information* and the associated adverse selection problem may in its extreme lead to total market failures. The *strategic interdependence of agents* in an economy, i.e., the dependence of players' optimal strategies upon the strategies of other agents,[462] may result in multiple equilibria.[463] Intermediaries are institutions that can coordinate economic agents to overcome market inefficiencies and disequilibria.[464]

### 3.4.1 Effects on asymmetric information

Missing information about the quality of products offered in the market may lead to market failure, as *Akerlof's 'market of lemons'* exemplifies.[465] In general, several instruments exist to overcome or mitigate the effects of asymmetric information (Section 2.3.1.4). Intermediaries may help to overcome market failures caused by informational asymmetries[466] by acquisition of information about the quality of products available in the market.[467] The intermediary can acquire *expertise* in a certain market,[468] and exploit this investment by becoming a *guarantor of quality*,[469] i.e., selling or mediating only objects (products or services) of high quality. The effect on the market is that low-quality suppliers will lose their market share and only suppliers of high-quality products can stay in the market.

---

[457]  Cf. [Bhattacharya/Thakor 93, p. 14].
[458]  Cf. [Yavas 95].
[459]  Cf. Section 2.4.
[460]  Cf. [Bhattacharya/Thakor 93] and Section 2.3.1.3.
[461]  Cf. [Cooper 88].
[462]  Cf. [Rasmusen 89, p. 21], [Holler 93, p. 1]
[463]  Cf. [Cooper 88].
[464]  Cf. [Yavas 95, p. 18].
[465]  Cf. [Akerlof 70] and Section 2.4.2.
[466]  Cf. [Garella 89], [Gehrig 93].
[467]  Cf. [Marvel 84], [Biglaiser 93], [Biglaiser 94].
[468]  The intermediary becomes an expert in the particular market, cf. [Biglaiser 93] and Section 3.2.3.2.
[469]  Cf. [Biglaiser 94] and Section 3.2.3.2.

Therefore, the average quality offered on the market increases.[470] A second effect is that prices charged for the same goods or services will assimilate, i.e., intermediaries have a price smoothing role for the market as well.[471] Thus the acquisition and dissemination of information by the intermediary can be a remedy to principal-agent problems formerly present in a market with asymmetric information. As a result of intermediary activities, the price system[472] will better reflect the actual information available on the market.

### 3.4.2  Coordination in presence of externalities

One example of externalities giving rise to a Pareto-inferior equilibrium is the activity of agents in bilateral search markets:[473] In a bilateral search market two types of agents, i.e., buyers and sellers, are actively searching for transaction partners. The chance of a successful match of two agents is dependent on the search effort invested by both types of agents. An increase of one agent's search effort increases the probability of a successful match, which increases the other agent's (the less active one) expected payoff as well. Therefore, the activities of the first agent have a positive externality. However, search effort causes private costs that cannot be internalized. Consequently, agents will chose a search intensity smaller than that maximizing the joint payoff. As a result, the economy will end in a sub-optimal equilibrium because of missing coordination between the market participants. In this situation an intermediary can be introduced as an *independent coordinator* in order to enable the economy to reach an equilibrium with a higher social welfare.[474]

### 3.4.3  Clearing the market

Transactions on markets require the existence and the availability of an appropriate partner for the transaction, i.e., the problem of the double coincidence of wants.[475] In case of high information costs for finding transaction partners or whenever demand has an element of randomness, intermediaries can provide immediacy of transactions, i.e., reduced waiting times and an increased probability of successful

---

[470]  Cf. Section 2.4.2.
[471]  Cf. [Peck 90] and [Demsetz 68, p. 35 fp.].
[472]  Cf. Section 2.4.1.
[473]  Cf. [Yavas 95].
[474]  Cf. [Yavas 95, p. 18].
[475]  Cf. Section 3.2.1 and [Spulber 96a, p. 143].

matches.[476] One main function of intermediaries is thus to find out *ways of clearing the market.*[477]

### 3.4.4 Summary

The effects of intermediation on markets are summarized in Table 8.

*Table 8:*    *Effects of intermediation on markets.*

| source of market inefficiency | intermediary activity | effect on market |
|---|---|---|
| information asymmetry and adverse selection | • acquisition and dissemination of information about product quality<br>• guaranteeing quality | • high product quality on the market<br>• smoothed prices |
| externalities: strategic interdependence of market participants | • coordination of agents | • equilibrium with higher social welfare can be realized |
| • no availability of transaction partners<br>• high search costs<br>• uncertainty of demand | • providing immediacy: liquidity and/or availability | • clearing the market |

## 3.5 Market microstructure

In the literature of financial intermediation the term *market microstructure* refers to the study of intermediation and the institutions of exchange, here it should be applied to markets in general. Acting on a market intermediaries are subject to competition. The effects of competition on markets for intermediary services and the resulting industrial structure will be discussed in the following.

### 3.5.1 Competition

Competition between market participants is a basic organizing principle in economics aiming at social welfare and progress.[478] In intermediation competition is always twofold: First, intermediaries contract on the supply and on the demand

---

[476]    Cf. [Cosimano 96], [Rubinstein 87], [Gehrig 93].

[477]    Cf. [Spulber 96a, p. 136].

[478]    Cf. [Bartling 80, p. 9 fp.].

market side and therefore have to compete in two rather than in one market. These markets are interrelated because success in one market implicitly affects the success in the other market.[479] For example, an intermediary who has established a large supplier network can offer a high probability for successful matches, automatically attracting a large number of consumers.[480] Second, intermediaries have to compete with other intermediaries and with direct exchange markets.[481]

As far as competition with direct transactions is concerned, the intermediary's profit is dependent on the ratio of the costs of direct transactions on the market and the price[482] charged for the intermediary services. If, for example, direct search for transaction partners is inexpensive, transactions are to a great extent performed directly between transaction partners and the intermediary only mediates a small share of all transactions occurring on the market. The intermediary's surplus is thus dependent on the *costs of direct transactions*, i.e., when search is more expensive the intermediary's return is larger[483] compared to a situation with lower search costs. On the other hand, if the intermediary charges a *high positive bid-ask spread*, a related search market, attracting shares of transactions formerly performed through the intermediary, arises.[484]

Most models[485] of intermediary competition treat price competition as the only form of competition. In practice, however, there are several different *forms of competition*.[486]

- *Price competition*: Different prices can only exist in imperfect markets.[487] The effects of price competition depend on the strength of the (oligopolistic) interdependency between the market participants.
- *Quality competition* is more probable the stronger the interdependencies in price competition are. Competition by means of quality includes the development of new products or services and the improvement or deterioration of existing products or services.

---

[479] Cf. [Yanelle 89a, p. 1].

[480] Cf. [Gehrig 96, p. 103].

[481] Cf. [Hänchen 85, p. 417], [Yanelle 89a, p. 2], [Cosimano 96]. See Section 4.5 as well.

[482] The intermediary's price for the services is either the height of the bid-ask spreads (merchant intermediary) or the fee charged for matching transaction partners (broker intermediary). For a formal treatment of the trade-off between the costs for direct search and the price charged by the intermediary see Section 4.3.2.

[483] Cf. [Spulber 96b, p. 579]. The statement was derived for merchant intermediaries who are setting bid and ask prices for potential transactions.

[484] Cf. [Gehrig 93, p. 113].

[485] A game theoretic treatment of price competition between intermediaries is given in [Yanelle 89a], [Yanelle 89b]. Treatments based on search models are given in [Gehrig 96], [Gehrig 93], [Spulber 96b].

[486] Cf. [Schmidt 93, p. 56-74].

[487] In atomic markets all prices are the same for identical goods (*law of indifference* by [Jevons 1871], cf. [Schumann 92, p. 212]).

- *Service competition* is closely connected with the sale of goods or services and is dependent on the type of goods or services.
- *Advertising competition*: Advertising can be informative or suggestive. The particular form of advertising depends on product characteristics and the phase of the product life cycle.[488]

The particular form of competition depends on the products or services offered and on the market structure. In general, the stronger the interdependency between market participants the smaller will be the price margin and the competition will be shifted towards other forms like quality or service competition.[489]

### 3.5.2  Industrial structure

In markets for intermediary services a tendency towards a natural monopoly is inherent.[490] A *natural monopoly* occurs whenever the joint costs of a single supplier of a good or service are smaller than the sum of costs resulting from any division of the provision among multiple suppliers.[491] The reason here is high fixed costs resulting from necessary investments for the installation of an intermediary business (cf. Section 3.2.2.2), for example, technologies, human capital, and reputation.[492] From the intermediary's point of view these investments are *competitive advantages* and *barriers to entry* for potential market participants.[493]

A detailed analysis has to take into account the activities of potential competitors in addition to effects resulting from high fixed costs. Gehrig[494] presented a *network competition model of broker intermediaries* who invest in trading facilities, i.e., supplier networks, and enter a price competition, i.e., a competition for commission charges. The size of the intermediary's supplier network determines the fixed costs, on the one hand, and the quality of the intermediary service on the other. The results of the model are:

- Given positive fixed costs, only a *finite number of competitors*, i.e., intermediaries, can be active in a market of finite size [Gehrig 96, p. 108].
- There is *always one globally active intermediary*, i.e., an intermediary who has established a supplier network reaching all possible suppliers in the market. The second and third largest intermediaries need to *differentiate* themselves from the largest one by offering a smaller network [Gehrig 96, p. 112].

---

[488]  Cf. [Kotler 88, p.347-376].
[489]  Cf. [Schmidt 93, p. 58].
[490]  Cf. [Demsetz 68, p. 42].
[491]  Cf. [Schumann 92, p. 295], [Gravelle 92, p. 223], [Varian 93, p. 410].
[492]  Cf. Section 3.2.3.2.
[493]  Cf. [Porter 92], [Schmidt 93, p. 62 fp.].
[494]  Cf. [Gehrig 96].

- A *global monopoly will always be challenged* by small intermediaries who need to acquire only small market shares to justify entry [Gehrig 96, p. 109].
- As the size of the largest networks grows, competition between the largest brokers intensifies and *prices converge to marginal costs* [Gehrig 96, p. 103].
- Smaller intermediaries will occupy *niche markets* [Gehrig 96, p. 101].

The main result of the model is that the *industrial structure* occurring in a market of brokerage services relying on a network of suppliers (or consumers) is that of a *natural oligopoly*[495] ('consisting of generally three larger intermediaries of similar size and smaller intermediaries occupying niche markets').[496] The model applies to a variety of real-world examples. The main focus, however, is on markets for *brokerage services* that attempt to find a matching trade on a commission fee basis. Examples are investment banks offering brokerage services for large-block transactions in the so-called 'upstairs market' of the NYSE.[497] Further examples are real estate brokers, head-hunters, and airline reservation systems.[498] In all these markets *networks of potential clients* play an important role, the model therefore gives some insight in the industrial structure of this broad class of intermediary services.

The results of the model implicitly reveal two main *intermediary strategies* in competitive market environments. One strategy is aiming to become a *globally active intermediary*, i.e., offering a network that reaches all potential suppliers and/or consumers. The other strategy is that of *specialization*, i.e., aiming to penetrate only a small but specialized share of the market.

---

[495]  Cf. [Shaked 83].

[496]  Cf. [Gehrig 96, p. 101].

[497]  *Large-block transactions* are not traded on the floor of the NYSE, but directly with large institutional investors mediated by large investment banks, cf. [Gehrig 96, p. 102].

[498]  Cf. [Gehrig 96, p. 102].

# 4 An economic model of information intermediaries

*Information intermediaries* are economic agents supporting the production, exchange, and utilization of information in order to increase the value of the information for its end-user or to reduce the costs of information acquisition. One possible role of information intermediaries, securing an adequate production and dissemination of information as independent market participants, was already mentioned in Section 2.5.2. The aim to make profit is the origin of their activities. The information processing activities of information intermediaries can generate an informational surplus or added value.[499]

The present chapter deals with an economic model of an information intermediary. The aim of the model is to develop a theoretical nucleus for the formal treatment of the economics of information intermediaries (Section 4.2). Within the basic model, derived in Section 4.3, fundamental economic aspects of information intermediaries will be analyzed, and some general results for the strategy of information intermediaries under given environmental conditions will be discussed (Section 4.4), as well as the effects of competition between information intermediaries (Section 4.5). Section 4.6 deals with the effects of information intermediaries on social welfare. The chapter starts with a short characterization of information intermediaries, an introduction to the theoretic approach followed in the present work, and a list of questions concerning the economics of information intermediaries (Section 4.1). The economic theory of search which is the basis for the intermediary model will be introduced subsequently (Section 4.2).

## 4.1 Introduction

### 4.1.1 Abstract characterization of information intermediaries

A characterization of information intermediaries can be based on the definition of intermediaries (Definition 2 in Section 3.1.3). The differentiating aspect of *information intermediaries* is that their activities focus on *information* instead of

---

[499] Cf. [Kuhlen 95, p. 9].

physical goods or financial assets. As already obvious in Section 2.1, information has to be integrated into a conceptual hierarchy of notions, having *knowledge* on its highest level (Figure 1 in Section 2.1.2). *Information* can be understood as the representation of knowledge, one level below knowledge in the conceptual hierarchy. The conception of information intermediaries refers to the notion of information, putting it in accordance with the definition of classical intermediaries given in Chapter 3 in the following way: Just as classical intermediaries information intermediaries mediate between the original supplier and potential consumers. The product, more generally, the object mediated and processed[500] by an information intermediary, is information, a message being the representation of knowledge originally produced by an author[501] different from the intermediary. What should be stressed here is: the activities of information intermediaries do not produce new knowledge,[502] but the intermediary's processing of information can bring out new information.[503] Examples for these intermediary activities are the transformation of one form of knowledge representation into another, or the collection and rearrangement of information from different sources to a new information product.[504] Thus the information intermediary also produces new information, i.e., new information products, and provides information services. The main difference to intermediaries mediating physical goods is that information is an immaterial good that can be copied for vanishing marginal costs, and that does not wear out by use (Section 2.1.5). An information intermediary can disseminate information once produced to a large number of end-users and thus exploit economies of scale.[505]

The activities performed by information intermediaries can be described by the following basic processes:

- *acquisition of information* (Section 2.2),
- *processing of information* (Section 2.1.6), and
- *dissemination of information* (Section 2.5).

---

[500] Cf. [Kuhlen 95, p. 259].

[501] In this context the *author of knowledge* has to be interpreted not only as an individual, but can also be an organization or an information system.

[502] The processing of information usually has a consequence for the information or knowledge of the system that processes the information (cf. Section 2.1.6 and [Kuhlen 95, p. 34 fp.]). However, the production of new knowledge is mainly the task of information producers, e.g., R&D or authors, and is not the primary task of information intermediaries.

[503] Kuhlen labeled it *new information products*, cf. [Kuhlen 95, p. 83 fp.].

[504] These types of information intermediaries are, for example, information brokers or news agencies, see Chapter 5.

[505] Cf. [von Ungern-Sternberg 84, p. 42], [Hänchen 85, p. 408].

Systems executing these functions can be grasped as *information processing systems* (Section 2.1.6).[506]

The central function and service of information intermediaries,[507] in the narrow sense of mediators of information, is the matching of end-user specific information needs with information available in any resource or information depot (Figure 10).[508]

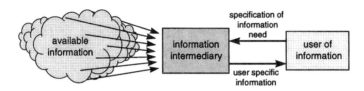

*Figure 10:*	*Fundamental function of information intermediaries in the narrow sense.*

The information intermediary reduces the end-user's search costs, including, for example, costs for communication, contact costs, costs for evaluation, and especially opportunity costs of time.[509] The fundamental function depicted in Figure 10 does not only apply to the search for information, but also to the search for physical products in a market.

Even if the information intermediary only mediates information that can be gathered by the individual information seeker as well, intermediation can be advantageous for the information seeker and the whole economy because of reductions in search costs.[510] The argument is that the information intermediary has the opportunity to spread the costs for carrying out information acquisition among a large number of users. In addition, the information intermediary usually performs these activities with higher efficiency due to specialization and can exploit economies of scale due to larger transaction volumes (Section 3.2.3). To exploit these economies of scale, the information gathered by the information intermediary has to be sold repeatedly. But, to achieve acceptance among potential clients, the services provided by the information intermediary have to focus the requirements

---

506	Real-life examples of information intermediaries can be found in several fields, for example, providers of stock price information, search engines, directory services, thematic oriented information collectors, or information brokers on the Internet. For a further discussion of information intermediaries on the Internet see Chapter 5 and [Resnick 95], [Sarkar 96].

507	In addition, the intermediary may do processing and formatting on the information, see Section 5.1.3.

508	For a characterization of *available information* see Section 1.1.

509	According to [Sass 84, p. 62] 'The primary function of information middlemen is to reduce the resources expended in transferring information. This is accomplished by either lowering the costs of transferring information or constraining the amount of information transferred.' See the description of search costs in Section 4.2.1 as well.

510	Cf. [Resnick 95] and Section 4.6.

of the end-user of the information. Hence, the services have to be personalized to the particular end-user to a certain degree.[511]

A further constituting aspect of information intermediaries is that they are independent economic agents performing their activities by order and for account of other market participants and with the aim to maximize their profit.[512] The basic characteristics of *information intermediaries*[513] mentioned so far can be summarized in the following concluding definition.[514]

*Definition 3:*  *An information intermediary is an independent, profit maximizing economic information processing system performing its activities (information acquisition, processing, and dissemination) on behalf of other economic agents' information needs.*

The information intermediary's major incentive to offer the services is the aim to make profit. Acting on behalf of end-users of information, the intermediary's profit is obviously determined by the value the services can create for potential clients. Therefore, the valuation of the intermediary's service by potential clients has to be considered as the major determinant of the profit gained.[515] The potential clients' central question is whether to consult the information intermediary and pay a fee or search privately and incur search costs.[516] This question can be answered by comparison of the expected quality of the result and the expected search costs for private search processes with the quality offered and the fee charged by the information intermediary. Questions concerning the economics, strategy, and design of information intermediaries have to take into account this focal point.

---

[511]  Information can be, for example, disseminated in form of information packages, cf. [Nink 91, p. 131 fp.], another form would be a personalized information service, see Section 5.3.

[512]  See the corresponding discussion in Section 3.1.

[513]  In the following the term intermediary will be used as a short form of the term information intermediary.

[514]  The definition does not cover pure technological systems like gateway services, services for protocol conversion [Zbornik 96, p. 147], or network bridges [Martin 89, p. 168 fp.] that mediate between systems on a pure technological basis, cf. [von Westarp 97]. These systems are not economic agents and do not primarily have a profit maximizing aim.

[515]  Cf. [Kotler 88, p. 18].

[516]  The information intermediary competes with personal search processes of potential clients, cf. Sections 3.5.1, 4.3.2.3, and 4.4. See [Gehrig 93, p. 99, 107] as well.

### 4.1.2 Theoretic approach to the economics of information intermediaries

Theoretic approaches to intermediation are the subject of various disciplines in economics literature, each focusing the particular functions and services offered by intermediaries in their special application area (Section 3.1). The information processing activities of intermediaries are usually only treated implicitly, i.e., in connection with the basic functions and services. However, a number of models from different application areas treat some aspects of information intermediaries. Detached from their special application area the different theoretic approaches can be roughly categorized as follows:

- *Marketmaking models*: Intermediaries are independent agents, buying and selling in the market (Section 3.3). Buyers and sellers express their valuation for particular objects traded on the market via bid and ask prices. Intermediaries 'process' this information that is distributed on the market, for example, by setting bid and ask prices themselves, and by buying and selling objects to match supply and demand. Practical models of this kind are discussed in: [Myerson 83], [Rubinstein 87], [Biglaiser 93], [Gehrig 93], [Roy 94], [Cosimano 96], and [Yavas 96]. The intermediaries introduced in these models are not information intermediaries in the narrow sense of Definition 3 because the mediation and processing of information is only one necessary activity derived from the primary activity of buying and selling.

- *Matching models*: Intermediaries perform the matching of opposite market sides in *bilateral search markets* in return for a fee. For example, buyers and sellers, or firms and workers search for each other in the market. Agents acting on these search markets can find each other directly or via the intermediary. Examples can be found in [Yavas 94] and [Gehrig 96].

- *Advertising models*: Information intermediaries mediate, i.e., forward, bundle, and process, information from sellers to potential buyers, being an alternative to the direct transfer of information from sellers to potential consumers in form of advertising messages, cf. [Sass 84, p. 33 fp.]

- *Search models*: An 'informational intermediary' collects information, for example, about the quality of products in stores offering these products, and subsequently sells the information to consumers who would otherwise have to perform their own search.[517] Examples can be found in [von Ungern-Sternberg 84] and [Hänchen 85]. These examples treat the problem of describing differentiated products (price, spatial differentiation, quality) by means of a *circular road model*.[518]

---

[517] Cf. [Hänchen 85, p. 413-414], [Anderson 96, p. 143 fp.].

[518] For circular road models see [Salop 79], [Novshek 80], [von Ungern-Sternberg 82], [von Ungern-Sternberg 84, p. 25].

All of these theoretic approaches to intermediation address the question whether the market participants use the intermediary or prefer direct contacts. In order to theoretically analyze the intermediary's role and efficiency in the different market settings, the optimal solutions for direct contacts have to be compared with contacts mediated by the intermediary.

The models stated above mainly differ in the way contacts between opposite market sides are incorporated without the intermediary: In market making models the underlying process is a *bilateral bargaining process.*[519] Matching models are founded on models of *bilateral search markets* with opposite agents actively searching for each other.[520] Advertising models take into account the dissemination of product information by firms and the firm's *advertising behavior,*[521] i.e., the push of information by the firms. Search models are based on models of *consumer search.*[522] These models incorporate a pull for information by consumers.

Putting together the different classes of intermediary models with the basic concept of information intermediaries (Section 4.1.1), it becomes obvious that the fundamental function of information intermediaries,[523] can be analyzed by means of a search model. The intermediary model presented by Hänchen/von Ungern-Sternberg[524] uses a fixed-sample-size search strategy in consumer search, which is not the optimal search rule.[525] In addition, the model is designed to focus questions concerning the effects of information intermediaries on market structure and efficiency. The present work, however, focuses questions concerning the economics, strategy, and design of information intermediaries and applies a slightly different model to be developed in the following sections.

In the present work the theoretic approach will be based on an economic search model as the optimal solutions for direct contacts between consumers of information and information sources. A risk neutral, monopolistic[526] information intermediary is introduced as an alternative source of information acquisition for the consumer. In the model the information intermediary performs acquisition and

---

[519] Cf. [Gehrig 93, p. 101 fp.], for a general treatment of bilateral bargaining processes see [Rubinstein 85], [Chatterjee 90].

[520] Cf. [Yavas 94, p. 406].

[521] Cf. [Bagwell 93].

[522] Cf. Section 4.2.1.

[523] The fundamental function of information intermediaries is search on behalf of clients, i.e., the matching of clients' information needs with a subset of available information (Figure 10).

[524] Cf. [Hänchen 85].

[525] See Section 4.2.1 and [Feinberg 77].

[526] The basic model introduces a risk neutral, monopolistic information intermediary to analyze the business of information intermediaries. Aspects of competition between information intermediaries offering comparable services will be analyzed in Section 4.5. The aspect of risk assessment of the information intermediary will be shortly addressed in Section 4.7.2.

direct sale of information.[527] The information is acquired by the intermediary by searching for suppliers, whose offers (products, services, information) exceed a specified level of quality requirements, from a population of suppliers with identical offers differing only in quality. Consumers can buy a reference[528] to suppliers that meet the quality requirements for a predestined fee from the intermediary, or consumers can perform their own search following an optimal search strategy. Due to the special properties of information (Section 2.1.5), the information intermediary has to produce the information only once and can copy and disseminate the information then freely.[529] The aim of the information intermediary is the maximization of the expected profit given the restrictions of the environment. To be applicable to the largest possible number of practical cases, the model abstracts from particular characteristics of the products, services, and information offered by the suppliers on the market and treats all offers simply as objects, the quality of which is described by a single attribute.[530]

### 4.1.3  Questions concerning information intermediaries

The basic concept of information intermediaries outlined so far poses a number of questions concerning the economics of information intermediaries. Especially the growing importance of information intermediaries to overcome problems of information overload and information asymmetries (Section 1.1) raises questions[531] about their strategy and design. The following list of questions concerning information intermediaries will be addressed in the basic model:

- *Basic questions*:
  - Is an independent information intermediary viable/profitable in the market for information?[532]
  - What kind of users (consumers of information) will consult the intermediary, and which will search personally?
  - How is the intermediary's viability and profitability influenced by the strategy chosen, i.e., the quality offered and the fee charged?

---

[527] Cf. Section 2.5.4.

[528] A reference can be, for example, the location of a supplier or an URL (uniform resource locator).

[529] The costs for search have to be borne only once, cf. [Hänchen 85, p. 408]. In the basic model it is assumed that the marginal costs for the dissemination of information are vanishing.

[530] See the description of objects by means of a product attribute in the simple search model introduced in Section 4.2.1.

[531] For some other questions concerning the optimal strategy of information intermediaries see [Rubinstein 87] and [Sass 84] as well.

[532] This is a basic question resulting from the demand for independent providers of information in markets for information to secure an efficient provision of information, cf. Section 2.5.2.

- How does the information intermediary affect the social welfare in the economy?
- What effects will competition among information intermediaries have on the intermediary's profitability and on the structure of the market for intermediary services?
- *Dependency on environmental conditions:*
  - What influences do search costs/communication costs have on the intermediary's profitability?
  - How does the a decreasing portion of relevant information in the set of all available information influence the business of the information intermediary?
  - How do consumers' preferences in a particular target market influence the business of the information intermediary?
- *Intermediary strategy:*
  - Given a particular environment, what is the optimal strategy for an information intermediary?
  - What general demands does the business of information intermediaries pose on the technologies applied to offer the services?
  - What influence does the intermediary's awareness on the market have on his/her efficiency?
  - What are the critical success factors for information intermediaries?

## 4.2 The economic theory of search

The model of the information intermediary is based on a microeconomic model of search. The aim of the present chapter is to introduce the microeconomic theory of search that enables us to describe situations of sequential decision making under uncertainty and with costly information procurement. Search processes are fundamental properties of economic markets.[533] The problem of search is a problem of disequilibrium and uncertainty.[534] The disequilibrium in the economic situation is mainly the result of costly information acquisition. Uncertainty can be caused by incomplete knowledge about the true state of the environment.[535] Stigler[536] pointed out the role of information in economic situations, and he examined search strategies in consumer search for information about the prices of products offered by different suppliers [Stigler 61] and in employee's job search for the highest wages [Stigler 62]. Since this first introduction of search problems to economic research, theory has been developed further and was applied to a multitude of economic

---

[533] Cf. [Lippman 79, p. 10].

[534] Cf. [Hey 81b, p. 2].

[535] Cf. Section 2.1.1.3.

[536] A review of Stiglers basic search models can be found in [Gastwirth 76] and [Telser 73].

problems. A number of authors[537] have extended Stigler's simple search model, that has only considered prices or wages as relevant characteristics, to models that take other characteristics as, for example, product quality into account. McCall, Salop, Lippman/McCall, and Yoon[538] have applied search theory to the analysis of job search and unemployment, Rosenfield/Shapiro/ Butler[539] have investigated the problem of selling an asset by applying search models. Several other more general decision problems have been studied with the aid of search theory, for example, by Weitzman, Morgan, and Hansson/Holt/ Mayer.[540]

In Stigler's simple search model the amount of search expended by a decision-maker depends on two factors: the expected return of the search process, and the costs[541] of the search activities. If the individual expects the return of search to be high, he/she will reject offers that are below this expectation and will continue searching. On the other hand, if the costs for search are high, the individual will tend to limit the activities spent in search.

In general terms, the *search problem* can be defined as follows: the decision-maker wishes to find a 'good' object out of a large collection of objects but wishes to spend only a minimum amount of resources for search, i.e., the decision-maker wants to maximize the expected reward from search.[542] Search problems of this kind are described in a series of economics literature, e.g., [McCall 65], [McCall 70], [Marschak 66], [Lippman 76], [Gastwirth 76], and [Hey 81b]. Solutions to such search problems aim to find an optimal strategy for the behavior of the decision-maker. This is to find values for the optimal intensity of search and information gathering under different environmental conditions, and the optimal procedures for acquiring the information.

In the following sections the basic structure of search models will be introduced (Section 4.2.1), a formal description of a simple search model will be given (Section 4.2.2), and some extensions to the simple search model will be discussed (Section 4.2.3).

## 4.2.1 The basic assumptions and structure of search models

In economics literature search models have been applied to several economic situations and different assumptions about the states of the decision-maker and his/her environment have been made. The mathematical foundations of the optimization

---

[537] Cf. [MacQueen 64], [Kihlstrom 74b], [Wilde 80], [Hey 81a], [von Ungern-Sternberg 82], [von Ungern-Sternberg 84], and [Janko 85].
[538] Cf. [McCall 70], [Salop 73], [Lippman 76], and [Yoon 81] respectively.
[539] Cf. [Rosenfield 83].
[540] Cf. [Weitzman 79], [Morgan 83], [Hansson 90].
[541] Search costs are a part of the costs of a transaction, see Section 3.2.2.2.
[542] The expected reward from search is determined by the utility of the best object found in the search process minus the costs spent for search.

problem and the different assumptions for search models will be reviewed in this section.

Search is a process of information acquisition about objects' characteristics and attributes (Section 2.2). To cope with the complexity involved in real-life search processes, a theoretic treatment has to abstract from the diversity of conditions of the particular case.[543] The present treatment of search processes constructs a simple, formal search model.[544]

An individual, referred to as the *decision-maker* or as the *searcher*, is seeking for an object[545] with a high value[546] of one particular attribute[547] in a population of almost identical objects differing only in that certain attribute value. The attribute value can be interpreted as representing the value of the object's quality, i.e., the higher the attribute value, the higher is the quality of the object.[548]

The searcher makes a sequence of observations, one at a time, $X_1, X_2, X_3,...$ of a random variable $X$ representing the objects' attribute values. The index stands for the number of the observation made. All observations are drawn from a known, constant distribution with the *cumulative distribution function* (CDF) $F(X)$. The searcher's reward is the maximum value of the random variable $X$ observed in the whole search process. Every single observation costs a constant amount $c>0$, independent of the way[549] the observations are generated. The search costs for a single observation accumulate all costs for the acquisition of information about the opposite market side,[550] i.e., for determining an object's value of the particular attribute under consideration. Hence, search costs include the costs for communication with the supplier, costs for determining the object's attribute value, and the

---

[543] In general, a theory has to abstract a small number of 'common and crucial elements' to explain a class of phenomena, cf. [Nagel 63, p. 213].

[544] Cf. [Hey 81b, p. 56, fp.] and [DeGroot 70, p. 272 fp.].

[545] These objects can be products, services, or information.

[546] In another formulation of the search model the searcher is looking for a product with a low price, i.e., the searcher samples from a known distribution of prices for products being all of the same quality. See, for example, [Hey 79b].

[547] To simplify matters only one attribute is introduced to describe the objects under investigation. In a more general setting a vector of attributes can be assumed to describe the objects' characteristics, cf. [Kihlstrom 74a, p. 416].

[548] The quality of an object can be conceived as 'the amount of a desirable attribute it possesses,' cf. [Kihlstrom 74a, p. 415].

[549] This is to say, the costs $c$ of a single observation are independent from the type of the search process, e.g., a sequential search or a fixed-sample-size search, and independent from the succession of the observations. In other terms, search is performed with a *standard sequential search technology*, i.e., marginal search costs are constant during the search process, cf. [Stiglitz 89, p. 783-784].

[550] Cf. Section 3.2.2.2.

searcher's opportunity costs of time.[551]

The searcher is assumed to be risk neutral, and the net reward will be the maximum utility[552] of all objects observed minus the sum of all search costs incurred in the whole process of search.

The assumptions of this simple search model, referred to as the *basic search paradigm (BSP)* in [Schotter 81], can be summarized as follows:

- observations of a random variable $X$ are drawn from a known, constant distribution with CDF $F(X)$ of objects' attribute values, representing the object's quality;
- a single observation costs a given constant amount $c>0$;
- the searcher is risk neutral and only aims to maximize the expected profit;
- the time horizon of the search problem is infinite; and
- the searcher has perfect recall to previous observations, i.e., an observation $X_j$ made in a previous step can be recalled and accepted if poorer results are determined in subsequent observations.

With these assumptions the decision-maker's optimization problem is to find the optimal strategy for the search process, i.e., to find an optimal stopping rule[553] that tells the searcher when to stop searching and what the expected-net reward will be following this strategy. The optimal *stopping rule* gives the searcher a *reservation-value* $x^*$ for the random variable $X$ and the following instruction for the search process, referred to as the *optimal search strategy* (Figure 11):

---

[551]  Cf. [McAfee 88, p. 100]. The most important part of the search costs is usually the cost of time, cf. [Stigler 61].

[552]  In this description of a simple search problem we speak about the utility of an object searched by the decision-maker and refer to the utility offered by the value of a single attribute of the object. In a more general description one has to take into account a vector of attributes and calculate the utility of the object by considering the contribution of every single attribute to the searcher's utility. See, for example, [Kihlstrom 74a, p. 415].

[553]  In statistics' literature economic search problems are referred to as *stopping problems* or *sequential decision problems*. See, for example, [DeGroot 70, p. 324].

- Stop searching if the currently observed value $X_i$ of the random variable is greater than the reservation value $x^*$.

- Continue search otherwise.

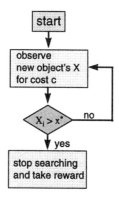

*Figure 11:     One step of search in the optimal search strategy.*

Theory derives methods to determine the reservation value $x^*$ and therewith the optimal search strategy for a wide class of different search problems. These differ in the assumptions about the searcher or about the searcher's environment.[554] The simple model of search claims that people perform search by using a *sequential decision procedure* with a somehow determined *reservation value* as a stopping rule. Feinberg/Johnson[555] have shown the superiority of a sequential decision rule over fixed-sample-size decision rules.[556] In a sequential decision procedure the searcher sequentially observes the value of a random variable and stops as soon as the value exceeds the reservation value. Whereas in a fixed-sample-size decision rule, the number of observations is determined before the process of search starts. Schotter/Braunstein[557] investigated the behavior of decision-makers in a situation comparable to the one given by the assumptions of the BSP; they found that people performing search actually behave as if they were setting a reservation value prior to search. The reservation values in these experiments were not calculated in a mathematical model, but determined from assumptions the searchers had made about their environment or simply by intuition.

A proof of the existence of an optimal search strategy for several classes of sequential decision problems is given by DeGroot[558] and will not be repeated here. Kohn/Shavell and Wilde[559] showed the existence and uniqueness of reservation values and thereupon the existence of an optimal search strategy in consumer

---

[554] The mathematical description of the search model and the determination of reservation values will be presented in Section 4.2.2.

[555] Cf. [Feinberg 77].

[556] McAfee/McMillan show that a sequential search mechanism is optimal in the class of all search mechanisms, cf. [McAfee 88].

[557] Cf. [Schotter 81].

[558] Cf. [DeGroot 70, p. 290 fp.].

[559] Cf. [Kohn 74], [Wilde 80].

search models. For the basic search model presented above the optimal search strategy is derived in [Hey 81b. p. 56-66] and formally proved in [Hey 79a].

## 4.2.2 The formal description of the simple search model

The aim of the current section is to derive mathematical foundations for the simple search model (BSP) and the solution of the model, based on the assumptions set up in the previous section. The model of the information intermediary, to be developed in Section 4.2, is based on this formulation.

### 4.2.2.1 The reservation value in the optimal strategy

According to Section 4.2.1, the decision-maker needs to determine a reservation value $x^*$ to formulate the optimal stopping rule. The reservation value can be derived from the following consideration:[560] At some stage during the search process, let be $X_m$ the maximum value of the random variable $X$ observed so far. The decision-maker can then stop searching and take the reward $X_m$ ignoring all search costs incurred until then or can take another observation. The expected additional net reward from one further observation in the search process, if $X_m$ already observed, is then given by:

*(eq. 9)*
$$G(X_m) = [X_m \cdot F(X_m) + \int_{X_m}^{\infty} x \, dF(x) - c] - X_m$$

The terms in the expression can be interpreted as follows:
- In the first term $F(X_m)$ is the probability that the next observation will yield a value $X_j \leq X_m$. In this case the searcher's reward will remain $X_m$, because the observed attribute value was not larger than the maximum of all observations made so far, which is $X_m$.
- The second term describes the expected reward in case the value observed is larger than $X_m$. In this case we have to integrate over the probability density function (PDF) $f(x)$ to find the expected reward.
- The observation causes costs $c$. The subtraction from the expected reward of the additional observation gives the searcher's net reward.
- To calculate the additional reward of one further observation, one subtracts the value $X_m$, already certain to the searcher, from the net reward.

Using integration by parts[561] (eq. 9) results in:

*(eq. 10)*
$$G(X_m) = \int_{X_m}^{\infty} [1 - F(x)] dx - c$$

---

[560]  Cf. [Hey 81b, p. 57 fp.].
[561]  For the simplification of (eq. 9) see Appendix B.

(eq. 11)    $$\frac{\partial\, G(X_m)}{\partial\, X_m} = -\left[1 - F(X_m)\right] \le 0 \quad \forall\; X_m \le \min\{x, F(x) = 1\}.$$

The function $G(X_m)$ is monotonously decreasing (see (eq. 11)), and has one extreme value at $G(+\infty) = - c < 0$. Together with the plausible assumption $G(-\infty) > 0$ (which is simply a condition that implies that some search is preferable to none) it follows that the integral equation

(eq. 12)    $$G(X_m) = 0 \quad \Leftrightarrow \quad \int_{X_m}^{\infty} [1 - F(x)]\, dx = c$$

has exactly one solution[562] for $X_m$.

The unique solution to (eq. 12) is the reservation value $x^*$ in the optimal strategy of the simple search problem (Section 4.2.1). For an observation with $X_m = x^*$ the expected additional reward of a further observation is zero $(G(x^*) = 0)$, so, the searcher is indifferent between stopping and continuing search. But, if the observation $X_m$ exceeds the reservation value $x^*$, the searcher will stop and take the observation as reward.[563] In (eq. 12) the integral represents the expected return from one additional observation; in equilibrium this is equal to the marginal costs $c$ for generating that observation. The integral equation (eq. 12) for the reservation value $x^*$ is a functional equation[564] that in some cases, depending on the complexity of distribution function $F(X)$, can only be solved numerically.

### 4.2.2.2 The searcher's utility

According to Section 4.2.1, an object is described by an attribute value $X_i$, which can be interpreted as the object's quality. Hence, the searcher's valuation of an object can be described as the valuation of the attribute value it possesses.[565] This valuation can be numerically expressed by a utility function, i.e., the representation of the searcher's preference ordering of the attribute values.[566] To take into account individual differences in the valuation of a particular product and its attributes between searchers, we have to introduce a function $U_j(X_i)$ to represent the valuation of the $j^{th}$ searcher for a value $X_i$ of the random variable $X$ observed.[567] If $U_j$ is a monotonous function[568] things become simple and the function $U_j(X_i)$ can be

---

[562]  Cf. [Hey 81b, p. 58].

[563]  According to the optimal search strategy stated in Section 4.2.1, the searcher will continue sampling until a value $X_m > x^*$ was observed.

[564]  Cf. [Wilde 80].

[565]  Cf. [Kihlstrom 74a].

[566]  Cf. [Gravelle 92, p. 74-76].

[567]  Cf. [Hey 81b, p. 63].

[568]  Even for functions $U(X)$ that are neither monotonously increasing nor decreasing an optimal search strategy can be developed, see [Hey 79a].

introduced in the formulation of the search model. A couple of transformations[569] of (eq. 12) results in:

(eq. 13)    $$\int_{x^\bullet}^{\infty} [1 - F(x)] \, dU_j(x) = c$$

The function $U_j(X_i)$ can be interpreted as the searcher's utility function,[570] or - as it will be done in the basic model of the information intermediary - as the $(j^{th})$ searcher's *willingness to pay for a particular value of the product attribute*. In this case the function $U_j(X_i)$ the function is a projection from the domain of attribute values $X_i$ to monetary units, i.e., it gives the individual's measure of the object's attribute in monetary units.

### 4.2.2.3 The searcher's net reward from an optimal strategy

Section 4.2.1 revealed that the searcher's net reward is the utility of the maximum value observed minus the total search costs. Denote the expected-net reward depending on an arbitrarily chosen reservation value $x$ by $V_x$, then the following equation holds:[571]

(eq. 14)    $$V_x = -c + \int_{x}^{\infty} U_j(x') \, dF(x') + V_x \, F(x) \cdot$$

The first term is the cost of an observation. The second term is the expected reward if the observation is greater than $x$, considering the probability that the observation is greater than $x$. The third term is the expected-net reward if the observation is less than, or equal to $x$ multiplied by the probability that the observation is less than, or equal to $x$. Solving (eq. 14) yields:

(eq. 15)    $$V_x = \frac{\left[ -c + \int_{x}^{\infty} U_j(x') \, dF(x') \right]}{[1 - F(x)]}$$

The optimal reservation value that maximizes the net reward $V_x$ can be derived from (eq. 15) through:

(eq. 16)    $$\frac{\partial V}{\partial x}(x^*) = 0 \cdot$$

which results after some transformations[572] in:

---

[569]    See Appendix C.
[570]    Cf. [Berger 80, p. 41 fp.], [DeGroot 70, p. 90].
[571]    Cf. [Hey 81b, p. 59], [Hey 79a].
[572]    See Appendix D.

*(eq. 17)*      $V_{x^*} = U_j(x^*).$

The result states the expected-net reward $V_{x^*}$ following the optimal search strategy is equal to the searcher's valuation of the optimal reservation value. The reservation value $x^*$ can be determined from (eq. 13). This result, called the *indifference property*,[573] will be used in Section 4.3.1.2 to derive the expected-net reward of an individual searcher in the basic model of an information intermediary.

## 4.2.3  Extensions to basic search models

The assumptions of the basic search model presented in Section 4.2.1 and 4.2.2 are quite severe in order to make the solution of the search problem mathematically tractable. Further research has led to an extenuation of the assumptions in order to make the model applicable to a wider class of problems. The present section summarizes the most important extensions.

### 4.2.3.1  Recall and the time horizon in the sequential decision process

In the basic search model the searcher can sample new observations forever, i.e., the time horizon of the problem is infinite. In addition, the searcher has perfect recall to previous observations, i.e., at any stage in the search process the decision-maker can chose the outcome of an observation $X_j$ made in a previous step.

If the time horizon of the problem is infinite, the possibility of recall extends no additional advantage to the decision-maker over sampling without recall,[574] since the reservation value $x^*$ remains constant during all stages of the search process, regardless of the number of observations. Consequently, the decision-maker can decide immediately after an observation was made whether to accept an object or to continue search. However, in some situations the time horizon is finite,[575] and future rewards are discounted at a constant rate.[576] In this search problem the reservation value becomes time dependent $(x_t^*)$.[577] In particular, the reservation value decreases as the horizon approaches, because the probability of finding a better

---

[573]  Cf. [Hey 81b, p. 60].

[574]  The reason is that the observations are independent and identically distributed, cf. [DeGroot 70, p. 335].

[575]  Assume, for example, that a single observation requires a certain period of time, and the decision-maker does only have a given amount of time applicable for search, cf. [Hey 81b, p. 66].

[576]  Cf. [Hey 81b, p. 67]. The interpretation for this can be that the searcher aims to realize the result of search as early as possible.

[577]  Cf. [Hey 81b, p. 70-74].

object in the remaining steps of search is decreasing.[578] In this case a searcher who has the opportunity of recall, is obviously better off than without recall, because of the opportunity to go back to higher values obtained in earlier observations, that were originally rejected when the reservation value $x_i^*$ was still higher.

### 4.2.3.2 Adaptive search models

According to the basic assumptions, the distribution of objects' attribute values is publicly known with certainty.[579] In real-life situations, learning about the environment is an important characteristic of rational behavior. In terms of the search model, learning refers to an accumulation of information about the characteristics of the underlying probability distribution. These search problems are labeled *adaptive decision models*.[580]

During the adaptive search process, information about the probability distribution is drawn from observations $X_i$ of the random variable $X$ itself.[581] With every new observation the decision-makers revise their assessment of the distribution, i.e., the reservation value $x^*$ in the optimal search strategy depends on the searcher's current assessment of the distribution. For a normal distribution the accumulation of information about the distribution can be described by means of the precision $p_t$[582] and the mean $m_t$ of the distribution. These parameters vary with increasing evidence about the distribution, and the reservation value as well as the optimal search strategy depend on these parameters:[583] $x_t^*(m_t, p_t)$.

### 4.2.3.3 Multistage search models

The previous section has shown the effects of uncertainty about information on the macro-level of the model on the search process. This is the information about the probability distribution of the objects' attribute values. In addition to that, uncertainty can occur on a micro-level of the search process as well. The information about an object's attribute value $X_i$ gathered in a superficial observation leaves the searcher uncertain about the true value $Y_i$ of the attribute until a precise evaluation of the object is conducted. To reduce the uncertainty, the searcher has to perform a

---

[578] Cf. [Hey 81b, p. 75-76].

[579] In this case we speak of a *static decision problem*. As an alternative interpretation of the publicly known distribution of attribute values, one can assume that the subjective assessment of the distribution remains fixed throughout the search process, cf. [Hey 81b, p. 80].

[580] Cf. [DeGroot 70, p. 336, fp.], [Rothschild 74], [Kohn 74], [Hey 81b, p. 80 fp.].

[581] A second source of information would be the observation of an external variable, cf. [Hey 81b, p. 93]. In this case a Bayes analysis can be applied, see Section 2.1.4.

[582] The precision of a distribution is defined as the reciprocal of the variance, cf. [Hey 81b, p. 85].

[583] Cf. [Kohn 74], [Hey 81b, p. 96].

second costly step of *evaluation*[584] (for costs $c_E > 0$) in addition to the observation (for costs $c$) in the search process. The problem can be modeled by means of a multivariate distribution $F(X, Y)$ in which the two dimensions of the distribution are correlated.[585] The first dimension $(X)$ of the distribution can be interpreted as the attribute value revealed by the supplier of the object; the second dimension $(Y)$ is the true attribute value found in a thorough evaluation of the object.

In the first stage of the search process the searcher observes the attribute $X_i$ of some random object, the decision-maker can then:[586]

- accept the object at once and receive the reward $E(Y \mid X=X_i)$,
- reject the object and continue search or
- evaluate the object's true attribute value $Y_i$.

The decision when to accept the object immediately, when to reject it, and when to test depends on the value $X_i$ observed in the first step, the value $Y_i$ investigated in the evaluation, and the correlation between the two values. In Figure 12 the search process is described schematically considering the optimal strategy. The reservation values $x^*$, $y^*$, $v^*$ of the different decisions in one step of the search process can be determined from a formal analysis of the two-stage search model; for a detailed description see MacQueen, Hey, and Janko/Taudes/Frisch.[587]

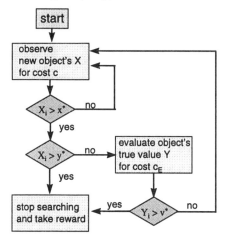

*Figure 12:*    *Sampling in the two-stage search process; based on [Janko 85, p. 4].*

---

[584]  Investment in activities that reveal information about the *experience characteristics* of products is called evaluation, cf. [Wilde 80, p. 1265]. According to Nelson, experience characteristics of products are those product attributes that are usually revealed 'by way of experience,' i.e., through purchase and use of the product, cf. [Nelson 70].

[585]  Cf. [Hey 81b, p. 76], [MacQueen 64], [Janko 85].

[586]  Cf. [Janko 85, p. 3].

[587]  Cf. [MacQueen 64], [Hey 81a], [Janko 85].

## 4.3 Model of an information intermediary

The present section introduces the basic assumptions and theoretic foundation of the model of a risk neutral, monopolistic information intermediary. First, the two markets the intermediary is operating in are introduced: (a) the supply market offering objects, i.e., products, services, or information, with a distribution of quality, and (b) the set of consumers with their individual preferences for different quality levels. Second, the intermediary's processes will be described: the acquisition of information in the supply market, and the sale and dissemination of information among potential consumers. The combination of the two processes results in the intermediary's optimization problem.

### 4.3.1 The intermediary's market environment

The information intermediary operates in a given market environment which imposes restrictions[588] on potential actions and accordingly on performance. The intermediary has no direct influence on the circumstances and parameters of the environment, but the intermediary can indirectly influence the environment by the decision which market to enter. In addition to these static influences of the environmental circumstances, the environment itself can be subject to changes[589] which then will influence the intermediary and the intermediary's performance as well.

#### 4.3.1.1 The suppliers' market side: sources of information

The basic model of an information intermediary has to abstract from particular characteristics of the products, services, or information offered by suppliers[590] so that the model remains as generally applicable as possible and mathematically tractable.[591] Hence, all offers are simply treated as objects that can be described by a single attribute[592] $X_i$, in which the subscript $i$ stands for one specific object. The distribution of the objects' attribute values is given by the CDF $F(X)$. The object's attribute value $X_i$ can be interpreted as the object's quality (Section 4.2.1). The particular objects under consideration can be products, services or information.

---

[588]    See, for example, [Laux 91, p. 23 fp.].
[589]    These changes can be, for example, changes in the preferences of consumers in a certain market due to technological progress. See, for example, [Illing 97, p. 11].
[590]    Suppliers will also be conceived as sources of information following the conception that 'sources of information are all persons, objects or processes that can supply information,' cf. [Gabler WI-LEX 88, p. 2544]. See Section 2.2 as well.
[591]    Cf. [Nagel 63, p. 213].
[592]    Cf. Section 4.2.1 and [Kihlstrom 74a].

As indicated in Section 1.2, the model has to cover information intermediaries operating in markets for information like the Internet. If we are concerned with search for information about a special topic in this environment, we are confronted with an enormous amount of available information.[593] However, relevant for a particular problem under consideration is only a very small portion of all available information. Additionally, the higher the demand on the relevance of the information, the smaller will be the portion of information matching the requirement.[594] The attribute value $X_i$, describing a particular object (or information) available on the market, can also be interpreted as the relevance of the object for a given decision problem under consideration. In this context the 'quality of an object' can be better labeled as *the relevance of the information for the particular topic under consideration*,[595] i.e., the higher the value of $X_i$, the more relevant is the particular information for the topic or decision problem under consideration.[596] This implies that for each particular topic under consideration a particular CDF $F(X)$ exists. On the Internet one can assume that the density of 'high' qualities, i.e., the density of relevant information, is strongly decreasing with magnitude. In the following, this circumstance will be expressed by means of an *exponential distribution*[597] taken as a special instance of the distribution of objects' attribute values.

The probability density function (PDF) $f(X)$ and the cumulative distribution function (CDF) $F(X)$ with the parameter $\lambda$ are then given by:[598]

*(eq. 18)*      $$f(X) = \lambda \cdot e^{-\lambda \cdot X},$$

*(eq. 19)*      $$F(X) = \left[1 - e^{-\lambda \cdot X}\right].$$

The parameter $\lambda$ is a measure for the concentration of values around the origin of the system of coordinates. The higher the value $\lambda$ is, the more the density of the probability is concentrated around zero (Figure 13). This property makes the expo-

---

[593]   Cf. Section 1.1 and [Kreibich 86, p. 26 fp.], [Kaminsky 77, p. 39 fp.].

[594]   Cf. [Zelewski 87].

[595]   See Section 2.1.1.3.

[596]   For example, the methods of Information Retrieval (IR) apply statistical methods to determine the relevance of a particular document to a certain topic. See, for example, [Akman 96], [Reimer 97], [Knorz 97], and Section 2.1.3. Following such techniques, the attribute value $X_i$ can be interpreted as a measure for the frequency of a term's occurrence in a particular document, which is the information item $i$.

[597]   The exponential distribution used here is a special case of the *Poisson distribution* $(\lambda^k / k!) \cdot e^{-\lambda \cdot x}$ with $k=1$, cf. [Bronstein 89, p. 663].

[598]   Cf. [Feller 70, p. 8, 14 fp.], [Bronstein 89, p. 665].

nential distribution an ideal candidate to describe the distribution of information relevant to a particular topic in a large network like the Internet.[599]

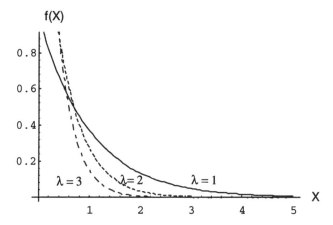

*Figure 13:*    *Probability density function f(X) of the exponential distribution for three different values of the parameter* λ *(λ=1, 2, 3).*

### 4.3.1.2  The consumers' market side

In Section 4.2.2.2 the searcher's utility from an object possessing a particular attribute value was introduced. In the model the utility function $U_j(X_i)$ will be used to describe consumers' willingness to pay for objects' attribute values $X_i$. To simplify matters, it is assumed that consumers are risk neutral; consequently, a linear utility function[600] $U_j(X_i)$ describes the $j^{th}$ consumer's valuation of a particular attribute value:

*(eq. 20)*      $U_j(X_i) = \beta_j \cdot X_i.$

The parameter $\beta_j$, measuring attribute values in monetary units,[601] is a measure for the $j^{th}$ consumer's willingness to pay for a particular attribute value. Between two or more consumers from the population of all consumers there is generally a difference in their individual willingness to pay for a particular attribute value. However, for the population as a whole we can also assume similarities in consumers' attitudes towards quality. This can be expressed by a distribution of the parameter $\beta$. In the following, a normal distribution $N[\mu_\beta, \sigma_\beta]$ with PDF $h(\beta)$ and CDF $H(\beta)$ is assumed to hold for the parameter $\beta$. The mean $\mu_\beta$ of the distribution is the medium value of the willingness to pay in the population, i.e., a larger value of the

---

[599]   The exponential distribution of objects' attribute values can be interpreted as a representation of the problem of *information overload* mentioned in Section 1.1.

[600]   Cf. [DeGroot 70, p. 22, 100], [Laux 91, p. 183 fp.].

[601]   The unit of the willingness to pay $\beta$ is *[monetary units / unit of attribute value]*.

mean $\mu_\beta$ expresses that in the population the willingness to pay for a particular attribute value is relatively higher than in a population with a lower mean. The standard deviation $\sigma_\beta$ of the distribution expresses the heterogeneity (or diffusion) of the population, i.e., a larger standard deviation $\sigma_\beta$ expresses that the preferences in the population are more heterogeneous (or diffused) than for smaller values of $\sigma_\beta$.[602]

The two parameters ($\mu_\beta$ and $\sigma_\beta$) describe the characteristics of the consumers' market side on an abstract level. A particular market can be described by a specific choice of the two parameters, but the relation to observable criteria of particular groups of consumers[603] is not given therewith. This abstract characterization of a market only gives the framework for the description and does not limit the application of the model to a particular form of description of the market as would be done, for example, by use of particular segmentation variables. From this point of view, a comparison of two (or more) different target markets of the information intermediary can be performed via the two distribution parameters. For example, a combination of $\mu_\beta = 'high'$ and $\sigma_\beta = 'low'$ may be the description of the market of business users of information from all industries, whereas the combination of $\mu_\beta = 'low'$ and $\sigma_\beta = 'low'$ can be interpreted as the market of private users of information from all demographic groups. This interpretation already involves a relation between observable characteristics of consumers (business vs. private users of information) and the distribution parameters of the model. In general, the model is completely detached from this interpretation.

With the utility function (eq. 20) of an individual consumer and the expected-net reward from search following an optimal search strategy (eq. 17) we are now able to calculate the consumer's expected-net reward from search in the simple search model of Section 4.2.2:

*(eq. 21)*     $$V_{x^*} = U_j(x^*) = \beta_j \cdot x^* = \beta_j \cdot x^*(\beta_j).$$

In Figure 14 the expected-net reward from search following an optimal search strategy is plotted against the parameter $\beta$, expressing the expected-net reward from personal search as a function of the willingness to pay $\beta$. The plot is slightly convex, expressing the fact that the marginal growth of the expected-net reward from search increases with an increase of the willingness to pay $\beta$ for a particular attribute value.

---

[602]    In a consumers' market it is common to distinguish between *homogeneous, diffused,* or *clustered* preferences for a set of product attributes, cf. [Kotler 88, p. 283]. In the model homogeneous preferences can be described by small values of $\sigma_\beta$, the diffusion of preferences can be described by increasing values of $\sigma_\beta$.

[603]    In general, consumer markets can be segmented by geographic, demographic, psychographic, and behavioral variables, cf. [Kotler 88, p. 286 fp.]. See [Hüttner 94, p. 104 fp.] and [Nieschlag 91, p. 14, 618 fp.] as well.

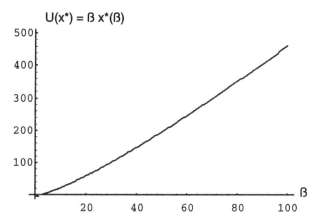

$$U(x^*) = \beta\, x^*(\beta)$$

*Figure 14:*  *Expected-net reward from search following an optimal strategy as a function of the willingness to pay β (c=1).*

## 4.3.2 The information intermediary

### 4.3.2.1 Basic characterization

The model of an information intermediary focuses the mediation of information and therewith the reduction of search costs as the intermediary's main service[604] for potential clients. The intermediary gathers information on the suppliers' market bearing the costs for search. The information intermediary is assumed to apply the same search technology and therefore bear the same costs for a single observation as individual information seekers. The sources of information are assumed to reveal their attribute values honestly. The information sold by the information intermediary is a reference[605] to an object available on the market that has an attribute value exceeding a given minimum level set by the intermediary. The information intermediary sells[606] this information to a number of consumers so that search costs can be spread[607] among all clients and, in addition, a positive profit

---

[604]  To keep matters simple and the model mathematically tractable the model only covers this fundamental, and in reality highly significant, service of the information intermediary (Section 4.1.1 and Figure 10).

[605]  In case of products, the reference can be the brand name and the supplier, in case of online available information the reference can be an URL.

[606]  The intermediary sells the information directly, an alternative method of selling information would be the indirect sale via services provided by the intermediary, cf. Section 2.5.4.

[607]  Search costs have to be borne only once, cf. [Hänchen 85, p. 408].

can be achieved. In this model the intermediary acts as a pure coordinator[608] in the market, i.e., the intermediary only performs the matching of demand and supply for objects (products, services, information) available in the market.[609] To take into account the consumers' opportunity to choose between personal search for information and consulting the intermediary, the intermediary's offer (or service) will be compared with the expected results from search performed by the individual consumer.[610] Further, the information intermediary is assumed to be risk neutral[611] and operates in the market only on behalf of his/her own profit maximization aim. Besides, the intermediary affects the market with the services offered as was discussed in Section 3.4 and, as will be shown, is one result of the model (Section 4.6).

In real-life examples the information intermediary operates in a given environment, already described in the previous section. The intermediary opening a new business has the choice of a particular market to enter. Once installed, the intermediary usually has little opportunity to exert any changes on the environmental conditions. The intermediary has to maximize the expected profit by application of an optimal strategy under the environmental restrictions given.[612]

Acting in the suppliers' and consumers' market, the intermediary has two main processes to perform, the *acquisition of information* and the *sale of information* (Section 4.1.1). The intermediary's behavior in the two processes can be described by two decision variables. In the acquisition of information the intermediary searches for objects and has to decide about the minimum attribute value $X^I$ to be accepted during search. This attribute value will be the 'object quality offered by the intermediary.' In the sale process the intermediary has to decide about the fee[613] $F^I$ consumers are charged to receive the reference to an object with at least the minimum attribute value $X^I$. Hence, the information intermediary 'guarantees' that the object referenced has at least the attribute value $X^I$. The sale and dissemination of the information is assumed not to cause marginal costs, i.e., the fee $F^I$ charged contributes to the information intermediary's revenue without further reductions.[614]

---

[608] Cf. Section 3.3.2 and [Baligh 67, p. 123 fp.].

[609] According to Section 3.3.2, matching of demand and supply is typical for a broker intermediary, who does not take over risk and does not buy and sell on his/her own behalf.

[610] The information intermediary competes with consumers' personal search processes, cf. [Gehrig 93, p. 99, 107].

[611] The intermediary's objective is therefore the maximization of the expected profit, cf. [Laux 87, p. 48].

[612] See, for example, [Baligh 67, p. 110 fp., 128 fp.], [Myerson 83].

[613] The fee $F^I$ is measured in monetary units.

[614] If the transfer of the information causes marginal costs $C'_D$, the resulting revenue obtained for every sale of the information will be reduced to $(F^I - C'_D)$ see Section 4.4.4.3.

The model takes into account only one cycle of information acquisition and dissemination by the information intermediary; the repeated execution of search processes by the intermediary (Section 3.2.3.2), is therefore assumed only implicitly.

Figure 15 depicts the intermediary's activities in the two markets schematically. On the suppliers' market side the object with $X_7 \geq X'$ is accepted by the intermediary, and on the consumers' market side a subset of all consumers (indicated in gray) chooses to go to the intermediary and buy a reference to the '$X_7$ - object' for the fee $F'$.

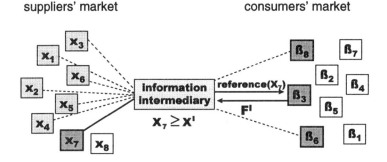

*Figure 15:*    *Schematic description of the intermediary's activities in the basic model.*

With the two decision variables $X'$ and $F'$ the intermediary's profit $P'$ is determined by the revenue $R'$ minus the search costs $C'$ incurred:

*(eq. 22)*        $P' = P'(X',F') = R'(X',F') - C'(X')$.

The intermediary is assumed to be risk neutral, therefore the intermediary's optimization problem is simply stated as:

*(eq. 23)*        $\underset{X',F'}{Max} \; P'(X',F') = \underset{X',F'}{Max} \; \left[ R'(X',F') - C'(X') \right]$.

The basic model of the information intermediary only considers costs $C'(X')$ incurred in the search for information. Other fixed costs, for example, investments in technologies applied by the intermediary to search for information or to communicate with clients or information sources, would bring a further negative contribution to the profit $P'$ in (eq. 22). With the introduction of fixed costs in the model critical values of the other parameters of the model can be determined. These critical values would indicate a threshold for which the information intermediary becomes profitable, i.e., for which $P'>0$. However, the model is not designed to perform numeric tests so that, for reasons of simplicity, fixed costs will be omitted in the basic form of the intermediary model. $C'$ and $R'$ will be derived in the following sections.

#### 4.3.2.2 *The intermediary's acquisition of information*

The intermediary searches in the suppliers' market for an 'acceptable quality', i.e., for an object with an attribute value of at least $X'$. In terms of the model, the intermediary searches by sequentially observing objects' attribute values drawn from the distribution of attribute values $X$ described by the CDF $F(X)$ (eq. 19). In this satiating search the probability of finding an object with an attribute value equal to or exceeding $X'$ is given by:

(eq. 24)
$$\int_{X'}^{\infty} dF(q) = \int_{X'}^{\infty} \frac{dF(q)}{dq} dq = \int_{X'}^{\infty} f(q) dq = \left[1 - F(X')\right] \cdot$$

The expected number of observations to be drawn from the distribution until an object with $X \geq X'$ is found, is given by:[615]

(eq. 25)[616]
$$\sum_{n=1}^{\infty} n \cdot F(X')^{n-1} \cdot \left[1 - F(X')\right] \;=\; \frac{1}{\left[1 - F(X')\right]} = e^{\lambda \cdot X'} \cdot$$

Therefore the total costs of the intermediary's search process are the costs of a single observation $c$ times the expected number of observations:

(eq. 26)
$$C'(X',c) = \frac{c}{\left[1 - F(X')\right]} = c \cdot e^{\lambda X'} \cdot$$

The search costs are a linear function of the costs for a single observation $c$, and an exponentially increasing function of the minimum quality level $X'$ guaranteed by the intermediary and the parameter $\lambda$ of the exponential distribution. The dependency of the intermediary's search costs on these parameters can be deduced from:

(eq. 27)
$$\frac{\partial}{\partial c} C'(X',c) = \frac{1}{\left[1 - F(X')\right]} = e^{\lambda X'} \quad > 0,$$

(eq. 28)
$$\frac{\partial}{\partial X'} C'(X',c) = \frac{c \cdot f(X')}{\left[1 - F(X')\right]^2} = c \cdot \lambda \cdot e^{\lambda X'} \quad > 0,$$

(eq. 29)
$$\frac{\partial}{\partial \lambda} C'(X',c) = \frac{\partial}{\partial \lambda}\left(\frac{c}{\left[1 - F(X')\right]}\right) = \frac{\partial}{\partial \lambda}\left(c \cdot e^{\lambda X'}\right) = c \cdot X' \cdot e^{\lambda X'} \quad > 0 \cdot$$

The dependency of the search costs on the parameters involved are portrayed in Figure 16 and Figure 17 for some special parameter values.

---

[615]   Cf. [DeGroot 70, p. 270].

[616]   The last transformation in the expression is:
$$\frac{1}{\left[1 - F(X')\right]} = \frac{1}{\left[1 - \left[1 - e^{-\lambda \cdot X'}\right]\right]} = e^{\lambda x' \cdot}$$

The intermediary's search costs are increasing with the minimum quality level $X^I$ offered by the intermediary. This is caused by the decreasing density of objects with higher attribute values in the distribution of attributes on the suppliers' market side (Section 4.3.1.1). Figure 16 reveals that a further decrease of the density of acceptable attribute values (qualities), described by an increasing value of the parameter $\lambda$ of the exponential distribution (Figure 13), results in an increase of the intermediary's expected search costs for a given value of $X^I$. Additionally, an increase in costs $c$ for a single observation (Figure 17) results in an increase of the expected search costs.

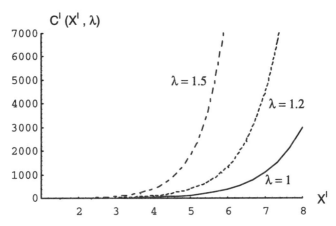

*Figure 16:*    *Dependency of the intermediary's expected search costs $C^I(X^I,\lambda)$ on the parameter $\lambda$ of the exponential distribution and the quality level $X^I$ ($c=1$).*

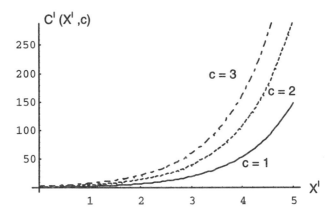

*Figure 17:*    *Dependency of the intermediary's expected search costs $C^I(X^I,c)$ on the costs $c$ for a single observation and the quality level $X^I$ ($\lambda=1$).*

### 4.3.2.3 The intermediary's clientele

In the model the intermediary sells the reference to an object with an attribute value of at least $X^I$ to consumers for a fee $F^I$. As indicated in the schematic picture of the intermediary's activities (Figure 15), not all consumers prefer to consult the information intermediary. Some consumers still prefer to perform their own search, because it provides them a higher expected-net reward than the price-quality combination offered by the intermediary. The expected-net reward from search is given by (eq. 21) in Section 4.3.1.2. The $j^{th}$ consumer's reward from buying the intermediary's information is given by:

(eq. 30)        $U_j^{Intermediary} = \beta_j \cdot X^I - F^I.$

The individual consumer prefers consulting the intermediary than performing personal search if:

(eq. 31)        $U_j^{Intermediary} = \left( \beta_j \cdot X^I - F^I \right) \quad > \quad U_j(x^*) = \beta_j \cdot x^*.$

This is the information seeker's *make or buy decision*. The individual's purchase decision is based on the values $X^I$ and $F^I$ quoted by the information intermediary. The information intermediary is assumed to honestly reveal the true reference to an object with a quality level of at least $X^I$, if consulted by the consumer.

Both sides of the *individual's make or buy condition* (the inequality in (eq. 31)) are plotted against the consumers' willingness to pay $\beta$ in Figure 18.

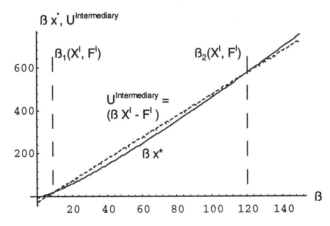

Figure 18:     *Comparison of the expected-net reward from personal search ($\beta \cdot x^*$) and the reward from using the intermediary $U^{Intermediary}$ (dashed line) plotted against the willingness to pay $\beta$ ($X^I=5$, $F^I=25$ and $\lambda=1$, $c=1$).*

The comparison of the two possibilities of consumers' information acquisition about the suppliers' market shows: For a given set of the decision variables ($F^I$ and $X^I$) and a given environmental parameter $\lambda$ only consumers with a medium willingness to pay $(\beta_1 < \beta < \beta_2)$[617] are better off, if they buy the information from the intermediary instead of searching personally. Consequently, these will consult the information intermediary. Consumers with a willingness to pay $\beta = \beta_{1:2}(X', F')$ are just indifferent between searching themselves and consulting the intermediary.

Consumers with a very high willingness to pay $(\beta > \beta_2)$ prefer to perform their own search because they have a very high valuation of quality. The quality level $X'$ offered by the intermediary, and therewith the net-reward $U^{Intermediary}$ achievable, is not high enough to make them better off than in their own search. For example, investors may require a rather high quality of market information (higher than the quality level $X'$ offered by the information intermediary) to make their investment decisions, because the information under consideration completely determines the outcome of their decision.[618] Therefore, these information seekers will prefer to perform their own search if the quality level offered by the information interme-diary is relatively low compared to their requirements. Consumers with a very low willingness to pay $(\beta < \beta_1)$ prefer to perform their own search, too, but for a slightly different reason. The reward $(\beta \cdot X')$ achievable with the quality level offered by the information intermediary's is too low to compensate them for the fee $F'$ charged for the information. Hence, these consumers will perform their own search, because they will be satisfied after only a few observations taken and incur very small search costs in their personal search processes. For example, people only roughly interested in the development of a particular market, require a rather low quality of information and thus will perform personal search in order to avoid the fee charged by the information intermediary.[619] The users of the information inter-mediary in this example will be information seekers for whom the information offered by the information intermediary only partly determines their personal decision problems. For these information seekers the information under consideration is only a smaller portion of all information required for the decision problem so that the price-quality combination offered by the information interme-diary is the best alternative for information acquisition for these information seekers.[620] However, it should be clear that the information intermediary can also

---

[617]   The values $\beta_1$ and $\beta_2$ are dependent on $X'$, $F'$, and $\lambda$.

[618]   In the terms of the basic model of decision theory (Section 2.1.4) the information under consideration would completely determine the action to be chosen by the decision maker. Therefore, the quality of the information required in this situation is relatively high, resulting in a relatively high willingness to pay $\beta$ for a particular quality level.

[619]   For these information seekers the information offered by the intermediary has no rele-vance for a particular decision problem, therefore, the quality of the information can be relatively low.

[620]   In this case the information obtained from the information intermediary has a propor-tionately small influence on the outcome of the decision so that a lower quality of the information is acceptable in return for relatively small costs for information acqui-sition.

satisfy the quality requirements of information seekers with a relatively high willingness to pay if a higher quality level $X^I$ will be offered.

Figure 18 reveals how variations in the intermediary's decision variables ($X^I$ and $F^I$) can be interpreted. An isolated increase of the quality level $X^I$ offered by the intermediary shifts the reward $U^{Intermediary}$ to higher values, this broadens the region of values $\beta$ for which $U^{Intermediary} > \beta x^*$. The range of values of the willingness to pay $\beta$ for which the intermediary is advantageous will increase as a result. The opposite effect is induced by an increase of the fee $F^I$ charged by the intermediary. The region of values $\beta$ for which $U^{Intermediary} > \beta x^*$ is reduced. The cause of these effects is the slight convexity of the expected-net reward from personal search following an optimal search strategy (Figure 14).

*Result 1:    Consumers with 'medium valuations' (willingness to pay) for quality buy information from the intermediary. Consumers with either high or low valuations (willingness to pay) prefer to search personally.*

The result stated herewith is different from results obtained in matching models. Yavas, for example, developed a matching model of a bilateral search market with buyers and sellers who have the opportunity to trade through an intermediary.[621] He found that only sellers with high valuations and buyers with low valuations trade through the intermediary. The intermediary in that case was a matchmaker as well. However, the main difference to the present model is that in bilateral search markets both market partners actively search for each other, and that valuations are expressed in form of bid and ask prices. In the search model presented here the sources of information are passive and only one market side invests in search.

### 4.3.2.4  Solutions to the intermediary model

Two values of the consumers' willingness to pay $\beta_1(X^I, F^I)$ and $\beta_2(X^I, F^I)$, for which consumers are indifferent between consulting the intermediary and performing personal search, were introduced in Figure 18. These values have to be determined from (eq. 31) together with the reservation value $x^*$ derived from the simple search model (eq. 13). This yields the following system of two equations that have to be solved simultaneously:

*(eq. 32)*
$$\left|\begin{array}{l} U^{Intermediary} = \left(\beta \cdot X^I - F^I\right) \quad = \quad U(x^*) = \beta \cdot x^* \\ \displaystyle\int_{x^*}^{\infty} \left[1 - F(x)\right] \cdot \beta \, d\, x = c \end{array}\right| .$$

---

[621]    Cf. [Yavas 94, p. 406, 408]. See Section 4.1.2 as well.

Using (eq. 20) and (eq. 19) and carrying out the integration[622] the system can be simplified to:

(eq. 33)

$$\left| \begin{array}{l} (\beta \cdot X' - F') = \beta \cdot x^* \\ \dfrac{1}{\lambda} \cdot e^{-\lambda \cdot x^*} \cdot \beta = c \end{array} \right| .$$

According to Figure 19 the system has 0, 1 or 2 solutions for $\beta$ depending on the choice of the decision variables[623] $X'$ and $F'$.

If the system (eq. 32) has 2 solutions, the situation is described by Figure 18 where consumers with a medium willingness to pay consult the intermediary. In case the system has only one solution (given by a combinations of decision variables in the left part of the diagram[624]) the intersection $\beta_1$ of the two curves in Figure 18 would lie below $\beta=0$, indicating that it is preferable for all consumers with a medium and low willingness to pay $\beta$ to consult the intermediary. If the system has no solution, the line $U^{Intermediary}=\beta X'-F'$ lies below the curve $U=\beta x^*$ for all values of $\beta$, expressing that the intermediary does not offer a service valuable to any consumer, and therefore has no clients at all.

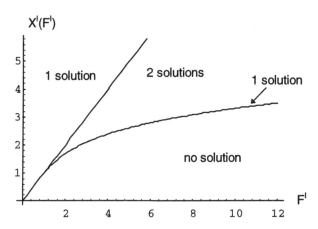

Figure 19:     *Number of solutions for $\beta_1$, $\beta_2 > 0$ to (eq. 32) for ranges of the decision variables $X'$ and $F'$ ($\lambda=1$, $c=1$), see Appendix E.*

---

[622]
$$\int_{x^*}^{\infty}[1-F(x)]\,dU(x) = \int_{x^*}^{\infty}[1-F(x)]\cdot\beta\,dx = \int_{x^*}^{\infty}e^{-\lambda x}\cdot\beta\,dx = \beta\cdot\left(\frac{-1}{\lambda}\cdot e^{-\lambda x}\right)\Bigg|_{x^*}^{\infty} = \beta\cdot\frac{1}{\lambda}\cdot e^{-\lambda x^*}.$$

[623] For a derivation of the ranges of parameters in Figure 19 see Appendix E.

[624] There is a second rather artificial case with only one solution to the system, described by the concave curve in Figure 19. In this case the two equations in the system (eq. 33) intersect tangentially.

### 4.3.2.5  The intermediary's expected revenue

According to the results of Section 4.3.2.3 the intermediary's clientele, i.e., the expected number of clients the intermediary will have for a certain choice of decision variables $F'$ and $X'$, can be derived by 'summing up' all consumers for whom condition (eq. 31) holds. Given the distribution $H(\beta)$ with PDF $h(\beta)$ for the willingness to pay $\beta$ within the population of consumers, and assuming that the number of potential users[625] of the information intermediary in the population is $N$, the expected number of consumers who will consult the intermediary is given by the integral of the PDF $h(\beta)$ over the interval $[\beta_1(X',F'), \beta_2(X',F')]$:

$$(eq.\ 34) \qquad E[N_{clients}] = N \cdot \int_{\beta_1(X',F')}^{\beta_2(X',F')} h(\beta)\,d\beta \cdot$$

The expected number of clients $E[N_{clients}]$ expresses how often the information intermediary can sell the information once gathered, i.e., the degree of reuse of the information.[626] In the following it will be assumed that the marginal costs for the dissemination of the information are vanishing. Therefore, the intermediary's expected revenue $R'$ is simply derived as the fee $F'$ charged times the expected number of clients:

$$(eq.\ 35) \qquad R'(X',F') = F' \cdot E[N_{clients}] = F' \cdot N \cdot \int_{\beta_1(X',F')}^{\beta_2(X',F')} h(\beta)\,d\beta \cdot$$

The intermediary's expected revenue $R'(X',F')$ as a function of the quality offered $X'$ and the fee charged $F'$ are plotted in Figure 20 and Figure 21 respectively. The revenue and, consequently, the expected profit is dependent on the characteristics of the consumers' market as well (eq. 35). The dependency on the parameters $\mu_\beta$ and $\sigma_\beta$ describing the distribution of the consumers' willingness to pay will be discussed in detail in Section 4.4.3.

With an increase in the quality level $X'$ offered by the information intermediary the number of consumers for whom the reward from buying the intermediary's information (the left hand side of the inequality in (eq. 31): $U^{Intermediary} = \beta X' - F'$) is larger than the expected reward from a personal search ($U(x^*) = \beta x^*$) is increasing. Consequently, the expected number of clients $E[N_{clients}]$ and accordingly the intermediary's expected revenue $R'(X',F')$ is increasing with an increase in $X'$ (Figure 20). Higher fees $F'$ charged by the intermediary reduce the reward $U^{Intermediary}$ that consumers can realize by consulting the intermediary. Therefore, the expected

---

[625]  The number $N$ of potential users can be different from the total number $N_0$ of consumers in the market for whom the intermediary's service might be advantageous ($N = u\ N_0,\ 0 \le u \le 1$). Differences may occur if the intermediary service can only be accessed with particular technologies, or if the information intermediary is not known to all consumers in the market, see Section 4.4.4.3.

[626]  Cf. Section 3.2.3.2.

number of clients and the intermediary's expected revenue decreases with an increase of the fee $F^l$ (Figure 21).

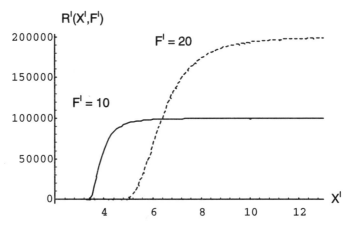

Figure 20:    *Dependency of the intermediary's expected revenue $R^l(X^l, F^l)$ on the quality level $X^l$ for two different fees $F^l=(10, 20)$ ($c=1$, $\lambda=1$, $\mu_\beta=4$, $\sigma_\beta=1$, $N= 10000$).*

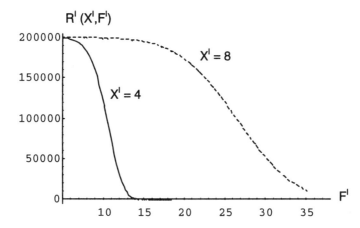

Figure 21:    *Dependency of the intermediary's expected revenue $R^l(X^l, F^l)$ on the fee $F^l$ for two different quality levels $X^l=(4, 8)$ ($c=1$, $\lambda=1$, $\mu_\beta=4$, $\sigma_\beta=1$, $N=10000$).*

### 4.3.3 The intermediary's optimization problem

Using (eq. 26) and (eq. 35), the intermediary's expected profit (eq. 22) can be stated as:[627]

(eq. 36)
$$P^I(X^I,F^I) = R^I(X^I,F^I) - C^I(X^I)$$
$$= F^I \cdot N \cdot \int_{\beta_1(X^I,F^I)}^{\beta_2(X^I,F^I)} h(\beta)\, d\beta - \frac{c}{\left[1 - F(X^I)\right]}.$$

The boundaries $\beta_1(X^I,F^I)$ and $\beta_2(X^I,F^I)$ of the integration can be derived from condition (eq. 31) in Section 4.3.2.3.[628] The intermediary's expected profit $P^I$ as a function of the quality level $X^I$ is plotted in Figure 22.

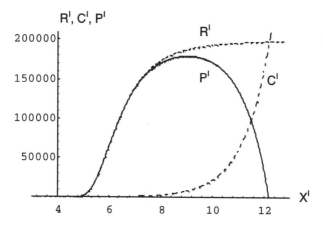

*Figure 22:*     *Expected revenue $R^I$, search costs $C^I$, and profit $P^I$ of the intermediary as a function of the quality level $X^I$ ($c=1$, $\lambda=1$, $F^I=20$, $\mu_\beta=4$, $\sigma_\beta=1$, $N=10000$).*

With an increase of the quality $X^I$ offered by the intermediary, the expected revenue $R^I$ increases as was already shown in Figure 20. However, the search for higher qualities $X^I$ results in higher search costs $C^I(X^I)$. The superposition of these two influences results in the graph shown in Figure 22. The dependency of the intermediary's expected profit $P^I$ on the two decision variables $X^I$ and $F^I$ is depicted in Figure 23 and Figure 24 respectively.

---

[627] The expected search costs, revenue, and profit are expressed in monetary units.
[628] For the numerical derivation of $\beta_1(X^I,F^I)$ and $\beta_2(X^I,F^I)$ see Section 4.3.2.4.

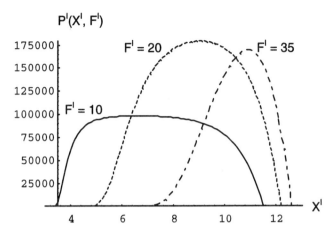

*Figure 23:*    Dependency of the intermediary's expected profit on the quality level $X^I$, plotted for three different fees $F^I=(10, 20, 35)$ $(c=1, \lambda=1, \mu_\beta=4, \sigma_\beta=1, N= 10000)$.

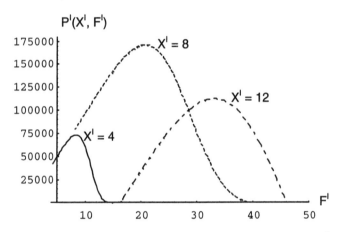

*Figure 24:*    Dependency of the intermediary's expected profit on the fee $F^I$, plotted for three different quality levels $X^I=(4, 8, 12)$ $(c=1, \lambda=1, \mu_\beta=4, \sigma_\beta=1, N= 10000)$.

For a fixed fee $F^I$ the dependency of the intermediary's expected profit yields what was already depicted in Figure 22. Different values of the fee $F^I$ in a variation of the quality level $X^I$ (Figure 23) and different values of the quality level $X^I$ in a variation of $F^I$ (Figure 24)[629] reveal that an optimal choice $(X^I,F^I)$ of decision variables must exist.

---

[629]    For a variation of the fee $F^I$ the expected search costs $C^I(X^I,c)$ are fixed by the minimum quality $X^I$ offered by the intermediary. Consequently, the intermediary's expected profit only varies due to changes of the expected revenue from variations of the fee $F^I$.

*Result 2:*  *For given environmental conditions (c, $\lambda$, $\mu_\beta$, $\sigma_\beta$, N) and a given fee $F^I$*
*(quality level $X^I$) the information intermediary's profit can be maximized*
*by a particular quality level $X^I_{opt}$ offered (fee $F^I_{opt}$ charged).*

This leads to the intermediary's optimization problem:

$$\underset{X^I,F^I}{Max}\, P^I(X^I,F^I) = \underset{X^I,F^I}{Max}\, \left[ R^I(X^I,F^I) - C^I(X^I) \right]$$

(eq. 37)

$$= \underset{X^I,F^I}{Max}\, \left[ F^I \cdot N \cdot \int_{\beta_1(X^I,F^I)}^{\beta_2(X^I,F^I)} h(\beta)\, d\beta - \frac{c}{\left[ 1 - F(X^I) \right]} \right].$$

The *intermediary's optimal strategy*, i.e., the combination of decision variables
$(X^I,F^I)$ maximizing the profit $P^I(X^I,F^I)$, can be derived from (eq. 36) by setting the
gradient of $P^I$ equal to zero:[630]

(eq. 38)    $$\vec{\nabla}\, P^I(X^I, F^I) = \left( \frac{\partial\, P^I(X^I, F^I)}{\partial\, X^I},\, \frac{\partial\, P^I(X^I, F^I)}{\partial\, F^I} \right) = \vec{0}.$$

The partial derivatives in (eq. 38) have to be derived by means of implicit
functions, this is done in Appendix F. However, the mathematics and the functions
involved only allow the numerical solution of (eq. 38) for $X^I$ and $F^I$. The results
presented below were obtained by numerically solving (eq. 37) and (eq. 38)
respectively, i.e., numerically determining maximum values of $P^I$ for $X^I$ and $F^I$.

## 4.3.4 Strategies of the information intermediary

The conditions stated in (eq. 38) can be applied in several ways. On the one hand,
for a given set of environmental parameters (c, $\lambda$, $\mu_\beta$, $\sigma_\beta$, N) the optimal choice of
both decision variables ($X^I$ and $F^I$) can be obtained. This is the determination of a
maximum of $P^I(X^I,F^I)$ (labeled: *profit-maximizing strategy*). On the other hand, one
of the intermediary's decision variables can be fixed and the other variable can be
chosen to maximize the expected profit (labeled *fixed-quality-level strategy*
$(P^I(X^I=const.,F^I))$ and *fixed-fee strategy* $(P^I(X^I,F^I=const.)))$.[631] This is equivalent
with an intersection through the region of possible decision variables. These
strategies can either be interpreted as the requirements (in quality level or in fee)

---

[630]    This is the necessary condition for the existence of a local extreme value. The sufficient condition for a local maximum would be that the Hesse-Matrix of $P^I$ is negative
definite, cf. [Heuser 88, p. 310 fp.].

[631]    In the fixed-fee and the fixed-quality-level strategy the profit is maximized as well,
however, the restriction that one of the intermediary's decision variable is fixed usually
results in profits smaller than in the profit-maximizing strategy. See the comparison of
the different strategies in Figure 30 and Figure 34 as well.

formulated by potential users of the information intermediary, or as the intermediary's commitment to a particular quality level or a particular fee respectively. An example of the optimal choice of the fee $F'_{opt}(X')$ under given environmental conditions is in Figure 25. The bottom part of Figure 25 depicts the resulting expected profit $P'$ following the optimal choice $F'_{opt}(X')$.

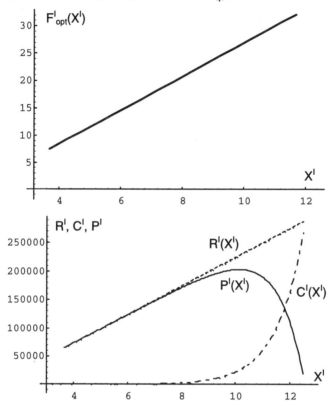

*Figure 25:*    *Optimal choice of fee $F'_{opt}$ (upper part), and expected search costs, revenue, and profit of the information intermediary charging the optimal fee $F'_{opt}$ (bottom part) as a function of $X'$ for given environmental conditions ($c=1$, $\lambda=1$, $\mu_\beta=4$, $\sigma_\beta=1$, $N=10000$).*

The optimal fee is increasing with the quality level $X'$ offered by the intermediary. The explanation can be derived from Figure 18. With increasing quality level $X'$ more consumers prefer to buy the information from this intermediary, this leads to an increased revenue $R'$. As a result, the fee $F'$ charged by the intermediary can be augmented as far as is justified by the increase in quality level. The optimal fee $F'_{opt}$ is already taken into account in the derivation of the revenue and profit in the bottom part of Figure 25. The increase of the quality level, however, results in increased search costs $C'(X')$, so the intermediary's expected profit will decrease for values larger than an optimal value $X'_{opt}$.

The corresponding example of the optimal adjustment of the quality level to the choice of a fee $F^I$ charged $X^I_{opt}(F^I)$ is given in Figure 26.

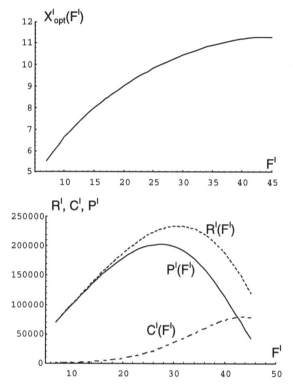

*Figure 26:*    Optimal choice of the quality level offered $X^I_{opt}$ (upper part), and expected search costs, revenue, and profit of the information intermediary offering the optimal quality level $X^I_{opt}$ (bottom part) as a function of $F^I$ for given environmental conditions ($c=1$, $\lambda=1$, $\mu_\beta=4$, $\sigma_\beta=1$, $N=10000$).

The search costs $C^I$ are indirectly dependent on the fee $F^I$ via the optimal quality level $X^I_{opt}$. The optimal quality level $X^I_{opt}$ is again taken into account for the derivation of $R^I$, $C^I$, and $P^I$. The optimal quality level $X^I_{opt}$ offered is restricted in its increase because of exponentially increasing search costs $C^I(X^I)$ (eq. 26).

The basic model of an information intermediary will be discussed with regard to influences of environmental conditions on the expected profit and the strategy of the information intermediary in Section 4.3. It should be clear that it is advantageous for the information intermediary[632] to react on variations of environmental conditions by adjusting the decision variables $F^I$ and $X^I$, and. From the intermediary's point of view, the profit-maximizing strategy is preferable to any other

---

[632]    It is advantageous for the information intermediary in the sense that a higher expected profit can be obtained.

strategy. In the following discussion of the basic model besides the profit-maximizing strategy only the fixed-quality-level strategy will be examined in detail.[633]

### 4.3.5 Summary of the assumption of the basic model

The assumptions of the basic model of an information intermediary are the following:

- All actors behave rationally,[634] and all actors are risk neutral, i.e., decisions are taken in order to maximize the expected profit or the expected utility.
- All actors have symmetric and certain information about the market environment.[635]
- Information seekers only differ in their willingness to pay for a particular quality level (Section 4.3.1.2).
- The information intermediary and individual information seekers apply an optimal search strategy (Section 4.2.1), and incur the same search costs for a single observation in the search process.
- Information seekers buy information from the information intermediary if the quality level offered and the price charged is preferable to a personal search process.
- Information sources reveal their information honestly.
- The information sold by the information intermediary is a reference to an object available on the market that has an attribute value of at least the quality level set (guaranteed) by the information intermediary.
- Information can be copied and disseminated without marginal costs.
- Information is acquired once by the information intermediary and sold to all consumers consulting the information intermediary.
- The model is static, i.e., only one period of information acquisition and dissemination by the information intermediary is taken into account.

---

[633] A fixed-fee strategy will not be analyzed in detail. The effects obtained for a fixed-quality-level strategy mainly correspond to the ones obtained for a fixed-quality-level strategy: If the optimal fee $F'_{opt}$ charged in fixed-quality-level strategy is decreasing under the influences of variations in environmental conditions, the optimal quality level $X'_{opt}$ will be increasing under the same variation and vice versa.

[634] Cf. [Gravelle 92, p. 6-8], [Feess 97, p. 198 fp.].

[635] This does not refer to the information gathered in the search process, but only to the environmental conditions, i.e., the parameters: $c$, $\lambda$, $\mu_p$, $\sigma_p$, $N$.

## 4.4 The influence of environmental conditions on the intermediary's strategy

The intermediary's expected profit $P^I(X^I,F^I)$ is influenced by the two decision variables the intermediary is able to control, and is dependent on the conditions of the environment. These conditions are:

- The costs for a single observation, i.e., the search costs ($c$).
- The distribution of qualities on the suppliers' market side ($\lambda$).
- The distribution of consumers' willingness to pay ($\mu_\beta$, $\sigma_\beta$).
- The number of potential consumers on the market for information ($N$).

The dependency of the optimal strategy[636] on the environmental parameters can be expressed by:

*(eq. 39)*     $$\vec{\nabla} P^I(X^I,F^I) = \left(\vec{\nabla}_{X^I,F^I} P^I\right)(c,\lambda,\mu_\beta,\sigma_\beta,N) = 0$$

The analysis is based on the intermediary's optimization problem introduced in Section 4.3.3. For a given set of environmental parameters ($c$, $\lambda$, $\mu_\beta$, $\sigma_\beta$, $N$) the intermediary's optimal strategy (eq. 38) will be derived, and the dependency of the strategy on the parameters will be discussed (eq. 39). The discussion will follow the succession of the above mentioning of environmental parameters. The general results of the model are exemplified by choice of a particular set of environmental conditions and the separate variation of each particular parameter from the set of parameters, i.e., the results are derived under the *ceteris paribus* (c.p.) assumption. Therefore, the variation of a single environmental parameter has to be understood as a *sensitivity analysis* within the scope of a particular environmental scenario.[637]

The model aims to treat the basic relations and interconnections of information intermediaries - it is not designed to perform numeric tests with real-life data bases. So the model applies only to relative comparisons of results obtained within the model.[638]

### 4.4.1 Search costs: c

The costs $c$ for a single observation in the search process are the same for consumers and for the information intermediary indicating that both use the same

---

[636] In this context, the term *optimal strategy* is used to indicate the intermediary's optimal reaction to a given set of environmental conditions.

[637] Cf. [Hinterhuber 92, p. 77, 188, 205 fp.].

[638] The numerical values displayed in the results have to be conceived as an aid to compare the different plots and not as an attempt to derive predictions with numerical accuracy.

search technology.[639] These search costs are to a great extent determined externally
(Section 4.2.1), search costs accumulate:
- the costs for contacts with potential information sources (e.g., communication costs, online costs, travel costs),
- costs for the evaluation of the quality of objects offered by a particular information source, and
- the opportunity costs of time (e.g., wages for the information seeker, missed
  profits).

The influence of search costs $c$ on the intermediary's expected profit $P^I$ is twofold.
First, the intermediary's expected search costs $C^I(X^I,c)$ are dependent on the costs $c$
of a single observation (Figure 17). Second, the intermediary's expected revenue
$R^I(X^I,F^I)$ is dependent on the costs $c$. The boundaries of the integration $(\beta_1(X^I,F^I)$
and $\beta_2(X^I,F^I))$ in (eq. 35) are implicitly dependent on $c$ via the determination of the
reservation value $x^*$ in the optimal search strategy of personal search processes (eq.
13).

### 4.4.1.1 Fixed-quality-level strategy

The influences of the search costs $c$ on the optimal choice of the intermediary's fee
$F^I_{opt}(X^I,c)$ and the resulting profit $P^I(X^I,c)=P^I(X^I,F^I_{opt}(X^I,c),c)$ for a fixed quality level
$X^I$ are plotted in Figure 27 and Figure 28 respectively. Figure 28 depicts the intermediary's expected profit as a function of $c$ for the optimal fee $F^I_{opt}$ for each setting
of the variables $X^I$ and $c$.

After the commitment to a fixed quality level $X^I$, the intermediary has to adjust the
fee $F^I_{opt}(X^I,c)$ to variations of the search costs $c$. For an isolated increase of these
costs the information intermediary augments the fee $F^I$ due to the profit maximization aim. The magnitude of the effect of this rise in prices on the profit, however, depends on the quality level $X^I$ offered (Figure 28) and on the other environmental conditions, i.e., the values of the other environmental parameters. Nevertheless, the intermediary can augment or at least preserve the expected profit by
adjusting the fee to altered search costs. This indicates the relative advantage of the
information intermediary's service over personal search of the information seekers.
The situation characterized herewith applies to information intermediaries with a
long-term commitment to a particular quality level. These information intermediaries have the fee charged as the only decision variable to react to changes of
environmental conditions. The analog case of a long-term commitment to a fee
charged would result in a reduction of the quality level offered by the intermediary
following the profit maximization aim.

---

[639]  An extension to this assumption may be different search costs for consumers' personal
search and the intermediary's search process (Section 4.4.1.3). This would indicate
different search technologies for the single information seeker and the information
intermediary as well as learning-curve effects of the intermediary.

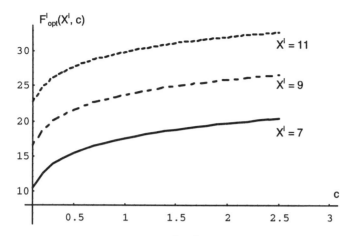

*Figure 27:*    Optimal choice of the fee $F'_{opt}(X')$ as a function of the search costs c ($\lambda=1$, $\mu_\beta=4$, $\sigma_\beta=1$, $N=10000$, $X'=(7, 9, 11)$).

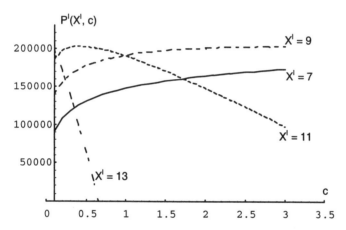

*Figure 28:*    Expected profit of the information intermediary as a function of the search costs c for the optimal choice of the fee $F'_{opt}(X')$ ($\lambda=1$, $\mu_\beta=4$, $\sigma_\beta=1$, $N=10000$, $X'=(7, 9, 11)$).

### 4.4.1.2 Profit-maximizing strategy

If the information intermediary has the opportunity to fully adjust and vary both decision variables ($X'$ and $F'$), an optimal strategy can be applied. In this case the profit-maximizing strategy determined from (eq. 39) is to reduce the quality level $X'_{opt}$ for increases of the search costs c (Figure 29). The optimal fee $F'_{opt}$ charged by the information intermediary as well as the expected profit $P'$ obtained following this strategy are independent of the search costs c and thus omitted here. The strategy can be made plausible by referring again to Figure 18 and (eq. 13). For increasing search costs $c$ the reservation value $x^*$ is decreasing, this leads to a decreasing expected-net reward $(\beta x^*)$ for consumers' personal search processes. With no alteration of the intermediary's decision variables the result would be an increase of the expected number of clients. But the increase in $c$ leads to augmented search costs $C'(X,c)$, requiring the intermediary to adjust the quality level $X'$ offered as well.

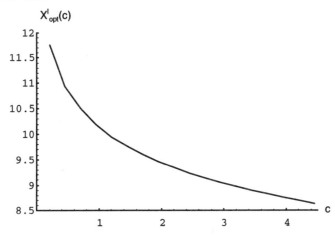

*Figure 29:*     *Optimal choice of the quality level $X'$ as a function of the costs $c$ for a single observation ($\lambda=1$, $\mu_\beta=4$, $\sigma_\beta=1$, $N=10000$).*

A comparison of the three possible strategies of the information intermediary (Section 4.3.4) is depicted in Figure 30, which has to be understood as a sensitivity analysis. The decision variables $X'$ and $F'$ in the fixed-fee and fixed-quality-level strategies are determined for the starting point of $c_0=1$. The expected profit $P'(c)$ is then calculated for the three different strategies as a function of $c$ with the other environmental conditions kept constant. The profit-maximizing strategy and the fixed-fee strategy both result in the independence of the expected profit of the costs $c$ for a single observation, whereas the fixed-quality-level strategy is unfavorable, because of its strong dependence on $c$. If the quality level is kept fixed, an increase of costs $c$ from the starting point $c_0=1$ results in higher expected search costs $C'$ of the intermediary. In contrast, a decrease of the costs $c$ below $c_0$ makes personal search processes of information seekers preferable to the price-quality combination offered by the intermediary, consequently resulting in reduced expected revenue of the intermediary. However, if the quality level is variable, as is the case in the fixed-fee and the profit-maximizing strategy, the intermediary can adapt search effort to the altered environmental conditions and c.p. preserve the expected profit.

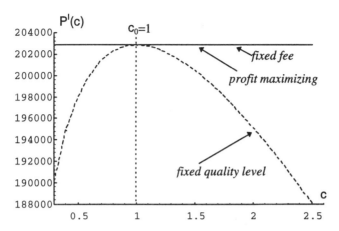

*Figure 30:*     *Comparison of the different strategies for variations of the costs c for a single observation ($\lambda=1$, $\mu_\beta=4$, $\sigma_\beta=1$, $N=10000$).*

### 4.4.1.3  Discussion

The major impacts of the costs for a single observation on the strategy of the information intermediary can be summarized as follows:

*Result 3:*   *An increase in the costs c per single observation c.p. leads to*
- *no alteration of the intermediary's expected profit and a decreasing quality level offered in case of a profit-maximizing strategy, or*
- *an altered expected profit in case of a fixed-quality-level strategy.*

The decrease of communication costs through the emergence of new information and communication technologies is heavily discussed in economics and information systems literature.[640] However, as indicated above communication costs are not the sole influencing factor for the costs of search for information; opportunity costs of time are another major influence.[641] The tendency towards the globalization of businesses and intensified competitive pressures even strengthens the effects of time in the search process of the single information seeker. Detached from the results of the model this can lead to an increased demand for services provided by information intermediaries.

Real-life information intermediaries, beyond those covered by the basic model, can obtain further competitive advantages in comparison to single information seekers. Advantages can be achieved by asset specific *investments in higher efficiency of search*, for example, investments in information technologies supporting the search process, efficient techniques and methods for the evaluation of the objects under

---

[640]   Cf. [Picot 94a], [Brynjolfsson 94].
[641]   Cf. [McAfee 88, p. 100], [Stigler 61] and Section 4.2.1.

consideration, and knowledge about the information to be searched. These investments result in a reduction of the costs for a single observation for the information
intermediary compared to an individual information seeker, if a comparable
quality of the result is assumed. A further source of search cost reductions for the
information intermediary is *learning-curve effects* due to larger transaction
volumes than the individual information seeker can achieve.[642]

In terms of the model different search costs have to be taken into account: the
intermediary's search costs $c^{Intermediary}$ and search costs for an individual information
seeker $c^{Individual}$, with: $c^{Intermediary} < c^{Individual}$.

### 4.4.2 Distribution of qualities: $\lambda$

The model assumes an exponential distribution of the objects' attribute values,
which were interpreted as the objects' quality. On markets for information it can
be assumed that the higher the quality, i.e., the relevance of the information,[643] the
lower is its density within the available information.[644] The density of relevant
information within all information available on the market is determined by:

- the density of adequate information sources, and
- the density of relevant information available from these sources.

The information intermediary, on the one hand, exploits the situation by offering
services on the market. On the other hand, the intermediary's profit achievable is
significantly dependent on the density of relevant information available on the
market: First, the intermediary's search costs $C'(X',\lambda)$ increase with decreasing
density of relevant information, i.e., with an increase of the parameter $\lambda$ (Figure
16). Second, the intermediary's revenue $R'(X',F')$ is dependent on the parameter $\lambda$
via the boundaries $(\beta_1(X',F')$ and $\beta_2(X',F'))$ of the integration in (eq. 35).[645] With an
increase of $\lambda$ the expected return $(\beta x^*)$ for consumers' personal search processes is
decreasing. This results in an outward shift of the boundaries $(\beta_1$ and $\beta_2)$ of the
integration in Figure 18 (or (eq. 35) respectively) and an increase in the intermediary's expected revenue.

---

[642] Cf. Section 3.2.3.1 and [Nink 91, p. 88]. Learning-curve effects would result in a
*convex search technology*, i.e., decreasing marginal search costs with increasing
number of samples, cf. [Stiglitz 89, p. 785].

[643] The objects offered on the market can be interpreted as information. The quality of the
objects is then interpreted as the relevance of the information for the particular problem
(Sections 4.3.1.1 and 4.3.2.3).

[644] Cf. [Zelewski 87].

[645] See the corresponding argumentation in Section 4.4.1.

### 4.4.2.1 Fixed-quality-level strategy

The parameter $\lambda$ influences the optimal choice of the intermediary's fee $F'_{opt}$ and the expected profit $P'(X',\lambda)=P'(X',F'_{opt}(X',\lambda),\lambda)$ for a fixed-quality-level strategy, these are depicted in Figure 31 and Figure 32 respectively. In case of a fixed-quality-level strategy an increase of the parameter $\lambda$ has an effect comparable to the influence of search costs $c$ on the optimal fee $F'_{opt}$ and the profit $P'$. In both situations the expected-net reward $(\beta x^*)$ for consumers' personal search processes is decreasing with an increase of the particular parameter ($c$ or $\lambda$).[646] Offering a fixed quality level, the intermediary can adjust the fee $F'_{opt}$ for an increase of the particular parameter in order to compensate for the exponentially increasing search costs $C'(X',\lambda)$ (Figure 31). However, this adjustment is only limited in its effect, because with a rising fee a growing number of consumers will prefer to perform personal search due to unfavorable price-quality combinations offered by the information intermediary. Consequently, the expected number of clients $E[N_{clients}]$ will decrease, leading, together with increasing search costs $C'(X',\lambda)$, to a steep decline of the expected profit $P'$. Figure 32 reveals the significant dependency of the intermediary's profit on the parameter $\lambda$ on a logarithmic scale on the axis of ordinates.

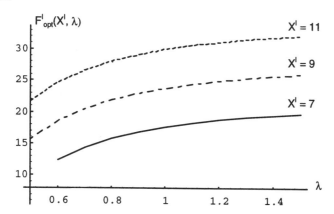

*Figure 31:*    *Optimal choice of the fee $F'_{opt}(X')$ as a function of the distribution parameter $\lambda$ ($c=1$, $\mu_\beta=4$, $\sigma_\beta=1$, $N=10000$, $X'=(7, 9, 11)$).*

---

[646] However, the difference between the two parameters is that search costs $c$ have a linear effect and the distribution parameter $\lambda$ has an exponential effect on the intermediary's profit. This distinction already becomes obvious from (eq. 27) and (eq. 29).

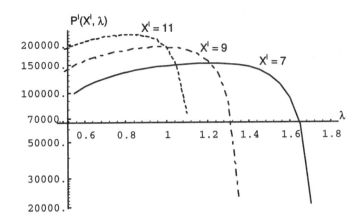

*Figure 32:*    *Expected profit of the information intermediary as a function of λ for the optimal choice of the fee $F'_{opt}(X')$ with logarithmic scale on the axis of ordinates (c=1, $\mu_\beta$=4, $\sigma_\beta$=1, N=10000, X'=(7, 9, 11)).*

### 4.4.2.2 Profit-maximizing strategy

The profit-maximizing strategy of the information intermediary is to adjust the quality level $X'$ and the fee $F'$ simultaneously. For a decreasing density of acceptable qualities available on the market the intermediary has to lower the quality level and the fee in order to maximize the expected profit. The optimal choice of the decision variables $X'_{opt}(\lambda)$ and $F'_{opt}(\lambda)$ as well as the expected profit $P'_{opt}(\lambda)=$ $P'(X'_{opt}(\lambda),F'_{opt}(\lambda))$ are depicted in Figure 33. The resulting profit is an envelope to the group of curves with different fixed quality levels depicted in Figure 32.
The simultaneous reduction of quality level $X'$ and fee $F'$ within this strategy is plausible by considering the search costs $C'(X',\lambda)$ in combination with the intermediary's competition with personal search activities of potential clients. The (exponentially) increasing search costs exert cost pressures on the intermediary, and the quality level offered cannot be kept up for a decreased density of acceptable qualities available on the market. For a given market of potential consumers (with given $\mu_\beta$ and $\sigma_\beta$) the intermediary can only react by reducing the fee $F'$ as well, because at any time consumers have the opportunity to perform their personal search if the price-quality combination becomes unfavorable. The magnitude of the effect is again dependent on the particular values of the other environmental parameters. The effect obtained for a variation of $\lambda$ for different environmental conditions, however, is the same as depicted in Figure 33.

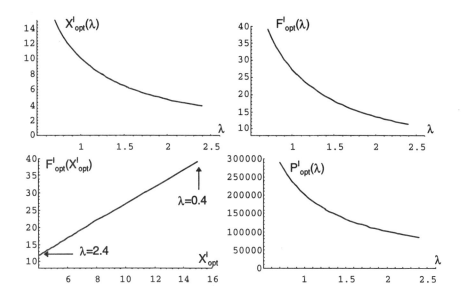

*Figure 33:*     *Description of the information intermediary's profit-maximizing strategy (optimal strategy) for a variation of $\lambda$ ($c=1$, $\mu_\beta=4$, $\sigma_\beta=1$, $N=10000$).*

The comparison of the three possible strategies is given in Figure 34.

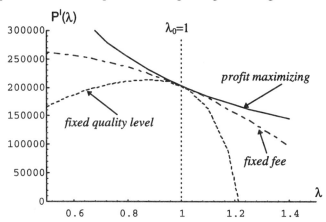

*Figure 34:*     *Comparison of the different strategies for variations of the density of relevant objects ($c=1$, $\mu_\beta=4$, $\sigma_\beta=1$, $N=10000$).*

The decision variables $X^I$ and $F^I$ in the fixed-fee and fixed-quality-level strategies are determined for the starting point of $\lambda_0=1$. The figure reveals that under variations of the density of relevant objects the profit-maximizing strategy is preferable to the fixed-fee strategy, and the fixed-fee strategy is preferable to the fixed-quality-level strategy concerning the intermediary's expected profit. If the quality level offered by the information intermediary is fixed, a variation of the parameter $\lambda$ has significant influences on the expected profit: Either the expected search costs $C'$ increase (for $\lambda > \lambda_o = 1$) or personal search processes of the information seekers become preferable to the intermediary's offer, resulting in a reduced revenue of the intermediary (for $\lambda < \lambda_o = 1$). In case of a fixed fee charged by the intermediary the quality level can be adapted to variations of $\lambda$ resulting in a smaller dependence on the parameter concerning the expected profit.

### 4.4.2.3 Discussion

The major impacts of the density of objects with an acceptable quality available on the market on the strategy of the information intermediary can be summarized as follows:

Result 4:    *For a decreasing density of objects with acceptable quality on the market the optimal reaction of the information intermediary is c.p.*
  - *to reduce the fee charged in case of a fixed-quality-level strategy, or*
  - *to simultaneously reduce the quality level offered and the fee charged in case of a profit-maximizing strategy.*

The possible reactions of the information intermediary on a decreasing density of relevant information are not satisfying from the consumers' point of view, especially considering the fundamental function of information intermediaries.[647] Within the limits of the model the information intermediary only has the opportunity to give way to altered environmental conditions by adjusting the fee and the quality level offered. Consequently, the intermediary has to bear a decline of the expected profit. Going beyond this basic model, the information intermediary has a number of opportunities to alleviate this dilemma. One measure would be the investment in the reduction of costs $c$ for a single observation (Section 4.4.1.3) in order to compensate for the higher search costs $C'$ resulting from the reduced density of relevant objects. An example is given in Figure 35. The figure depicts the cost reduction $\gamma(\lambda) = (1 - (c^{Intermediary}/c))$ for a single step in the search process of the information intermediary necessary to maintain the profit $P'_{opt}(\lambda = 1)$ gained for the decision variables $(X'_{opt}(\lambda = 1)$ and $F'_{opt}(\lambda = 1))$ optimal in the starting point of the increase of the parameter $\lambda$. A value $\gamma(\lambda) = 0.2$ means that the information intermediary has to reduce the costs $c^{Intermediary}$ for a single observation to 80% of the starting value to maintain the quality level $X'$ and the fee $F'$ for the service.[648]

---

[647]    The fundamental function of information intermediaries taken into account here is *search on behalf of clients*, see Section 4.1.1 and especially Figure 10.

[648]    The information intermediary's search costs are: $c^{Intermediary} = c(1 - \gamma(\lambda))$.

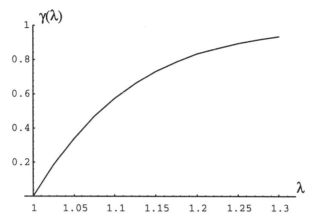

*Figure 35:*     Compensation of decreasing density of high quality on the market (increase
of $\lambda$) by cost reductions for a single observation of the information intermediary ($c=1$, $\mu_\beta=4$, $\sigma_\beta=1$, $N=10000$).

Another argument takes into account the intermediary's numerous repetitions of
search processes, not yet represented in the model. Due to repeated searches it
pays off for the information intermediary to *specialize on a particular topic* and
*invest in expertise* in a particular market.[649] Knowledge about the suppliers' market
enables the information intermediary to make a selection of appropriate information sources before undertaking search. This restricts the number of information
sources and increases the density of relevant information in the information to be
taken into account during the search process.

Another step might be the *establishment of vertical and horizontal networks* or
other forms of cooperation with information sources and other information intermediaries.[650] These networks can be relational, technological, or both. Vertical
networks can be established with information sources known to offer high quality,
which restricts the number of information sources to be taken into account before
the actual search process starts. However, these networks require permanent
control of the information sources involved as well as expansion and improvement.
Horizontal networks can be established with other information intermediaries
focusing other thematic areas. Using these relational intermediary networks the
single information intermediary may cover a broader thematic area with the
services offered. Besides this, the intermediary's search process can be improved
by intermediary networks if information about markets and market participants,
i.e., information about the information sources available on the market, is
exchanged between the cooperating intermediaries.

A further opportunity might be the provision of *value-adding services* that justify a
higher price to be charged for the service offered by the intermediary. If the

---

[649]   See Section 3.2.3.2 and [Nink 91, p. 89].
[650]   Cf. [Nink 91, p. 159 fp.].

production of these value-adding services does not completely use up the additional revenue generated, the information intermediary may compensate the losses in profit, or subsidize the search process with the remaining profit to retain the quality level offered.[651]

### 4.4.3 The valuation of quality in the consumers' market

The intermediary model takes into account differences in consumers' attitudes towards quality. These differences are expressed by consumers' different willingness to pay for a particular quality level, either achievable by personal search or by purchasing information from an information intermediary. On an abstract level, the whole population of consumers is described by a normal distribution of the willingness to pay with mean $\mu_\beta$ and standard deviation $\sigma_\beta$ (Section 4.3.1.2). The influences of these parameters on the intermediary can be interpreted in two slightly different ways: First, the intermediary installing a new service or entering a new market has the choice of a particular *target market*.[652] In terms of the model this market can be described by a particular combination of the two parameters ($\mu_\beta$ and $\sigma_\beta$).[653] Second, the information intermediary's expected profit in a selected target market is influenced by variations of consumers' attitudes towards quality. The influences of variations of the two parameters on the intermediary's expected profit and the optimal strategy will be discussed separately in the following sections. Subsequently, the intermediary's choice of a target market will be analyzed.

The two parameters of the PDF $h(\beta)$ of the willingness to pay $\beta$ influence the intermediary's expected profit via the expected number of clients $E[N_{clients}]$ (eq. 34). The boundaries of the integration ($\beta_1(X',F')$ and $\beta_2(X',F')$) are independent of the two distribution parameters ($\mu_\beta$ and $\sigma_\beta$), the influences are solely determined via the integrand $h(\beta)$.

The factors determining the willingness to pay in the particular target market are multifarious. In principle the information intermediary has to relate the attributes describing the particular target market under consideration with the two parameters of the distribution of the willingness to pay (Section 4.3.1.2). The following

---

[651]    This claim indicates a high demand for automation in the information intermediary's production process. This can be achieved by application of information technologies. However, the services of information intermediaries have a significant share of analytical processing of information, usually requiring human actors, cf. Section 5.1.3.

[652]    The intermediary's service addresses a particular group of information seekers in the market for information, this group is designated as the *intermediary's target market* (other designations could be *target audience* or *market segment*).

[653]    In this case the values of $\mu_\beta$ and $\sigma_\beta$ describing the consumers' market side can be conceived as indirect decision variables of the information intermediary, because the intermediary can indirectly arrange these variables by choosing a target market to enter. See Section 4.4.3.3 as well.

discussion of the consumers' market side is completely detached from particular segmentation variables.[654]

### 4.4.3.1 *Mean of the distribution of consumers' willingness to pay:* $\mu_\beta$

The parameter $\mu_\beta$ describes the mean value of consumers' willingness to pay for a certain quality level on the target market of the information intermediary. In general, the higher the mean value $\mu_\beta$ of the distribution, the higher should c.p. be the information intermediary's expected profit. This expectation is confirmed by the results of the model.

#### 4.4.3.1.1 *Fixed-quality-level strategy*

The influences of a variation of the parameter $\mu_\beta$ on the optimal fee $F'_{opt}(X',\mu_\beta)$ and the resulting expected profit $P'(X',\mu_\beta)=P'(X',F'_{opt}(X',\mu_\beta),\mu_\beta)$ for a fixed-quality-level strategy are depicted in Figure 36 and Figure 37 respectively.[655] With an increase of the mean $\mu_\beta$ of the distribution the intermediary's expected profit is increasing with a slope dependent on the quality level $X'$ (Figure 37). The boundaries of the integration in (eq. 34) are independent of the mean $\mu_\beta$, a variation of $\mu_\beta$ shifts the whole distribution to higher values of the willingness to pay (Figure 18). Due to a higher willingness to pay for a particular quality level in the whole market the intermediary can charge higher fees $F'_{opt}$ (Figure 36) without loosing clients to personal search processes.

---

[654]    For possible segmentation variables see, for example, [Kotler 88, p. 287], see Section 4.3.1.2 as well.

[655]    The willingness to pay $\beta$ is per definition a positive value (Section 4.3.1.2). The distribution function $h(\beta)$, however, does not exclude negative values of $\beta$. Therefore parameters of $\mu_\beta$ and $\sigma_\beta$ are chosen to comply with $\int_{-\infty}^{0} h(\beta)\,d\beta < 0.1\,\%$ : In Figure 36, Figure 37, and Figure 38 the plots start at $\mu_\beta=3$.

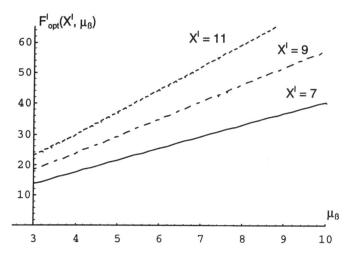

*Figure 36:*    Optimal choice of the fee $F'_{opt}(X')$ as a function of the distribution parameter $\mu_\beta$ (c=1, $\lambda$=1, $\sigma_\beta$=1, N=10000, X'=(7, 9, 11)).

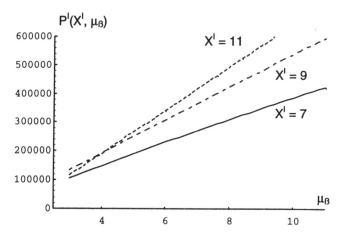

*Figure 37:*    Expected profit of the information intermediary as a function of $\mu_\beta$ for the optimal choice of the fee $F'_{opt}(X')$ (c=1, $\lambda$=1, $\sigma_\beta$=1, N=10000, X'= (7, 9, 11)).

### 4.4.3.1.2 Profit-maximizing strategy

Following a profit-maximizing strategy the effects on the information intermediary's expected profit and optimal fee are the same as in the previous section
(Figure 38).

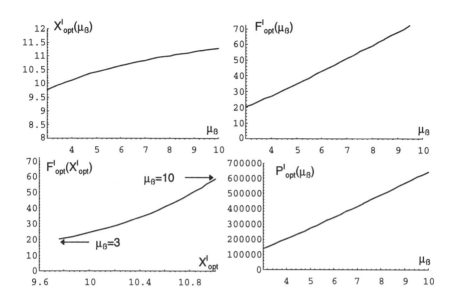

*Figure 38:*     *Description of the information intermediary's profit-maximizing strategy (optimal strategy) for a variation of $\mu_\beta$ ($c=1$, $\lambda=1$, $\sigma_\beta=1$, $N=10000$).*

The comparison of the three different strategies (not depicted for the variation of $\mu_\beta$) reveals that the profit maximizing strategy is preferable to the fixed-quality-level strategy, and the fixed-quality-level strategy is preferable to the fixed-fee strategy.

### 4.4.3.1.3 Summary

The effects of a variation of the medium willingness to pay $\mu_\beta$ in the market on the strategy of the information intermediary can be summarized as follows:

*Result 5:*     *An increase of the medium willingness to pay in the intermediary's target market c.p. leads to an increase of the optimal fee charged and an increase of the expected profit.*

### 4.4.3.2  Standard deviation of the distribution of consumers' willingness to pay: $\sigma_\beta$

The parameter $\sigma_\beta$ describes the heterogeneity (or diffusion) of the consumers' market (or target market) selected by the information intermediary (Section 4.3.1.2). The smaller the value of the standard deviation $\sigma_\beta$ is, the more homogeneous is the market with regard to the willingness to pay for a particular quality level.

#### 4.4.3.2.1 Fixed-quality-level strategy

Following a fixed-quality-level strategy, the information intermediary has to adjust the optimal fee $F'_{opt}(X',\sigma_\beta)$ according to Figure 39. This results in an expected profit $P'(X',\sigma_\beta)= P'(X',F'_{opt}(X',\sigma_\beta),\sigma_\beta)$ as is depicted in Figure 40.[656]

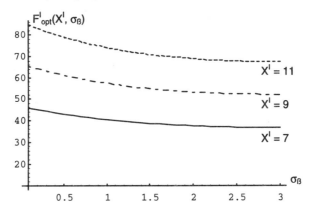

*Figure 39:*    *Optimal choice of decision variables $F'_{opt}(X')$ as a function of the distribution parameter $\sigma_\beta$ ($c=1$, $\lambda=1$, $\mu_\beta=10$, $N=10000$, $X'=(7, 9, 11)$).*

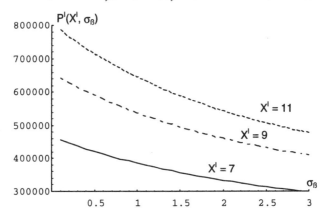

*Figure 40:*    *Expected profit of the information intermediary as a function of $\sigma_\beta$ for the optimal choice of the fee $F'_{opt}(X')$ ($c=1$, $\lambda=1$, $\mu_\beta=10$, $N=10000$, $X'=(7, 9, 11)$).*

---

[656]    The range of values for the standard deviation $\sigma_\beta$ is chosen in these figures to comply with $\int_{-\infty}^{0} h(\beta)\, d\beta < 0.1\%$. The value of the mean of the normal distribution is therefore set to $\mu_\beta=10$.

The optimal fee $F'_{opt}$ is slightly decreasing with increasing values of $\sigma_\beta$. The argumentation can be derived from Figure 18. The boundaries ($\beta_1$ and $\beta_2$) of the integration in (eq. 34) are independent of the standard deviation $\sigma_\beta$. For an increase of $\sigma_\beta$ considerable parts of the PDF $h(\beta)$, formerly lying within the boundaries of the integration, exceed the boundaries of the interval defined by $[\beta_1,\beta_2]$. These parts yield no contribution to the intermediary's expected number of clients $E[N_{clients}]$ (eq. 34) or the expected revenue $R'(X',F')$ (eq. 35). For a fixed quality level the adjustment of the fee $F'$ to the variation of $\sigma_\beta$ cannot compensate for the loss of expected clients of the information intermediary. This means that for a decreasing homogeneity of the consumers' market addressed by the service the intermediary has to take into account reduced expected profits.

### 4.4.3.2.2 Profit-maximizing strategy

The results for a profit-maximizing strategy for a variation of the homogeneity of the intermediary's target market are summarized in Figure 41. The effect is comparable to the one described in the fixed-quality-level strategy. However, the difference is that in the profit-maximizing strategy the expected profit exceeds the profit achievable with a fixed quality level offered.

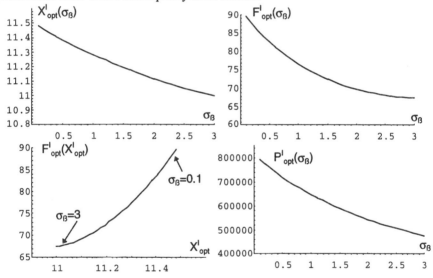

*Figure 41:*    *Description of the information intermediary's profit-maximizing strategy (optimal strategy) for a variation of $\sigma_\beta$ (c=1, $\lambda$=1, $\mu_\beta$=10, N=10000).*

The comparison of the different strategies (not depicted for the variation of $\sigma_\beta$) reveals that the profit-maximizing strategy is preferable to the fixed-quality-level strategy, and that the fixed-quality-level strategy is preferable to the fixed-fee strategy.

### 4.4.3.2.3 Summary

The influences of variations of the homogeneity of the target market, i.e., the standard deviation $\sigma_\beta$, on the information intermediary's profit and optimal strategy can be summarized as follows.

*Result 6:    An increase of the heterogeneity (the standard deviation $\sigma_\beta$) of the willingness to pay in the intermediary's target market c.p. leads to a decreasing optimal fee and a decreasing profit in fixed-quality-level and profit-maximizing strategies. In profit-maximizing strategies the optimal quality level is decreasing as well.*

### 4.4.3.3 Discussion

The services of the information intermediary have to concentrate on a particular group of potential consumers in order to focus the effort and reduce the costs.[657] In marketing-management[658] consumers' markets are usually described by multi-dimensional characteristics.[659] The aim is to identify market segments with groups of consumers as homogeneous as possible.[660] Consumers in these market segments have comparable preferences for one or more attributes of products offered therein. A narrow market segmentation, i.e., the identification of a multitude of consumer characteristics, is advantageous for information acquisition about consumers' wants and subsequent penetration of the market segments.[661] However, it reduces the number of potential consumers in a particular market segment. This simple argument indicates that a universally valid rule for market segmentation cannot be given.[662]

In the intermediary model the consumers' market side is not described by multi-dimensional characteristics, but on a more abstract level by the distribution of preferences for a particular product attribute, i.e., the willingness to pay for a particular quality level (Section 4.3.1.2).[663] This description allows to model the fundamental underlying decision about the breadth (or the narrowness respectively) of the target market to be chosen by the information intermediary.

---

[657]    Cf. [Nink 91, p. 89].

[658]    Cf. [Kotler 88], [Nieschlag 91], [Hüttner 94].

[659]    Cf. [Kotler 88, p. 286 fp.], [Nieschlag 91, p. 835 fp.]. See Section 4.3.1.2 as well.

[660]    Cf. [Hüttner 94, p. 106].

[661]    Cf. [Hüttner 94, p. 106-108].

[662]    Cf. [Hüttner 94, p. 107].

[663]    The correlation between a particular *market for information* and the mean value $\mu_\beta$ of the willingness to pay in that market cannot be given in general. It has to be determined through analysis of the particular market under consideration.

The mean value $\mu_\beta$ is mainly determined by the information intermediary's decision about a particular market to enter[664] (e.g., a market for technological information vs. a market for information about products and markets, cf. Sections 2.1.1.3 and 2.2.1) as well as the decision about the target audience (e.g., business users vs. private households, cf. Section 4.3.2.3). The degree of market segmentation (no market segmentation vs. complete segmentation or anything between)[665] determines the homogeneity of the target market and therefore the value of the standard deviation $\sigma_\beta$.

The previous analysis has revealed that for fixed-quality-level strategies and profit-maximizing strategies the intermediary's profit

- increases with an increasing mean $\mu_\beta$ on the target market (Result 5), and
- decreases with an increasing standard deviation $\sigma_\beta$, i.e., with decreasing homogeneity of the target market (Result 6).

An information intermediary installing a new business or new services has the choice of a particular target market for the service. An example is given in Table 9.

*Table 9:     Example of different target markets described by the distribution parameters $\sigma_\beta$ and $\mu_\beta$ (c=1, $\lambda$=1, N=10000).*

|  | high homogeneity ($\sigma_\beta=1$) | low homogeneity ($\sigma_\beta=3$) |
|---|---|---|
| high mean willingness to pay ($\mu_\beta=16$) | $X^I_{opt}=11.8$<br>$F^I_{opt}=129.2$<br>$P^I(X^I_{opt}, F^I_{opt})=1120510$ | $X^I_{opt}=11.6$<br>$F^I_{opt}=112.4$<br>$P^I(X^I_{opt}, F^I_{opt})=887541$ |
| low mean willingness to pay ($\mu_\beta=8$) | $X^I_{opt}=11.0$<br>$F^I_{opt}=59.4$<br>$P^I(X^I_{opt}, F^I_{opt})=493828$ | $X^I_{opt}=10.7$<br>$F^I_{opt}=54.1$<br>$P^I(X^I_{opt}, F^I_{opt})=355265$ |

The example takes into account two values (*high* and *low*) for each of the distribution parameters ($\sigma_\beta$ and $\mu_\beta$) describing four different target audiences for the service. The table displays the intermediary's optimal strategy ($X^I_{opt}=X^I_{opt}(\mu_\beta,\sigma_\beta)$, $F^I_{opt}=F^I_{opt}(\mu_\beta,\sigma_\beta)$) for the given environment and the expected profit $P^I(X^I_{opt},F^I_{opt})$ achievable. In principle, the table recapitulates what was already found in Figure 38 and Figure 41. For a given mean value of the willingness to pay in the market it is advantageous for the information intermediary to concentrate on a homogeneous target market. The intermediary's expected profit is higher, the higher the mean value of the willingness to pay is in the selected target market. As a consequence information intermediaries aiming to finance the services via fees should c.p. direct the design of the service to markets with a high medium willingness to pay and high homogeneity if such choice is possible.

---

[664]   One criterion to select a target audience can be the focus on a particular industry, cf. [Nink 91, p. 89].

[665]   Cf. [Kotler 88, p. 280-308], [Hüttner 94, p. 104 fp.].

### 4.4.4  Number of potential users in the market: N

Besides the distribution of the preferences in the consumers' market (Section 4.4.3) the number $N$ of potential users belonging to a particular target market is a determining factor of the information intermediary's expected number of clients $E[N_{clients}]$ (eq. 34) and therefore of the expected profit. The number $N$ of potential users can be different from the total number $N_0$ of all consumers in the market if, for example, the intermediary's service can only be accessed with particular technologies, cf. Section 4.4.4.3.

#### 4.4.4.1  Fixed-quality-level strategy

If the quality level offered by the information intermediary is fixed, a variation of the number $N$ of potential users has no effect on the optimal fee $F'_{opt}$, it is $F'_{opt}(N)=const.$. This can be seen in (eq. 38) and (eq. 68) in Appendix F: the second component of the gradient $\vec{\nabla} P'(X', F')$, i.e., the equation $\partial P'(X', F')/\partial F' = 0$, is independent of $N$. The plot for $F'_{opt}(N)$ is therefore omitted here. The dependency of the expected profit on the number of potential users $N$ is depicted in Figure 42. The effect is simply that of the linear increase of $N$ described by (eq. 36).

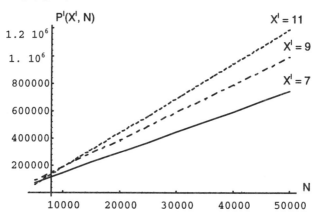

Figure 42:    *Expected profit of the information intermediary as a function of N for the optimal choice of the fee $F'_{opt}(X')$ (c=1, $\lambda$=1, $\mu_\beta$=4, $\sigma_\beta$=1, X'=(7, 9, 11)).*

### 4.4.4.2 Profit-maximizing strategy

The profit-maximizing strategy for a variation of the number $N$ of potential consumers is described in Figure 43.

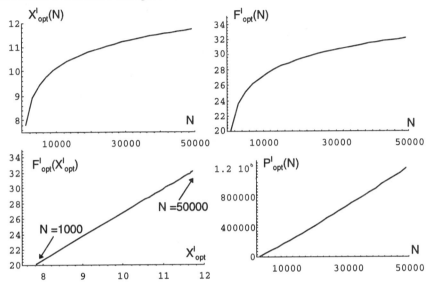

*Figure 43:*     *Description of the information intermediary's profit-maximizing strategy (optimal strategy) for a variation of $N$ ($c=1$, $\lambda=1$, $\mu_\beta=4$, $\sigma_\beta=1$).*

The comparison of the different strategies (not depicted for the variation of $N$) revealed that the profit-maximizing strategy is preferable to the fixed-quality-level strategy, and that the fixed-quality-level strategy is preferable to the fixed-fee strategy.

### 4.4.4.3 Discussion

The main influences of variations in the number $N$ of potential users are summarized as follows:

*Result 7:* *An increase of the number of potential users of the information intermediary c.p. leads to an increase of the expected profit.*

The findings very generally show that the larger the market for information the more it pays to enter the market as an information intermediary, because the information has to be produced only once and can be copied (nearly) without further marginal costs[666] but each in return for a fee. In this context, the intermediary's expected number of clients $E[N_{clients}]$ (eq. 34) can be interpreted as the degree of reuse of the information once gathered. The more the information intermediary can exploit economies of scale by reusing the information, i.e., sell the information multiply, the higher will be the expected profit.

The number of potential users is associated with the previous discussion of the intermediary's target market (Section 4.4.3), a particular target market has a particular number of consumers. However, other characteristics of the consumers' market can determine the number of potential users as well. These are, for example, the availability of a particular communication technology to access the services offered by the information intermediary,[667] the existence of special knowledge or skills necessary to use the services, and the awareness of the information intermediary on the market. These characteristics, not directly described through the parameters $\mu_\beta$ and $\sigma_\beta$, determine the actual number of users of the information intermediary as well. If, for example, the services of the information intermediary were attractive for $N_0$ consumers, but only a share of $u$ ($0 \leq u \leq 1$) of them fulfills the requirements necessary to access the services, the number of potential users of the information intermediary would be only $N=uN_0<N_0$. The percentage $u$ of all users (or consumers) in the target market being potential users of the information intermediary can be interpreted as the intermediary's *awareness on the market*,[668] i.e., the higher the percentage $u$ the more consumers know about the services offered by the intermediary. In the numerical treatment of the model a variation of $N$ is equivalent to a variation of $u$. The production of information usually causes high fixed costs (Section 2.2.3). If the intermediary has incurred fixed costs from providing the services, for example, asset specific investments, the model could determine a critical number $N$ of potential users (or of the percentage $u$) required to recover these costs.[669]

If the transfer of the information causes marginal costs $C'_D$, the resulting revenue obtained for every single user of the information intermediary will be reduced to $(F'-C'_D)$, and the expected revenue $R'$ will be reduced as well (Section 4.3.2.1). Therefore, the dissemination of the information by the information intermediary should ideally cause no or at least very small marginal costs. The Internet is an

---

[666] Cf. Section 2.1.5.

[667] Communication technologies are subject to network externalities which determines the spreading of these technologies among potential consumers, cf. [Markus 87], [Markus 92], [Hayashi 92], [Buxmann 96]. For example, if the access of the information intermediary's service requires access to the Internet, $N$ is the number of those consumers being part of the intermediary's target market who possess Internet access.

[668] The awareness in the market is obviously dependent on the intermediary's marketing effort. This and further influences on information search services are discussed in [Lindquist 78].

[669] The correlation between the critical number of users of the information intermediary and fixed costs is linear (eq. 36) and thus omitted here.

example of a market for information with a huge number of potential users of such services, and it offers the opportunity for inexpensive dissemination of information. The results of the model indicate that information intermediaries should aim to offer their services via communication channels, more generally, via media that possess a significant spreading and acceptance among potential consumers.[670] The result also indicates the importance of the awareness of the intermediary's services on the target market.

However, another effect can limit the number of users consulting the information intermediary. If a particular penetration of the market is achieved, the properties of information, i.e., the fact that information can be copied for vanishing marginal costs, and the availability of communication networks may result in an involuntary exchange of the information sold by the information intermediary between clients of the intermediary and non-clients.[671] This gives rise to the need for personalized (end-user specific) information products and services in order to avoid bypassing of the intermediary's fee.

If the information intermediary performs search for information on behalf of a *single user*, no economies of scale can be exploited, i.e., the information gathered cannot be sold repeatedly. In this case high efficiency of search (cf. Section 4.4.1.3), the specialization on a particular subject area and knowledge about appropriate information sources (cf. Section 4.4.2.3), and the focus on a target market with a high willingness to pay (cf. Section 4.4.3.3) will be of particular importance for the information intermediary. The information intermediary has two possibilities to account for the services offered. One possibility is a fixed fee for the complete contract, indicating that the quality of the result will be implicitly determined by the information intermediary (fixed-fee strategy). This procedure is appropriate if the sources of information to be taken into account in the search process are laid down before search.[672] The other possibility is a fixed fee per unit of time so that the client can weigh out the quality of the result with the costs incurred.[673]

---

[670] This claim is especially important for information intermediaries offering their service on the Internet. These intermediaries should base their services on commonly accepted technologies and standards (and not implement features that require special equipment or software). The effects of the spreading and acceptance of information technologies on its users are discussed in [Antonelli 92].

[671] This is a problem inherent in information products, cf. Section 2.5.1.

[672] For example, the information intermediary searches in a predetermined set of online-databases.

[673] Cf. [O'Leary 87, p. 27].

## 4.5 Competition between information intermediaries

The basic model of an information intermediary presented so far has focused a monopolistic information intermediary operating on the market for information. The intermediary had the opportunity to fully adjust the decision variables $X^I$ and $F^I$ to environmental conditions in order to maximize the expected profit. Competition existed only indirectly with personal search processes of potential consumers.[674] The present section introduces the case of *direct competition* between information intermediaries operating in the same market. First, a duopoly model of information intermediaries will be introduced to formally describe direct competition in the market for information (Section 4.5.1). Second, some basic effects of competition on the two information intermediaries will be discussed (Section 4.5.2).

### 4.5.1 Formal treatment of competition in the intermediary model

The basic model of an information intermediary, introduced in Section 4.2, was already based on the implicit treatment of competition. The information intermediary competes with personal search processes of potential consumers acting on the market for information (Section 4.3.2.3). The individual information seeker only consults an information intermediary if the net reward from using the intermediary exceeds (or at least equals) the expected-net reward from personal search (eq. 31). If more than one information intermediary operate in the market, the individual information seeker takes into account the additional price-quality combinations as further alternatives for information acquisition. Again the $j^{th}$ consumer on the market chooses the alternative that maximizes the expected utility $U_j$:

*(eq. 40)*     $U_j = Max[(\beta_j \cdot x^*), (\beta_j \cdot X_1^I - F_1^I), (\beta_j \cdot X_2^I - F_2^I), ...]$,

where $(X^I_{1}, F^I_{1})$ is the quality-price combination offered by intermediary 1. The consumer's decision problem reveals that within the basic model information intermediaries either compete in prices $(F^I)$, in the quality levels $(X^I)$ or in both. The intermediaries' market structure is an oligopoly,[675] and in case of only two competing intermediaries it is a duopoly, which will be taken into account in the following analysis. The intermediary's expected profit (e.g., $P^I_{1}$ for intermediary 1) now becomes dependent on the competitor's (intermediary 2) decision variables:

[674] Other sources of indirect competitions are, for example, intermediaries in related markets, cf. [Demsetz 68].

[675] The major implication is that the market participants are strategically interdependent, cf. [Varian 93, p. 447 fp.], [Varian 94, p. 286 fp.].

$P'_1 = P'_1(X'_1, F'_1, X'_2, F'_2)$. The expected profit of one of the two intermediaries (here for intermediary 1) can be expressed as follows (cf. (eq. 36)):[676]

$$P_1^I(X_1^I, F_1^I, X_2^I, F_2^I) = R_1^I(X_1^I, F_1^I, X_2^I, F_2^I) - C_1^I(X_1^I)$$

(eq. 41)

$$= F_1^I \cdot N \cdot \int_{\beta_1^{I_1}(X_1^I, F_1^I, X_2^I, F_2^I)}^{\beta_2^{I_1}(X_1^I, F_1^I, X_2^I, F_2^I)} h(\beta)\, d\beta - \frac{c}{\left[1 - F(X_1^I)\right]}.$$

The boundaries of the integration, $\beta_1^{I_1}(X_1^I, F_1^I, X_2^I, F_2^I)$ and $\beta_2^{I_1}(X_1^I, F_1^I, X_2^I, F_2^I)$, have to be determined by the following system being an extension to (eq. 32):

(eq. 42)

$$\left| \begin{array}{l} U_1^{Intermediary} = \left(\beta \cdot X_1^I - F_1^I\right) = \left\{ (\beta \cdot x^*), (\beta \cdot X_2^I - F_2^I) \right\} \\[2mm] \int_{x^*}^{\infty} \left[1 - F(x)\right] \cdot \beta\, d\,x = c \end{array} \right|.$$

System (eq. 42) determines those values $\beta_1^{I_1}$ and $\beta_2^{I_1}$ of the willingness to pay $\beta$ for which consumers are indifferent either between consulting intermediary 1 and consulting intermediary 2 or between consulting intermediary 1 and a personal search process (Figure 44). For intermediary 2 a corresponding set of functions and equations symmetric to (eq. 41) and (eq. 42) exists. If consumers have no preferences and if both intermediaries offer identical price-quality combinations, the market will be equally divided among the two intermediaries.[677] The expected joint revenue of both intermediaries will equal that of a single monopolistic intermediary and it will be divided equally among the two ($R_1^I + R_2^I = R^I$). However, the search costs $C^I$ have to be borne by both intermediaries. For different price-quality combinations offered by the two intermediaries, each intermediary serves consumers from a certain range of willingness to pay $\beta$ in the market. This is depicted for an arbitrary choice of the decision variables ($X'_1$, $F'_1$, $X'_2$, $F'_2$) in Figure 44.[678] The figure shows the utilities $U_1^{Intermediary}$ and $U_2^{Intermediary}$ that the two competing intermediaries offer to consumers in the market and the expected-net reward $\beta$ $x^*$ from personal search processes as a function of the willingness to pay $\beta$. In this particular case consumers with a low willingness to pay (region I in Figure 44) prefer to perform personal search, whereas consumers with a medium willingness to pay consult intermediary 1 (region II), and consumers with a high valuation of quality are best served by intermediary 2 (region III). The shaded areas under the PDF $h(\beta)$ represent the market shares of the two intermediaries.

---

[676]   A corresponding objective function exists for intermediary 2.
[677]   Cf. [Rasmusen 89, p. 262, 270], [Gibbons 92, p. 17].
[678]   The factor $\alpha$ is simply a scaling factor to achieve the simultaneous plot of the PDF $h(\beta)$ and the utility functions on the same axis of ordinates.

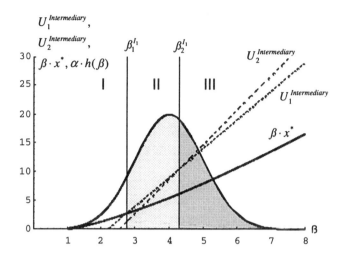

*Figure 44:*    Determination of the consumers' source of information acquisition, i.e., the boundaries of the integration in (eq. 41), for an arbitrary choice of decision variables $(X'_1=5,\ F'_1=11,\ X'_2=6,\ F'_2=15.3)$ $(c=1,\ \lambda=1,\ \mu_\beta=4,\ \sigma_\beta=1,\ N=10000)$.

The strategic interdependence revealed by Figure 44 has to be taken into account in the single intermediary's strategy.[679] Therefore, the intermediary's optimal decision variables $X'_{1opt}$, $F'_{1opt}$ now become dependent on the actions taken by the competitor: $X'_{1opt}=X'_{1opt}(X'_2,F'_2)$, $F'_{1opt}=F'_{1opt}(X'_2,F'_2)$.[680] Some basic games and strategies of the two competing intermediaries will be examined in the following (Section 4.5.2), but beforehand the underlying assumptions should be emphasized again:

- Consumers decide rational, i.e., according to their expected utility (eq. 31). This implies that consumers have no preferences for a particular source of information (Section 4.3.1.2).[681]
- Information about environmental conditions is symmetrically distributed among all market participants and known with certainty.[682] At all stages of the game the market participants have the same symmetric information.[683]

---

[679] Game theory provides a great variety of methods and approaches to treat strategic interdependence in oligopolistic markets. See, for example, [Rasmusen 89, p. 259 fp.], [Kreps 90], [Myerson 91], [Gibbons 92], [Holler 93].

[680] These functions describe the optimal reaction of intermediary 1 on a particular strategy of intermediary 2, the dependency on the environmental parameters, however, is omitted here for clearness.

[681] Cf. [Myerson 91, p. 6].

[682] This assumptions only refers to information about environmental conditions, but not to information gathered in the search processes.

[683] Cf. [Rasmusen 89, p. 53].

- All market participants know this (common knowledge[684]).
- The game is static, i.e., only one game is taken into account,[685] and non-cooperative.
- The information intermediaries operating in the market have identical search technologies, i.e., incur the same search costs $c$ for a single observation, and only differ in the fees charged and/or quality levels offered.[686]

## 4.5.2 Effects of competition

Within the model competition can come along either in form of price competition or in competition in the quality level offered;[687] this will be discussed in Section 4.5.2.1. Besides these special forms, competition can occur in price-quality combinations (Section 4.5.2.2).

### 4.5.2.1 Price competition and competition in the quality level

From the basic model mentioned above some general results for two cases of competition between the two information intermediaries can be obtained.

**Price competition**
If both intermediaries offer the same quality level ($X'_1=X'_2$), the two functions $U_1^{Intermediary}$ and $U_2^{Intermediary}$ will be parallels ((eq. 42) and Figure 44). In this case the intermediary charging the lowest fee will serve the whole market, and for equal fees $F'_1=F'_2$ the market will be divided equally among the two intermediaries. This can be expressed by the expected profit $P'_1$ for one[688] of the intermediaries (eq. 43):[689]

(eq. 43)
$$P'_1(X'_1,F'_1,X'_2,F'_2) = \begin{cases} -C'(X'_1) & \text{for } F'_1 > F'_2 \\ \frac{1}{2} \cdot R'(X'_1,F'_1)-C'(X'_1) & \text{for } F'_1 = F'_2 \\ P'(X'_1,F'_1) & \text{for } F'_1 < F'_2 \end{cases}^{690}$$

Neglecting search costs $C'(X'_{1,2})$ the possibility to capture the whole market by (slightly) undercutting the other's price leads to a unique *Nash equilibrium*

[684] Cf. [Rasmusen 89,p. 50], [Myerson 91, p. 63 fp.].
[685] Cf. [Feess 97, p. 387], [Holler 96, p. 32].
[686] Cf. Section 4.4.1.3.
[687] See Section 3.5.1 for other forms of competition.
[688] A corresponding equation holds for intermediary 2.
[689] Cf. [Rasmusen 89, p. 264].
[690] The expected search costs $C'$, the expected revenue $R'$, and the expected profit $P'$ of the individual information intermediary can be determined by the simpler formulas ((eq. 26), (eq. 35), and (eq. 36)) of the monopolistic case.

$F'_1=F'_2=0$ for pure price competition between the intermediaries.[691] However, both information intermediaries have to perform information acquisition to offer the quality level $X'_1=X'_2$, and incur costs $C'_{1,2}(X'_{1,2})= C'(X'_{1,2})$ for the search process. These costs are fixed for the information intermediaries in this case, because the information has to be produced (searched) only once and can be copied and disseminated without further costs (Section 4.3.2). In equilibrium a minimum fee[692] $F'_{min}(X'_1=X'_2)$ is charged by both intermediaries. This minimum fee $F'_{min}$ can be determined by $P'(X'_1,F'_{min})= R'(X'_1,F'_{min})-C'(X'_1)=0$ with $X'_1=X'_2$ (Figure 22 in Section 4.3.3).[693] The argumentation is based on the concept of the *Nash equilibrium*, i.e., a situation in which no player has incentives to deviate from his/her strategy given that the other players do not deviate.[694] For an arbitrary choice of fees $F'_{1,2}>F'_{min}$ one intermediary (say intermediary 1) can raise his/her expected profit, i.e., capture the whole market and gain the monopoly profit $P'(X'_1,F'_1=(F'_2-\varepsilon))>0$ (eq. 43), by reducing the fee to $F'_1=(F'_2-\varepsilon)$.[695] The other intermediary (in this argumentation intermediary 2) will obviously follow this price reduction, at least down to the same fee $F'_2=F'_1$, because he/she has the same incentive to undercut the fee charged by the first to capture the whole market and increase the expected profit. In equilibrium the fees $F'_1$ and $F'_2$ will therefore be equal.[696] The equilibrium fee can be determined as follows: A further reduction of the fee is desirable for the single information intermediary as long as the expected profit for serving the whole market will be positive for the reduced fee as well $(P'(X'_1,F'_1)>0)$. If the minimum fee $F'_{min}$ is already reached, a further reduction of the fee to $(F'_{min}-\varepsilon)$ would result in negative expected profits for serving the whole market $P'(X'_{1,2}(F'_{min}-\varepsilon))<0$. The minimum fee $F'_{min}$ is therefore the Nash equilibrium which can be determined by $P'(X'_1,F'_{min})= R'(X'_1,F'_{min})-C'(X'_1)=0$. As $R'(X'_1,F'_{min})= C'(X'_1)$ and the expected profit in equilibrium is $\frac{1}{2} R'(X'_1,F'_{min})-C'(X'_1)$ (eq. 43) the profit

---

[691] This is the basic *Bertrand equilibrium* of a duopoly obtained for pure price competition between the players neglecting any costs incurred, cf. [Rasmusen 89, p. 264].

[692] In the basic Bertrand model of a duopoly, where fixed costs are zero and the only costs are the marginal costs for production, in equilibrium prices equal marginal costs, cf. [Varian 93, p. 462], [Gravelle 92, p. 307], [Tirole 93, p. 209 fp.]. The effect that the profit is zero for price competition in a duopoly is often referred to as the *Bertrand paradox*, cf. [Tirole 93, p. 210].The equilibrium obtained here is different, because in the setting of the model search costs are fixed costs and marginal costs are zero.

[693] The expected profit for the monopolistic case $(F'_1 < F'_2$ in (eq. 43)) is set equal to zero to determine the minimum fee $F'_{min}$.

[694] Cf. [Rasmusen 89, p. 33], [Varian 93, p. 471].

[695] Cf. [Gravelle 92, p. 307], [Feess 97, p. 420].

[696] Cf. [Feess 97, p. 419].

achieved by both intermediaries in equilibrium[697] will be negative: $P^I_1(X^I_1, F^I_{min}, X^I_2, F^I_{min}) = P^I_2(X^I_2, F^I_{min}, X^I_1, F^I_{min}) < 0.$[698]

The result obtained for this special case of competition expresses that under the given assumptions (homogeneous products $(X^I_1 = X^I_2)$, competition only in prices, complete information, no consumer preferences, static game) the market for information intermediaries has a tendency toward a natural monopoly,[699] because the market entry of an identical information intermediary is not advantageous, neither for the entrant nor for the established intermediary.[700] This is exactly the case for the two competing information intermediaries who both produce the same information $(X^I_1 = X^I_2)$, and both have to bear search costs $C^I(X^I_{1,2})$. As information can be copied for vanishing marginal costs, the production and dissemination of the information by only one information intermediary would halve the costs.

**Competition in quality levels**
The second special case would be that both intermediaries charge the same fee $(F^I_1 = F^I_2)$ and only compete in the quality levels offered. Here the intersections of the functions $U_1^{Intermediary}$ and $U_2^{Intermediary}$ with the axis of ordinates will be equal and the two functions only differ in slope ((eq. 42) and Figure 44). The following argumentation corresponds to the one given above for the case of price competition: In this situation the intermediary offering the highest quality level will capture the whole market and the other will attract no demand.[701] Neglecting the intermediaries' search costs incurred to offer the particular quality levels this would lead to a Nash equilibrium of $X^I_1 = X^I_2 = \infty$. The existence of search costs $C^I_{1,2}(X^I_{1,2}) = C^I(X^I_{1,2}) > 0$, however, limits the quality levels $X^I_1 = X^I_2$ to a maximum quality level $X^I_{max}$ to be offered in equilibrium. This maximum quality level can be determined by the condition $P^I(X^I_{max}, F^I_{1,2}) = R^I(X^I_{max}, F^I_{1,2}) - C^I(X^I_{max}) = 0 \Rightarrow R^I(X^I_{max}, F^I_1) = C^I(X^I_{max})$ with $F^I_1 = F^I_2$. The Nash equilibrium yields $X^I_1 = X^I_2 = X^I_{max}(F^I_1 = F^I_2)$, and the intermediaries' profits are again negative: $P^I_1(X^I_{max}, F^I_1, X^I_{max}, F^I_2) = P^I_2(X^I_{max}, F^I_2, X^I_{max}, F^I_1) < 0.$

The main result obtained from the considerations concerning competition either in prices or in the quality level between two information intermediaries can be summarized as follows:

---

[697] Gehrig also obtained vanishing profits in equilibrium for price competition between two identical intermediaries in a market making model, cf. [Gehrig 93, p. 112].

[698] In a duopoly with zero fixed costs the equilibrium profit for pure price competition is zero, cf. [Rasmusen 89, p. 264], [Feess 97, p. 420].

[699] The same tendency exists for intermediaries in trade, as was shown in a market making model of an intermediary, cf. [Gehrig 93, p. 113]. See Section 3.5.2 and [Gravelle 92, p. 223], [Varian 93, 410] for natural monopolies.

[700] See the corresponding argumentation for the basic Bertrand model in [Feess 97, p. 420].

[701] For the case of competition in the quality level a profit function corresponding to (eq. 43) can be derived.

*Result 8:*    *Competition in a duopoly of information intermediaries, either purely in prices or solely in the quality level offered, results in negative expected profits for both intermediaries. The Nash equilibrium obtained in price competition (competition in the quality level offered) is a minimum fee determined by the common quality level offered (a maximum quality level offered determined by the common fee charged).*

The results obtained for these cases of competition are only special cases because competition in prices and in quality is artificially separated.[702] In real-life cases these two forms of competition usually occur in combination. This will be taken into account in the following section.

### 4.5.2.2  Competition in price-quality combinations

Simultaneous competition in prices and in quality has to be analyzed by means of the more complex function for the expected profit in (eq. 41). To start up with, a simultaneous game with discrete strategy space for the two information intermediaries will be discussed.

### 4.5.2.2.1  Simultaneous game with discrete strategy space

The simplest game of competition in price-quality combinations between two information intermediaries is given by a discrete strategy space[703] for the two information intermediaries. The two information intermediaries are assumed to operate simultaneously[704] in the market for information, i.e., both choose their strategy without knowing the other's choice, and both have symmetric information about the environment. The strategy space of the following basic game consists of four combinations of quality level and prices: $\{(X^I_{high}, F^I_{high}), (X^I_{high}, F^I_{low}), (X^I_{low}, F^I_{high}), (X^I_{low}, F^I_{low})\}$. In the game intermediaries perform information acquisition, i.e., the search process, and have to bear the search costs $C_{1,2}(X^I)$ in any case.[705] The payoff matrix for the game of the two information intermediaries, labeled intermediary 1 and intermediary 2, is depicted in Table 10 for an arbitrary choice of environ-

---

[702] Such a critique occurred for the Bertrand model of price competition, which has lead to the extension of the model into a combination of competition in prices and in quantities, cf. [Feess 97, p. 420, 429]. The extension is known as the Kreps/Scheinkman model, cf.[Kreps 83], [Feess 97, p. 420-421].

[703] The *strategy space* is the set of strategies available to a player, cf. [Rasmusen 89, p. 24].

[704] In *simultaneous games* players chose their strategies without knowing the other's choice. This has to be distinguished from *sequential games* in which players chose their strategies one after another, cf. [Varian 93, p. 448, 477 fp.].

[705] The assumption that search costs only have to be borne if the intermediary faces a demand greater zero, i.e., the information intermediaries only perform information acquisition on demand, does not alter the basic results obtained in Table 10.

mental conditions. The matrix shows the expected profits $((P^I_1 ; P^I_2)$, cf. (eq. 41)) of the two information intermediaries for the particular strategy chosen. The columns and rows shaded in light gray mark dominated strategies, which therefore can be neglected for the determination of the Nash equilibrium.[706] The Nash equilibrium is marked in darker gray in the matrix, it is the situation in which both intermediaries offer high quality $X^I_{high}$ and charge only low fees $F^I_{low}$. Obviously the equilibrium is *Pareto-inefficient*[707] for both intermediaries, but from the clients' point of view it is advantageous.[708]

Table 10:    *Payoff matrix for a simultaneous game of two information intermediaries competing in price-quality combinations. The variables are chosen arbitrarily:* $X^I_{high}=10$, $X^I_{low}=5$, $F^I_{high}=25$, $F^I_{low}=12.5$ $(c=1, \lambda=1, \mu_\beta=4, \sigma_\beta=1, N=10000)$.

|  | | intermediary 2 | | | |
|---|---|---|---|---|---|
| $(P^I_1 ; P^I_2)$ | | $X^I_{high}, F^I_{high}$ | $X^I_{high}, F^I_{low}$ | $X^I_{low}, F^I_{high}$ | $X^I_{low}, F^I_{low}$ |
| interme- | $X^I_{high}, F^I_{high}$ | (88943;88943) | (-22027;102563) | (199913;-148) | (199913;-148) |
| diary | $X^I_{high}, F^I_{low}$ | (102563;-22027) | (40268;40268) | (102563;-148) | (102563;-148) |
| 1 | $X^I_{low}, F^I_{high}$ | (-148;199913) | (-148;102563) | (-148;-148) | (-148;95434) |
|  | $X^I_{low}, F^I_{low}$ | (-148;199913) | (-148;102563) | (95434;-148) | (47643;47643) |

### 4.5.2.2.2 Sequential choice of strategies

The basic cases of competition were simultaneous games. In reality, however, situations that correspond with sequential games are of great importance, for example, the entry into monopolistic market,[709] or leaders and followers[710] in oligopolistic markets. Moreover, in the following the strategy space is continuous,[711] i.e., all combinations of prices and qualities are possible. As was introduced earlier in Section 4.3.3 the information intermediary can either follow a fixed-quality-level strategy or a profit-maximizing strategy. In case of a fixed-quality-level strategy the information intermediaries commit themselves to a quality level $X^I$, and the fee $F^I$ can be adjusted to maximize the expected profit $P^I_{1,2}$. In case of a profit-maximizing strategy both decision variables can be chosen in order to maximize the expected profit.

---

[706] Cf. [Myerson 91, p. 57-58].

[707] A Pareto-efficient strategy would be a situation in which no other strategy choice will make both players better off, cf. [Varian 93, p. 474].

[708] The apparatus of game theory can be applied to the basic payoff matrix to discuss further strategies and effects that can occur. See, for example, [Varian 93, p. 469 fp.]. This is omitted here in order to analyze the effects of continuous strategy spaces and sequential choices of strategies.

[709] Cf. [Kreps 90, p. 57], [Holler 93, p. 17].

[710] Cf. [Varian 93, p. 448 fp.].

[711] Cf. [Rasmusen 89, p. 76], [Holler 93, p. 61-62].

**Fixed-quality-level strategy**

The course of the process is as follows: first both intermediaries chose the quality level offered ($X^I_1$ and $X^I_2$), then one intermediary (denoted intermediary 1) chooses the fee charged ($F^I_1$) and the other (intermediary 2) chooses the optimal fee ($F^I_{2opt}$) as a reaction to intermediary 1's strategy. Subsequently all consumers chose their source for information acquisition (eq. 40), which determines the expected profit of the two intermediaries (eq. 41).

The optimal reaction of intermediary 2 ($F^I_{2opt}$) to the offer of intermediary 1 ($X^I_1$ and $F^I_1$) is depicted for an arbitrary choice of parameters in Figure 45. In addition, the expected profit of intermediary 1 ($P^I_1(F^I_1)$) and the expected profit of intermediary 2 ($P^I_{2opt}(F^I_1)$) are depicted in the figure as a function of the fee $F^I_1$ charged by intermediary 1.

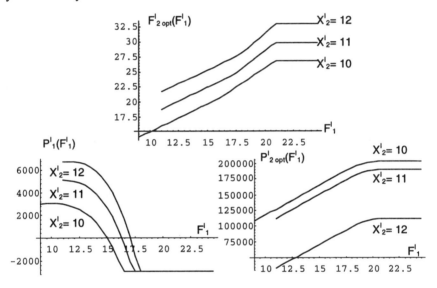

*Figure 45:*    *Optimal reaction of intermediary 2 ($F^I_{2opt}(X^I_1, F^I_1)$) to the strategy of intermediary 1 ($X^I_2=(10, 11, 12)$, $X^I_1=8$, $F^I_1=variable$, $c=1$, $\lambda=1$, $\mu_\beta=4$, $\sigma_\beta=1$, $N=10000$).*

The negative value of the expected profit for the leader $P^I_1(F^I_1)$ for high values of the fee $F^I_1$ charged is simply the value of the search costs $-C^I_1(X^I_1)$. The reason is that for high fees $F^I_1$, intermediary 1 looses all of his/her market share either to intermediary 2 or to personal search processes. For a particular quality level $X^I_2$ offered by intermediary 2 the optimal reaction is given by the optimal fee $F^I_{2opt}$ which can be determined from the maximization of the expected profit: $P^I_2(X^I_2,F^I_2,X^I_1,F^I_1) \rightarrow$ *Max!* $\Rightarrow \partial P^I_2(X^I_2,F^I_2,X^I_1,F^I_1)/\partial F^I_2 = 0$ for a fixed value of $X^I_2$ (see (eq. 41)).

The possibility to react with the optimal fee $F'_{2opt}$ to any strategy chosen by the leader (intermediary 1) gives the follower (intermediary 2) an advantage over the leader, who has to make the first move in the game.[712] This becomes clear by comparison of the magnitude of the expected profits achievable by intermediary 1 (the leader) and intermediary 2 (the follower), confer $P'_1$ and $P'_{2opt}$ in Figure 45.[713] A second effect observable in Figure 45 is that the consumers' market can be divided between the two information intermediaries so that both intermediaries can be economically viable, i.e., both gain positive profits. In particular, the expected profit $P'_1$ achievable by intermediary 1, who offers a low quality level $X'_1$, grows (a) with an increase of the quality level $X'_2$ offered by intermediary 2, and (b) with a decrease of the own fee $F'_1$ charged. This expresses that the division of the consumers' market side between the two information intermediaries is mainly produced by the quality level offered. Then consumers with a lower willingness to pay $\beta$ are served by the intermediary offering a lower quality level, whereas consumers with a higher willingness to pay prefer to go to the intermediary who offers a higher quality level.

**Profit maximizing strategy**
The course of the process is comparable to the one for a fixed-quality-level strategy, except for the fact that the follower (intermediary 2) chooses the profit maximizing strategy as a reaction: first the leader (intermediary 1) chooses a strategy ($X'_1$ and $F'_1$), then the follower (intermediary 2) chooses the optimal reaction to the leader's strategy ($F'_{2opt}$ and $X'_{2opt}$). The optimal reaction of intermediary 2 ($F'_{2opt}(X'_1,F'_1)$ and $X'_{2opt}(X'_1,F'_1)$) is determined from the maximization (eq. 38):

*(eq. 44)*
$$\vec{\nabla}_{X'_2,F'_2} P'_2(X'_2,F'_2,X'_1,F'_1) =$$
$$\left( \frac{\partial P'_2(X'_2,F'_2,X'_1,F'_1)}{\partial X'_2}, \frac{\partial P'_2(X'_2,F'_2,X'_1,F'_1)}{\partial F'_2} \right) = \vec{0}$$

An example of the optimal reaction of intermediary 2 on the strategy of the leader is depicted in Figure 46 for an arbitrary choice of decision variables and different quality levels offered by intermediary 1. In addition, the expected profit for the leader $P'_1$ and the follower $P'_{2opt}$ are depicted in the figure. The cracks in the two reaction curves ($F'_{2opt}(X'_1,F'_1)$ and $X'_{2opt}(X'_1,F'_1)$) of intermediary 2 occur in the vicinity of those strategies of intermediary 1 where the expected profit $P'_1$ vanishes. For cases in which intermediary 1 is still in the market intermediary 2

---

[712] A comparable result can be obtained for the more general case of price-leaders and price-followers in an oligopoly consisting of identical players. In this case the position of a price-follower is preferable to the position of the price leader, too. Cf. [Varian 94, p. 302].

[713] In all cases, including those not depicted in Figure 45, the expected profit of the follower (in this case intermediary 2) exceeds the expected profit of the leader (intermediary 1): $Max[P'_1(X'_1,F'_1,X'_2,F'_{2opt})] < Max[P'_2(X'_2,F'_{2opt},X'_1,F'_1)]$.

obviously has to follow a different reaction than for cases in which intermediary 1 can be expected to gain no demand. However, as both intermediaries are expected to have symmetric information, intermediary 1 will not choose strategies that would result in a total loss of the market share.

If the follower applies a profit-maximizing strategy, the follower's expected profit is larger than for a fixed-quality-level strategy and the leader's profit is further reduced compared to the situation depicted in Figure 45.[714] As above in the case of a fixed-quality-level strategy for the follower's reaction to the strategy of the leader, the market can be divided between the two intermediaries in case of the profit-maximizing strategy.

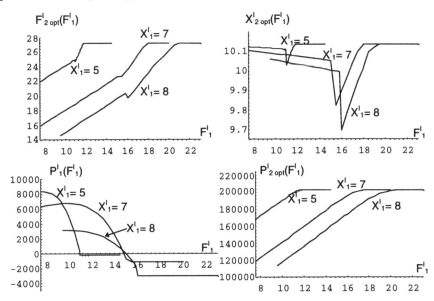

*Figure 46:*     *Optimal reaction of intermediary 2 $(F^l_{2opt}(F^l_p X^l_l), X^l_{2opt}(F^l_p X^l_l))$ to the strategy of intermediary 1 $(X^l_l=(5, 7, 8), F^l_l=variable, c=1, \lambda=1, \mu_\beta=4, \sigma_\beta=1, N=10000)$.*

The main result of the analysis can be summarized as follows:

*Result 9:*     *Competition in a duopoly of information intermediaries in price-quality combinations can lead to a division of the market between the two, so that both intermediaries can be economically viable.*

*The position of the follower is advantageous, because of the opportunity to optimally react on the leader's strategy.*

---

[714]     This becomes clear from the comparison of the numerical results obtained for the two situations (Figure 45 and Figure 46).

### 4.5.2.3  Discussion

The existence of fixed costs,[715] those have a relatively high proportion in the production of information (Section 2.2.3), and the market structure in the market for information intermediaries, give rise to a tendency toward a natural monopoly of the information intermediary if competition can only take place in one strategic variable (Result 8). Different from this case of competition purely performed via prices or via the quality level offered, the more realistic case of competition in price-quality combinations has revealed that, under the assumptions made, more than one intermediary can be economically viable in a market for information (Result 9). A comparable result will also be obtained, if the services provided by the intermediary require the installation and operation of some kind of network that causes costs.[716] Differentiation of the intermediaries can then be achieved by different network sizes and the market structure turns out to be a natural oligo‑poly.[717] These results correspond with general assertions about markets for information (Section 2.5.2) and markets for intermediary services (Section 3.5.2).

The results obtained in the analysis of competition between two information intermediaries have some implications for the optimal strategy of information intermediaries in markets for information. The possibility of direct competition between information intermediaries and especially the threat of entry of a competing information intermediary into the market of an established one has negative effects on the intermediary's performance and can, in special cases, become ruinous. The established information intermediary therefore has to take precautions to minimize the effects of competition and gain competitive advantages.[718] Appropriate measures in particular are, for example: reputation obtained from past performance (Sections 2.3.3 and 3.2.3.2), the provision of value-adding service to differentiate the own offer from that of others, and the investment in personal abilities as well as in search technologies to reduce the costs for information acquisition (Section 4.4.1.3). Another measure can be the installation of relational networks between independent information intermediaries in order to coordinate each other or, in a

---

[715] Sources of fixed costs can be, for example, costs for technologies applied by the information intermediary. In terms of the basic model of an information intermediary these costs would make a further negative contribution to the expected profit, cf. Section 4.3.2.1.

[716] Cf. [Gehrig 96] and Section 3.5.2.

[717] The result was found for price competition between broker intermediaries maintaining supplier networks of different sizes, cf. [Gehrig 96, p. 108 fp.], however, the model is applicable to a much broader class of problems, cf. [Gehrig 96, p. 102].

[718] The basic strategies, competitors within an industry can follow in general, were outlined by Porter [Porter 92, p. 62-66]: *Overall cost leadership* in production and distribution. *Differentiation*, i.e., concentration on achieving superior performance in some important customer benefit area valued by the market as a whole. *Focusing* the business on one or more narrow market segments. Cf. [Kotler 88, p. 57].

closer relation between the intermediaries, to build up market power or to diversify in different thematic areas.[719]

It should be clear that the results obtained depend on the underlying assumptions. In real-life cases further influences and effects that were not modeled in the basic intermediary model have consequences for the competitive situation of the information intermediary:

- *Asymmetric information*: Information about environmental conditions as well as about the other players' strategy will usually be distributed asymmetrically between the market participants.[720] The occupation of information about information sources, search techniques and technologies, and environmental conditions can be a competitive advantage of the information intermediary.
- *Product differentiation*: Value-adding services can be provided to differentiate the services offered from that of competing intermediaries.
- *Intermediary's reputation*: Past performance of an information intermediary can play an important role in the consumers' decision for a particular intermediary.[721] This induces that consumers do not only take their decision about the source of information acquisition with regard to prices and the quality level offered, but also according to *preferences* for a particular source of information.
- *Collusion and cartels*:[722] Information intermediaries can augment their profit by agreeing about prices and qualities, therefore, intermediaries may collude or form a cartel.[723]

## 4.6 Welfare effects through the information intermediary

The savings of economic resources, especially transaction costs, resulting from intermediation are one major justification of intermediaries in general (Section 3.2.3). Information intermediaries, as one special type of intermediaries, focus on information processing activities that they perform on behalf of other economic agents' information needs (Definition 3). One main function[724] of these activities is

---

[719] For a comprehensive discussion of *marketing strategies*, i.e., strategies for market-leaders and market-followers, in general see [Kotler 88, p. 308-346].

[720] Cf. [Rasmusen 89, p. 133 fp.], [Gibbons 92, p. 143 fp., 165 fp.].

[721] Cf. [Wilson 85], [Rasmusen 89, p. 94 fp.], and Section 3.2.3.2.

[722] *Collusion* refers to the case of cooperation between the players without any explicit agreement. The term *cartel* refers to cooperation of players according to explicit agreements, cf. [Feess 97, p. 431]. These situations can be analyzed by means of *repeated games*, cf. [Varian 93, p.475], [Feess 97, p. 431 fp.].

[723] Higher profits can be obtained if both intermediaries agree (by collusion or in a cartel) to charge higher prices than in the Nash equilibrium. See, for example, Table 10 and see [Varian 93,p. 462] as well.

[724] Information intermediaries perform various other functions and services, however, a central function is the mediation of information (Section 4.1.1).

the mediation of information focused in the basic model. Therefore, a central function of information intermediaries is the reduction of the costs for information acquisition (search costs),[725] being from a macroeconomics point of view an increase of social welfare. These effects on social welfare can be analyzed within the basic model of information intermediaries as will be shown in the following.

## 4.6.1 The social welfare function

The social welfare function $W$ for a situation without an information intermediary can be determined by summing up the utilities[726] of all consumers operating in the market for information:

*(eq. 45)* $$W = \sum_{j=1}^{N} U_j(x^*) = \sum_{j=1}^{N} \beta_j \cdot x_j^* \cdot$$

The searcher's utility is the monetary representation of the searcher's valuation of an object's attribute value (Section 4.2.2.2). It can be expressed as the expected-net reward following the optimal search strategy $(V_{x^*} = U_j(x^*) = \beta_j \cdot x_j^* = \beta_j \cdot x^*(\beta_j)$, (eq. 17) in Section 4.2.2.3). This can be determined by the particular willingness to pay $\beta_j$ of the single searcher ((eq. 20) in Section 4.3.1.2). In a population of searchers with willingness to pay $\beta$ for a particular quality level that can be described by means of a PDF $h(\beta)$ the sum in (eq. 45) can be transformed into an integration over $\beta$:

*(eq. 46)* $$W = N \cdot \int_0^\infty \beta \cdot x^*(\beta) \cdot h(\beta) \, d\beta \cdot$$

In (eq. 46) it is assumed that the number of consumers with $\beta \in [\beta_0, \beta_0 + d\beta]$ can be expressed by $N \cdot h(\beta_0) \cdot d\beta$, i.e., $d\beta$ is infinitesimal. The social welfare $W^{Intermediary}$ of those consumers in the economy using the information intermediary who offers a quality level $X'_{opt}$ and charges a fee $F'_{opt}$ can be determined correspondingly.

*(eq. 47)* $$W^{Intermediary} = \sum_{j=1}^{N} U^{Intermediary} = \sum_{j=1}^{N} \left( \beta_j \cdot X'_{opt} - F'_{opt} \right) \cdot IsUser(j) \cdot$$

Here, the information intermediary is assumed to follow a *profit-maximizing strategy*. The function *IsUser(j)* determines whether the $j^{th}$ consumer is a user of

---

[725] Cf. [Resnick 95] and Section 4.1.1.
[726] The welfare function of the whole economy sums up the different consumers' utilities, cf. [Varian 93, p. 532 fp.].

the information intermediary ((eq. 31) in Section 4.3.2.3).[727] For an infinitesimal $d\beta$ and PDF $h(\beta)$ this can be transformed into:

$$(eq.\ 48) \qquad W^{Intermediary} = N \cdot \int_{\beta_1(X^I_{opt},F^I_{opt})}^{\beta_2(X^I_{opt},F^I_{opt})} \left(\beta \cdot X^I_{opt} - F^I_{opt}\right) \cdot h(\beta)\ d\beta\ \cdot$$

The boundaries $\beta_{1;2}(X^I_{opt}, F^I_{opt})$ of the integration have to be determined via the system in (eq. 32). Further, the welfare of those consumers in the economy who prefer personal search to consulting the intermediary has to be taken into account to compare the two situations (Section 4.3.2.3):

$$(eq.\ 49) \qquad W^{search} = N \cdot \left[ \int_{0}^{\beta_1(X^I_{opt},F^I_{opt})} \beta \cdot x^*(\beta) \cdot h(\beta)\ d\beta + \int_{\beta_2(X^I_{opt},F^I_{opt})}^{\infty} \beta \cdot x^*(\beta) \cdot h(\beta)\ d\beta \right] \cdot$$

Hence, the increase of social welfare $\Delta W$ through the activities of the information intermediary can be determined by:

$$(eq.\ 50) \qquad \Delta W = \left(W^{Intermediary} + W^{search}\right) - W,$$

which is simply the difference between the social welfare achievable in an economy with the information intermediary minus the social welfare in the economy without the intermediary.

## 4.6.2  Welfare effects

The main effect of information intermediaries discussed in the present work are resource savings concerning costs for information acquisition. The major determinants of these costs of search are the costs $c$ for a single observation in the search process and the distribution of objects' attribute values available on the market. This is described by the distribution parameter $\lambda$ (cf. Section 4.3.2.2). The dependency of social welfare on these two parameters in an economy with an information intermediary and without the intermediary is depicted in Figure 47 and Figure 48. In both cases the information intermediary chooses a profit-maximizing combination $X^I_{opt}$ and $F^I_{opt}$ of the decision variables.

---

[727]
$$IsUser(j) = \begin{cases} 1 & for\ (\beta_j \cdot X^I_{opt} - F^I_{opt}) \geq \beta_j \cdot x^* \\ 0 & otherwise \end{cases}$$

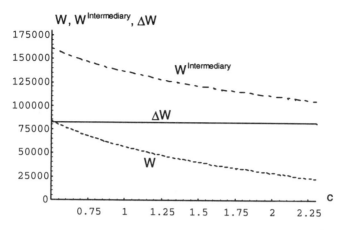

Figure 47:    Social welfare and welfare effects of the information intermediary as a
              function of the costs c for a single observation ($\lambda=1$, $\mu_\beta=4$, $\sigma_\beta=1$, $N=$
              $10000$).

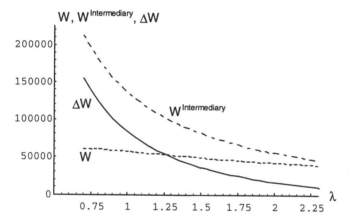

Figure 48:    Social welfare and welfare effects of the information intermediary as a
              function of the distribution parameter $\lambda$ ($c=1$, $\mu_\beta=4$, $\sigma_\beta=1$, $N=10000$).

For an increase of the costs $c$ for a single observation the social welfare is slightly
decreasing for an economy without an information intermediary ($W$) as well as for
an economy with an intermediary ($W^{Intermediary}$) (Figure 47). However, the decrease is
equivalent in both cases so that the resulting increase in social welfare through the
information intermediary $\Delta W$ is independent of the magnitude of the search costs
$c$. This independence results from the assumption that the information intermediary
and information seekers apply the same search technology (Section 4.3.2.1). In an
economy without an information intermediary increasing costs $c$ for a single observation lead to a decreasing expected-net reward ($\beta \cdot x^*$) for consumers' personal
search processes. This causes the decrease of welfare in the economy as a whole.

The information intermediary, following a profit-maximizing strategy, reduces the quality offered $X'_{opt}$ and retains the fee $F'_{opt}$ charged due to increased search costs $c$ (Section 4.4.1.2). The social welfare in the economy with an intermediary $W^{Intermediary}$ is therefore decreasing as well. Nevertheless, the activities of the information intermediary lead to enhancements of social welfare $\Delta W$ in all cases.

An increase of the parameter $\lambda$, i.e., the decrease of the density of high qualities on the market, leads to a slight decrease of social welfare $W$ in an economy without an information intermediary, and to a steep decrease of social welfare in an economy with an intermediary (Figure 48). As a result, the increase of social welfare through the information intermediary $\Delta W$ is decreasing with an increase of the distribution parameter $\lambda$. The cause is again the decrease of the expected-net reward $(\beta \cdot x^*)$ for consumers' personal search processes with an increase of $\lambda$ as well as the profit-maximizing strategy of the information intermediary (Section 4.4.2.2). The information intermediary adjusts the quality level $X'_{opt}$ and the fee $F'_{opt}$ to a decreasing density of high qualities (Figure 33), resulting in decreasing social welfare $W^{Intermediary}$ as well. However, in this case the intermediary leads to increased social welfare $\Delta W$ that asymptotically approaches zero for a further increase of the parameter $\lambda$.

If the information intermediary retains the quality level $X'$ offered and the fee $F'$ charged, social welfare will be increasing for decreasing density of high quality objects among all objects available.[728] The reason is that with an increasing value of the parameter $\lambda$ personal search processes become less preferable compared to the price-quality combination offered by the information intermediary. In this case the information intermediary can maintain the expected profit, for example, through learning-curve effects or investments in the reduction of search costs, i.e., the costs for a single observation (cf. Figure 35).

## 4.6.3 Discussion

The economic viability of a monopolistic information intermediary has already become obvious from the analysis performed in Section 4.4. Moreover, the above analysis reveals that from a macroeconomics' point of view the information intermediary is advantageous for the economy as a whole.[729] Hence, the intermediary's profit is justified through an increase in social welfare made feasible by the

---

[728] This result is not depicted here, but should be clear from (eq. 48), (eq. 49), and (eq. 50).

[729] The activities of the information intermediary, i.e., the dissemination of information about markets, will clearly have other consequences on the efficiency of the particular market (Section 2.4). These effects are not included herein, because the treatment of the economic welfare through the information intermediary only covers the effects concerning the search for information. Therefore, the present examination is only a partial analysis, cf. [Varian 93, p. 483], [Feess 97, p. 246 fp.].

activities.[730] In terms of the model the effect of an information intermediary on social welfare $\Delta W$ does only have positive values, i.e., the intermediary can only lead to an increase of social welfare. The argumentation is as follows: If the information intermediary is not advantageous to consumers, no information seeker will consult the intermediary but will instead perform personal search. This can be expressed by: $W^{Intermediary} \rightarrow 0 \Rightarrow W^{direct\ search} \rightarrow W \Rightarrow \Delta W \rightarrow 0$.

The fact that the information intermediary always has an augmenting effect on economic welfare is brought about by the (implicit) assumption of the basic model that all information about the environment is symmetrically distributed among all market participants (Section 4.3.5). That is to say, all information seekers have complete and perfect information about the environment as well as the information intermediary. In this situation economic agents, i.e., information seekers, will only consult the information intermediary if the combination of quality level $X^I$ offered and fee $F^I$ charged is advantageous to them (eq. 31). Perfect information about the environment enables the individual information seekers to come to their decisions with certainty and therefore chose the best alternative for information acquisition. This is either the purchase of information from the information intermediary or a personal search process. As a result, the information intermediary will solely augment social welfare in the whole economy, a reduction is not possible under these assumptions. If, on the other hand, the decision about the best alternative of information acquisition has to be taken by the information seeker under asymmetric information about the environment,[731] a sub-optimal choice may occur. Compared to a situation with symmetric information this would result in a loss of utility for the individual information seeker. Summed up over the whole economy, the asymmetric distribution of information about the environment among market participants gives rise to a potential for negative effects of the information intermediary.[732]

In practical cases asymmetric distribution of information can have multiple forms. For example, information asymmetries can concern information about the environment or information about other market participants. In addition, information can be asymmetrically distributed among all market participants

---

[730] Gümbel stated that the intermediary's profit is justified as a share of the resource savings (or reductions in transaction costs) produced together with the trading partners, cf. [Gümbel 85, p. 193]. See Section 3.2.4 as well.

[731] For example, the individual information seeker only has noisy information about the distribution parameter $\lambda$ (Section 4.7.3). Therefore, the information seeker can determine the reservation value $x^*$ for a private search process only with uncertainty. Consequently, the decision about the best alternative for information acquisition, obtained from (eq. 31) and involving the reservation value $x^*$, can only be taken under uncertainty.

[732] A similar result for asymmetric information among market participants was obtained by Yavas in the analysis of intermediaries (matchmakers) in bilateral search markets, cf. [Yavas 94, p. 426].

(including the information intermediary) or only between the information intermediary and information seekers. A situation with asymmetric information
between the information intermediary and potential clients can give rise to
principal-agent problems (Section 2.3.1).[733] From the information intermediary's
point of view, strategies including some kind of fraud can become advantageous in
the short-run. In the long-run, however, advantages from clients' repeated transactions with the intermediary may gain importance and thus eliminate strategies
that are optimal in the short-run.[734]

The previous discussion and the major results can be briefly summarized as
follows:

*Result 10:*    • *From a global point of view a monopolistic information intermediary
                   is advantageous for the economy as a whole if information about the
                   environment is symmetrically distributed among all market partici-
                   pants.*
                • *Asymmetric information about the environment gives rise to a
                   potential for negative effects of information intermediaries.*
                • *The magnitude of social welfare effects of intermediation can depend
                   significantly on environmental conditions.*

In the basic model the information intermediary is assumed to apply the same
search technology and therefore bear the same costs for a single observation as
individual information seekers (Section 4.3.2.1). In contrast, if the information
intermediary's costs for a single observation were considerably smaller than in
personal search processes, for example, because of higher experiences or advanced
search technologies (Section 4.4.1.3), the advantage of the information intermediary over personal search processes will be further increased. However, the distribution of the resource savings between the intermediary and the clients remains to
be solved (Section 3.2.4). An effect to be taken into account here is, for example,
competition between information intermediaries operating in the same market.

## 4.7 Extensions to the basic intermediary model

The model of an information intermediary presented in this chapter concentrated
on the analysis of the basic environmental influences on information intermediaries and their optimal strategy. The model was based on a couple of
assumptions (Section 4.3.5) and treated the information intermediary on a rather
abstract level. The aim was to work out the mediation of information and

---

[733]   See Section 2.3.2 as well.

[734]   For possible remedies to principal-agent problems see Section 2.3.3.

information filtering (Figure 10) as the major function and service of information intermediaries. In real-life examples these assumptions, e.g., complete knowledge about environmental conditions and asymmetric distribution of information, will be fulfilled only partly. So the model is idealized in this regard. A number of assumptions of the model can be attenuated or altered in the directions that are named below.[735] However, the underlying mathematics will become more complex through these extensions and the tractability of the model will suffer therefrom.

### 4.7.1 Distributions assumed in the model

The model employed two distributions to describe the two market sides of the information intermediary. The distribution of qualities on the suppliers' market side was described by an exponential CDF $F(X)$ (Section 4.3.1.1). This seemed appropriate for the description of a strongly decreasing density of relevant information in the market for information, however, other distributions can be appropriate for different types of markets. For example, a binomial distribution can be assumed if the variable $X$ describing the quality of the objects under consideration can only take integer values, or a normal distribution can be taken in case of a population with a given mean value of the quality.

The other distribution used in the model is the distribution of the willingness to pay for a particular quality level in the population with CDF $H(\beta)$. In this market a normal distribution seemed appropriate because it was plausible that consumers' preferences are similar but with a slight diffusion. Here, other distributions can be applied as well. For example, an uniform distribution can be used if the willingness to pay is equally distributed over an interval.

The effects of different distributions employed in the model are mainly numerical in result and may express other plausible assumptions or other applications of the model.[736] However, since the major aim of the model is to elaborate basic statements about the tendency of influences from environmental conditions on information intermediaries, it is appropriate to concentrate the analysis on the distributions selected in the basic model.

### 4.7.2 Risk assessment of the market participants

Consumers as well as the information intermediary were assumed to be risk neutral (Sections 4.2.1 and 4.3.2.1). This implies that both are only oriented on the expected reward or profit achievable, and that both ignore any risk inherent in their activities. Real-life economic agents are usually risk averse. This can be expressed

---

[735] The examination of possible extensions of the basic model can also be understood as a critical discussion of the basic assumptions of the model.

[736] It can be expected that the basic results of the model will be retained except for the magnitude of the effects.

by a concave utility function $(U''(X) \le 0 \ \forall X)$.[737] One possible example is that of absolute risk aversion expressed by the *Arrow-Pratt index of absolute-risk aversion* $R_A^U(X) = -U''(X)/U'(X)$.[738] For a constant, absolute-risk aversion $R_A^U(X) = R = const.$ this yields an exponential utility function $a - b \cdot \exp(-RX)$.[739] Taking these risk attitudes into account, the consumers' utility function (eq. 21) would have to be altered, and the information intermediary's decision problem has to maximize the expected utility instead of simply maximizing the expected profit.[740]

### 4.7.3 Information asymmetries between information intermediary and information seekers

The basic model assumed that potential clients of the information intermediary have the same information about the information sources on the market as the information intermediary has (Section 4.3.1.1). In terms of the model both have the same knowledge about the parameters of the distribution as well as about potential information sources. In practical applications, however, it can be assumed that the information intermediary has more experience and more knowledge about the information sources available on the market than the ordinary information seeker has. The model can take this extension into consideration by assuming different knowledge about the distribution parameter $\lambda$ for potential clients and the information intermediary. This can, for example, be expressed by assuming that the information intermediary takes the exact value of the distribution parameter $\lambda$ to determine the reservation value $x^*$ in the optimal stopping rule (Section 4.2.2.1). Whereas, the potential clients are assumed to have only knowledge of a noisy distribution parameter $\lambda_{client} = \lambda \cdot (1 + \varepsilon_\lambda)$, $\varepsilon_\lambda \in [-1, 1]$.[741]

In situations with an asymmetric distribution of information about the environment between the information intermediary and potential clients *principal-agent problems* can occur (Section 2.3.1).

The formal treatment of these effects would require the extension of the model toward a multi-period model to take into account the effects of repeated trans-

---

[737]    Cf. [Hey 81, p. 22], [Berger 80, p. 40 fp.].

[738]    Cf. [Hey 81, p. 23], [Eisenführ 94, p. 213].

[739]    Cf. [Hey 81, p. 24-25].

[740]    Cf. [Varian 93, p. 216 fp.], [Eisenführ 94, p. 202 fp.].

[741]    To accentuate effects that lead to higher expected search costs for potential clients, it can be assumed that: $\varepsilon_\lambda \in [-0.5, 1]$. The value of the parameter $\varepsilon_\lambda$ describes the magnitude of the difference in knowledge about the environment between the information intermediary and potential clients. It is an additional parameter describing the population of information seekers. The value $\lambda_{client}$ can be determined for each particular information seeker or for the whole population.

actions, and the application of game theoretic methods to analyze the interme-diary's strategic behavior.

### 4.7.4 Different search technologies of information intermediary and information seekers

As well as differences in the information distribution between the information intermediary and potential clients further differences in the search behavior can occur. In real-life cases these differences are, for example, caused by the interme-diary's advantages in experience resulting from higher transaction volumes (Section 3.2.3) or by application of different search technologies. In the model these differences can be expressed through different search costs $c$ for a single observation for the information intermediary ($c^{Intermediary}$) and for information users ($c^{Individual}$) (Sections 4.4.1.3 and 4.4.2.3).[742] One result of this effect will be an increase of the information intermediary's expected profit due to reduced costs $C$ for information acquisition. If the intermediary applies the increase in efficiency, for example, to improve the services offered, further competitive advantages can be gained. Another utilization can be the reduction of the fee charged for the service in order to attract a larger number of clients.

Another possible extension can be the assumption of learning-curve effects in the search process, for example, a *convex search technology*, i.e., decreasing marginal search costs (= costs for a single observation in the search process) for an increasing number of samples.[743]

### 4.7.5 Extensions of the underlying search model

The basic model of search (Section 4.2.1) underlying the basic model of an infor-mation intermediary can be extended in several directions (Section 4.2.3). Multi-stage search models can be employed to further differentiate between the process of search and a subsequent evaluation of promising objects. Adaptive search models can be applied to take into account learning processes concerning environ-mental conditions. Finite time horizons in search models emphasize the effects of time elapsing during the search process.

---

[742] The information intermediary can be assumed to incur lower costs for a single observation than information seekers.

[743] See [Stiglitz 89, p. 782-786] for search costs obtained from different search techno-logies.

### 4.7.6 Modeling the information processing activities of the information intermediary

The model focuses the mediation and filtering of information as the information intermediary's central function and services offered. Information intermediaries, conceived as economic information processing systems (Definition 3) perform further information processing activities. Examples are the evaluation of information, the bundling of information from different information sources, and storing of information for later use.[744] To fully model these activities it would be necessary to take into account the semantics of information processed by the information intermediary (Section 2.1.1.2). As a first approach, information can be represented by different messages received by the information intermediary. Information processing activities would then be modeled by storing, bundling, and rearranging the messages received and sending out new messages.[745] Such extensions give the opportunity to further analyze the information processing capacities, the thematic orientation and specialization of information intermediaries as well as the case of a merchant intermediaries for information, i.e., intermediaries buying and selling information on their own account (Section 3.3.2).

## 4.8  Summary

The *basic model of an information intermediary* opened some insight into the business and the strategies of this special kind of intermediaries. Furthermore, some basic principles as well as recommendations for the design and strategy of information intermediaries were derived. These will be briefly summarized in the following.

### 4.8.1  General results of the basic model

Within the scope of the model one major result is that a monopolistic information intermediary can be *economically viable* in the market for information, and therefore can satisfy the role of an independent provider of information to secure efficient information provision in the market, cf. Section 2.5.2. The service provided by the information intermediary leads to an *increase of social welfare*. The increase is dependent on the intermediary's strategy and on the environmental conditions.

Information intermediaries are limited in their activities by the possibility of personal search of the information seekers, which acts like a competitor and

---

[744]  See Sections 2.1.6 and 5.1.3.

[745]  Marschak, for example, conceives information systems as channels and introduces messages to be exchanged between different economic agents, cf. [Marschak 75].

disciplines the intermediaries (*indirect competition*), and by the threat of market entry of competitors (*direct competition*).[746] In case of direct competition in price-quality combinations between identical information intermediaries the follower has the advantage to adjust the strategy to the environment and the services offered by the leader. This has emphasized the necessity of differentiation of the service offered by the single information intermediary in order to gain competitive advantages and to strengthen the own position.

The information intermediary can follow several *strategies* (choices of price-quality combinations) to offer the service and to react to user requirements and environmental conditions. The simultaneous adjustment of prices and quality level to environmental conditions is the most preferable strategy. In a *fixed-quality-level strategy* the profit is highly dependent on the costs for a single observation in the search process and the density of high quality objects in the set of all available objects. It should only be applied if these determinants of the search process can be estimated in advance.[747] Following a *fixed-fee strategy* the information intermediary can adjust the search effort to environmental conditions (search costs and density of relevant information), determining the quality of the result.

The *business strategy*[748] of information intermediaries has to address influences from the supply market side (sources of information) as well as the demand market side (information seekers):

**The sources of information:** The density of relevant information among all information is a major influence on the profitability of the information intermediary, therefore knowledge about appropriate information sources is a core competency of the information intermediary. Reductions in costs for a single observation in the search process can compensate for a decreasing density of relevant information (Figure 35). Hence, efficient search tactics and search technologies are a further foundation of the business of information intermediaries.

**The target market of information seekers:** The services offered by the information intermediary have to focus a particular target market and specialize in a thematic domain. The expected profit is higher the more homogeneous the market of potential clients is and the higher the medium willingness to pay is in the market. The number of users, among other things, determined by the intermediary's awareness on the market and the preconditions to access the service, has to exceed a critical mass to recover fixed costs.

---

[746]  For the distinction of *direct* and *indirect* competition see [Gehrig 93, p. 107].

[747]  This result is based on the comparison of the different strategies of the information intermediary under variation of environmental parameters, confer Figure 30 and Figure 34.

[748]  In general, a typical strategy of intermediaries is to secure economies of scale and scope by achieving a dominant market share, cf. [Bakos 91a].

## 4.8.2 Critical success factors for information intermediaries

The analysis of the basic model covered several influences on the business of an information intermediary and revealed three main foundations of the information intermediary:

- The exploitation of economies of scale: cross-sectional (across customers) and temporal reuse of information,[749]
- the expertise in search for information, and
- domain specific knowledge.

These domains roughly correspond to the structural and functional sources of intermediary efficiency found for classical intermediaries in Section 3.2.3. In particular, the following *critical success factors for the business of information intermediaries* were revealed:

**Basic requirements**:

- Attraction of a critical number of users.
- Provision of a personalized service.
- Provision of value-adding services in addition to the service of information mediation.
- Focus on a thematic domain.

**Core competencies:**

- Knowledge and possession of optimal search tactics.
- Knowledge about potential clients, i.e., the preferences and information needs of information seekers in the target market.
- Technological knowledge (expertise) in the thematic domain of the service.
- Knowledge about information sources, their availability, and quality.

**Business specific investments:**

- Awareness of the service on the market.
- Good reputation on the market.
- Relations, i.e., relational networks, with adequate (high quality) information sources.
- Relational networks with information intermediation services in other thematic domains.
- Information infrastructure:
  - Adequate technologies to access relevant information sources.
  - Information technologies for efficient information processing and the management of knowledge.
  - Provision of commonly accepted and widespread access technologies to the services provided.

---

[749]    Cf. Section 3.2.3.2.

# 5 Concepts and design of information intermediaries

The present chapter associates the *basic model of an information intermediary* discussed in Chapter 4 with real-life concepts and applications as well as their technological realization. The basic model treated the business of information intermediaries on a rather abstract level and focused the fundamental function of information acquisition on behalf of other economic agents' information needs, i.e., the search for information or objects on behalf of a client (Figure 10 in Section 4.1.1).[750] This basic function is a common foundation of a broad class of real-life information intermediaries, for example, market research agencies,[751] rating agencies in financial markets,[752] news agencies, and information brokers.[753] The essential characteristic of all these enterprises in the market for information is that they conceive information as an economic commodity[754] and process information on behalf of their clients' information needs (Section 2.5.3). According to Definition 3 information intermediaries perform information processing activities and provide value-adding services that go beyond the basic function analyzed in the model. These activities and services will be discussed in Section 5.1.

With the emergence of electronic information and communication networks, i.e., open WANs like the Internet (Section 1.1), *network-based intermediaries* have tremendously gained importance.[755] Network-based intermediaries fall into many categories, some are the network-based counterpart of established businesses, others emerge as completely new businesses.[756] One possible categorization can

---

[750] The process of information mediation is initiated by the recipient of the information, i.e., the information seeker directs the information intermediary to search for specific information (pull of information). The other case (push of information), i.e., the information source directs the information intermediary to disseminate information to specific recipients, is not addressed by the model. See Section 4.1.2.

[751] Cf. [Knoblich 85, p. 571-573].

[752] Cf. [Büschgen 91, p. 579-580].

[753] Cf. [Knoblich 85, p. 570-573].

[754] This does not necessarily mean that the services are always performed for a fee charged from the client. However, it should indicate that the fundamental function of these enterprises lies on the mediation of information and not on the production of new knowledge.

[755] Cf. [Resnick 95], [Sarkar 96], [Bailey 97], [Whinston 97, 270-280].

[756] Cf. [Harrington 96].

follow the form of coordination the intermediary is supporting[757] (Figure 6). Within this conception network-based intermediaries can be roughly distinguished as those involved in transactions in market environments, i.e., in *electronic markets*,[758] and those in organizational environments, e.g., in *virtual organizations*.[759] Another dimension describes the services and functions performed by the intermediary. For example, network-based intermediaries operating in electronic markets provide services like aggregating demand, matching suppliers and customers of products, services, and information, and achieving trust.[760] These intermediaries will be discussed in Section 5.2.

A particular type of network-based intermediaries are information intermediaries that are network-based, in the following these will be referred to as *network-based information intermediaries*.[761] Network-based information intermediaries offer services for information search, filtering, and retrieval in electronic information and communication networks[762] and address the problem of information overload (Section 1.1). The environmental circumstances, basic matching technologies, and an abstract architecture of network-based information intermediaries will be discussed in Section 5.3.

The chapter closes with a discussion of economic aspects of network-based information intermediaries in Section 5.4.

## 5.1 Information intermediaries

Until now, information intermediaries were treated on a rather abstract level of the basic model (Section 4.1.1). In this section a more differentiated view on the functions (Section 5.1.1) as well as a on the different types (Section 5.1.2) of real-life information intermediaries will be given, and the information processing

---

[757] Cf. [Gebauer 96, p. 34-47].

[758] 'Electronic Commerce denotes any form of economic activity conducted via electronic connections,' cf. [Wigand 97, p. 260]. An *Electronic Market* (*EM*) is therefore one particular form of coordination within Electronic Commerce, this will not be discussed in detail, see [Picot 96, p. 331-341], [Kalakota 96], [Merz 96], [Wigand 97, p. 259-309], [Whinston 97, p. 1-57] for a review.

[759] For information and references about *virtual organizations* (*VOs*) see http://www.virtual-organization.net.

[760] Cf. [Bailey 97], [Bakos 91a], [Sarkar 96], [Bakos 97b]. Sarkar designated these intermediaries as *cybermediaries*, cf. [Sarkar 96].

[761] Fikes applied the term *network-based information brokers* to technologies and services that enable vendors and buyers to retrieve 'information about services and products via the Internet from multiple vendor catalogs and data bases for both human and computer-based clients,' cf. [Fikes 95].

[762] Cf. [Fikes 95], [Whinston 97, p. 294-304].

activities will be analyzed in more detail (Section 5.1.3). Information brokers will be examined as an ideal example of information intermediaries (Section 5.1.4).

### 5.1.1 Analysis of the information need and the need for intermediaries in markets for information

In the market for information the number of sources and suppliers of information as well as the amount of information is much larger than the single information seeker can handle, especially if not being specialized in the particular domain under consideration. Individual information seekers cannot contact every possible information source, nor can they estimate the accuracy and true value of the information offered. This implies two main causes for a need for intermediation in markets for information, one concerns the *amount* of available information,[763] the other concerns the *domain* of the information.[764] The reasons that account for the need for intermediation in markets for information are mainly the following:[765]

**Amount** of information:
- Contacting the original producer of knowledge is time-consuming and expensive.
- Information concerning a particular topic is distributed across different sources, each requiring special access technologies and/or search capabilities. And each source of information may be using a different type of representation for information or knowledge and a different organization of the information.[766]
- Only a small part of all information available is relevant to the problem or question under consideration and information may be provided redundantly, i.e., as multiple representations of the same knowledge (Figure 2).

The **domain** of information:
- Knowledge and special competencies are necessary to access the information sources.[767]
- The solution of complex problems usually requires knowledge and information from several thematic domains, e.g., different scientific disciplines.
- The representation of knowledge may be inadequate for the end-user.

---

[763] The density of relevant information in the information available (see Sections 4.3.1.1 and 4.4.2) expresses a comparable situation from the viewpoint of a particular problem or question under consideration. See Section 1.1 as well.

[764] These causes broadly correspond to two of the main foundations of information intermediaries, see Section 4.8.2.

[765] Cf. [Kuhlen 95, p. 259-260]. Kuhlen does not distinguish between reasons concerning the amount and those concerning the domain of information. See [Zelewski 87, p. 738], and [Birchall 94] as well.

[766] Cf. Section 2.1.3.

[767] For example, an online-database requires the searcher's ability to formulate queries.

- The end-user might be unable to clearly specify his/her demand for information.[768]

The discrepancy between information need of an individual facing a particular task and the information available is depicted by means of different sets in Figure 49.[769] Only a part of the information need that is subjectively felt can be articulated by the individual, and not all information actually available is accessible by the information seeker. In addition, the subjective information need is usually different from the information objectively required to fulfill the task under consideration, i.e., the information seeker may not be able to specify the complete information need in advance. As a result, the information that is actually applicable to the task (the *current information level*) is only the intersection of the three sets (depicted with hatch in Figure 49).

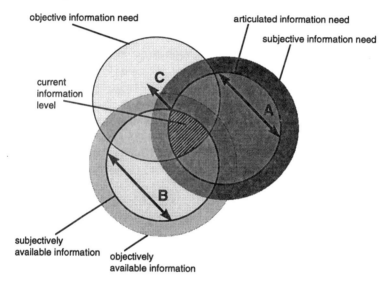

*Figure 49:*    *Information need, objectively and subjectively available information, and objective information need, based on [Kuhlen 95, p. 345] and [Picot 96, p. 106]. The arrows indicate the three basic value-adding functions of an ideal information intermediary.*

An ideal information intermediary has the task to expand the intersection between the three sets, i.e., the current information level, and produce an added value for the information seeker. This can be done in the following three directions:[770]

---

[768]   According to the theory of the *Anomalous State of Knowledge* (ASK), users can easier specify the anomaly in their personal state of knowledge than formulate a request to an information retrieval system, cf. [Belkin 82].

[769]   Cf. [Kuhlen 95, p. 344 fp.], [Picot 96, p. 106 fp.], [Wigand 97, p. 88 fp.].

[770]   Cf. [Kuhlen 95, p. 346-347].

- The information need that is subjectively felt but not articulated has to be discovered (indicated by arrow A in Figure 49).
- More information has to be made available to the individual, i.e., expansion of the subjectively available information (arrow B).
- Analysis of the objectively necessary information (arrow C).

Obviously, these value adding functions are only fulfilled by ideal forms of information intermediaries like information brokers (Section 5.1.4).[771] Other forms of information intermediaries will only partly fulfill these tasks. Nevertheless, the arguments given so far indicate a demand for information intermediaries in knowledge and information intense domains, like R&D.[772] This requires that the intermediary is highly specialized in the field under consideration,[773] e.g., in information from special disciplines in natural sciences[774] or information about existing patents.[775] In addition to the domain of technological information, the domain of market information[776] is an important business for information intermediaries, for instance, news agencies or agencies for business information.[777] According to the particular information need in these domains, information intermediaries provide different services to improve the availability and the application of information, and create an added value.[778]

## 5.1.2 General characterization of information intermediaries in markets for information

In real-life markets for information multiple forms of information mediation occur. Kuhlen distinguishes three basic *models of information mediation* (Figure 50). The models take into account that information is a representation (or reconstruction) of knowledge that was originally produced by scientists, inventors, or authors.[779] The upper part of the figure expresses the fact that a particular knowledge product, e.g.,

---

[771]    Langhein claimed that information intermediaries should aim to conceive themselves as *providers of problem solutions*, because information itself is usually an aid in the solution of problems, cf. [Langhein 85, p. 235-263].

[772]    Cf. [Grudowski 97, p. 826].

[773]    See Sections 4.8.2 and 4.4.2.3.

[774]    Technology transfer, cf. [Kuhlen 95, p. 338-339].

[775]    Cf. [Schmidt 92, p. 95].

[776]    For the distinction of technological information and market information see Section 2.1.1.3.

[777]    Cf. [Knoblich 85, p. 566-573].

[778]    For a characterization of *added values* obtained from information processing see [Kuhlen 95, p. 86-94].

[779]    Cf. [Kuhlen 95, p. 259-266], see Section 2.1.2 as well.

a scientific paper[780] written by an author, has to be processed before it can be accessed by a potential end-user. In this context processing of the knowledge product refers to activities like producing and publishing an abstract,[781] arranging and referencing the knowledge product in an existing classification,[782] and including the text in an information retrieval system.[783]

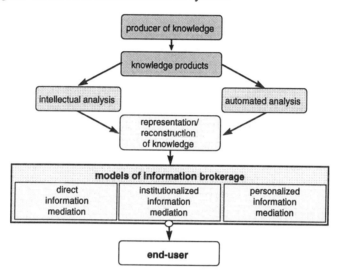

*Figure 50:     Framework for the basic models of information mediation, adapted from [Kuhlen 95, p. 262-266].*

In case of *direct* information mediation the end-user directly accesses the representation of knowledge provided by the original producer via communication networks or via end-user systems, for example, expert systems,[784] gateways, hypertext representations.[785]

The *institutionalized* form refers to knowledge depots that are operated by an institution. These knowledge depots, for example, libraries, and online-databases,[786]

---

[780] Of course, a scientific paper itself is a representation of knowledge, because it is the result of information processing done by the author, cf. [Kuhlen 95, p. 86]. This implies that the processes of intellectual and automated analysis indicated in Figure 50 can take place on multiple levels, however, the focus of the framework lies on the activities indicated in the text.

[781] For abstracting see [Kuhlen 95, p. 86-87], [Kuhlen 97].

[782] See Section 2.1.3.

[783] For the application of information retrieval systems in the organization of knowledge and information see [Kuhlen 95, p. 257-286].

[784] For expert systems as information intermediaries see [Drenth 91].

[785] Cf. [Kuhlen 95, p. 266].

[786] Cf. [Kuhlen 95, p. 263, 279-280].

store representations of knowledge (= information) and provide services to access the information. The end-user can access the information in the depot and is supported, if necessary, by an information specialist. The information specialist is usually associated with one particular knowledge depot and provides expertise about search tactics, information sources, and the access to the information in the particular knowledge depot. The specialist does not provide support concerning the contents of the information requested by the end-user.

*Personalized* information mediation refers to the activities of *information brokers*,[787] who access information sources, process the information, and provide an end-user specific information product. Information brokers will apply other forms of information mediation in their information processing activities, e.g., the information broker will search in a knowledge depot (Figure 52).

The foundation of the direct information mediation is mainly the exploitation of economies of scale, i.e., the reuse of information by multiple users. In the model of institutionalized information mediation *expertise in search* is additionally provided (by the information specialist), but the search and evaluation of the information is still an end-user task. In the case of personalized information mediation the information broker takes over most of the information processing activities for the end-user and offers a new, personalized information product. The foundation of personalized information mediation therefore is mainly determined by *expertise in search*, and *domain specific knowledge*.[788]

In general, the major foundation of the particular information intermediary, i.e., the exploitation of economies of scale, the expertise in search, and the domain specific knowledge,[789] can be taken as a criterion for the characterization of information intermediaries. Besides, the characterization can follow the general characterization of enterprises in markets for information (Section 2.5.3).

### 5.1.3 Information processing functions of information intermediaries

Information intermediaries were defined as *economic information processing systems* (Definition 3). The main elements of information processing systems and the functions performed were generally described in Section 2.1.6.[790] The major activities of information intermediaries within this framework are discussed in the following.

---

[787] For information brokers see [Kaminsky 81], [Zelewski 87], [O'Leary 87], and Section 5.1.4.

[788] See Section 4.4.2.3.

[789] Cf. Section 4.8.2.

[790] See [Bode 93, p. 101-111], [Kuhlen 95, p. 82-94], [Alter 96, p. 365] as well.

### 5.1.3.1 Receiving information

Information is usually dispersed in a variety of information sources, recently especially electronic information sources.[791] These information sources have several differentiating properties (Section 2.2). The most important properties in the present context are: the applicability to a particular question, the availability, the topicality, the quality and the credibility of the information provided, the mode of access, and the price charged for the information.[792] The success of the information intermediary, i.e., the quality of the result and the intermediary's profit, is to a large extent determined by the search strategy, the technology applied, and the knowledge about the characteristics of the sources of information (Section 4.8.2).

Therefore the acquisition of information requires[793]

- an appropriate technology[794] (possibly an account) to access the information sources,
- knowledge about the organization of information within the particular source,[795]
- the capability to utilize the information retrieval systems attached to the information sources,[796] and
- the ability to develop efficient search strategies, and identify and select relevant information.[797]

These requirements correspond to those derived from the basic model of an information intermediary.

### 5.1.3.2 Storing information

One foundation of information mediation is the transformation of information into a transferable *information product*.[798] This new information product can be stored for later reuse by the information intermediary. Another possibility is the storage of *meta-information*, for example, references to information concerning a

---

[791] For online available information sources see [Kuhlen 95, p. 267-331]. For examples of online-databases see [Staud 93] and for a review see [Staud 97].

[792] The quality level provided by the information sources and the costs charged for the information are considered in the basic model of an information intermediary as the parameters $\lambda$ and $c$, respectively (Sections 4.3.1.1 and 4.3.2.2).

[793] Cf. [Schmidt 97, p. 441].

[794] Cf. [Rowley 92, p. 335-337].

[795] Cf. Section 2.1.3.

[796] Cf. [Drenth 91, p. 125-128].

[797] Information is relevant for the information problem if it is new for the searcher, and if it allows to take conclusions that would be impossible without the information, cf. Sections 2.1.1.3, 2.1.1.4, and [Picot 96, p. 71 fp.].

[798] Cf. [Kuhlen 95, p. 84].

particular topic, by the information intermediary.[799] Examples for information intermediaries offering this meta-information as a service in electronic networks (the Internet) are directories, search-engines, and electronic product catalogs.[800]

### 5.1.3.3 Manipulating information

The manipulation of information is a central activity and major source of added values provided by information intermediaries. Three main forms of information processing can be distinguished:[801]

- The *synthetic processing* of information is the bundling of information from heterogeneous information sources. It implies the elimination of duplicate information and ensures that no relevant information is disregarded.
- The *synoptic processing* of information is the classifying and categorizing arrangement of the information to put the single object of information into a broader context. Examples are state-of-the-art reports[802] about the technological progress in a particular field, and management dossiers[803] combining different materials.
- The *analytic processing* of information is the condensation, valuation, and critical judgment of the information available for a particular topic. The result is a new information product that does not only reproduce existing information, but also gives an estimation of the quality of the information as well as recommendations for its application.

Examples for these forms of information processing are given in Figure 51.[804] The activities are arranged according to the demand on the information processing system concerning the understanding of the information as well as analytical capabilities.

---

[799]  Cf. [Rowley 92, p. 14-15], [Kuhlen 95, p. 104-105, 262].
[800]  Cf. [Rowley 92, p. 3-18], [Kuhlen 95, p. 481-487], [Lynch 97], [Jeusfeld 97, p. 493-494] and Section 5.3.5.
[801]  Cf. [Schmidt 92, p. 40-42], [Kuhlen 95,p. 351-353], [Schmidt 97, p. 441-442].
[802]  Cf. [Nink 91, p. 132 fp.], [Kuhlen 95, p. 352].
[803]  Cf. [Kuhlen 94].
[804]  See [Schmidt 92, p. 35] and [Alter 96, p. 365] as well.

**Synthetic information processing**
- *Collection* of information from different information sources. The information bundled to a new information product may still include redundant or contradictory information.

**Synoptic information processing**
- *Categorization* of information according to a given set of criteria. No redundancy check or consistency check is done.
- The *selection* of information aims to filter information from the set of available information according to predetermined search criteria. No cross-referencing to other relevant information that does not directly fit the search criteria is done.
- The *rearrangement* of information combines information selected from different information sources and eliminates redundant information to produce a new information product.

**Analytic information processing**
- The *analysis* of information additionally checks the consistency of the information that was gathered. The inference of new search criteria from the information to refine the selection or to find related information is another possible result.
- The *interpretation* of information relates the information gathered so far to other pre-existing information, domain specific knowledge, and environmental conditions and derives conclusions.
- *Appraisal* relates the information gathered and processed so far to a decision problem, evaluates alternative actions, and recommends a decision for the particular situation.

*increasing demand on information processing system*

*Figure 51:     Examples of information manipulating activities.*

### 5.1.3.4 Altering the internal structure of the system

The repeated execution of information processing activities accumulates experience in the information processing system, e.g., the information intermediary, which is obviously an alteration of the system 'information intermediary' that can be conceived as a learning process.[805] These experiences are an increase of the intermediary's domain specific knowledge, either disembodied or embodied knowledge,[806] can be conceived as a core competency of the information intermediary (Section 4.8.2), and will have consequences on future executions of the information processing activities. As a result, the costs and time expended for search may decrease with an increase of the number of searches performed by the intermediary (Section 4.4.1.3).

---

[805]  For learning processes see, for example, [Forsyth 86].
[806]  Cf. Section 2.1.2.

### 5.1.3.5  Sending out information

The information processed by the information intermediary is usually client-specific, so the presentation of the results has to address the client's information need and ability to interpret and apply the information. Two slightly different domains of information presentation can be distinguished:[807]

- *Formal methods* of information presentation cover all types of the medial preparation of the information, e.g., the presentation in form of time-graphs, diagrams, and animation.[808]
- *Pragmatic methods* focus the client's individual requirements of presentation. For example, a management report abstracts from technical details that are relevant for a study of the technological feasibility of a scientific method.

A further relevant aspect concerning the dissemination of the information is the medium the information is transferred with. It can be either stored on physical media or transferred via communication networks.[809]

## 5.1.4  Example: Information brokers

An *information broker*[810] is a typical example of an information intermediary in the market for information. The business of information brokers is mainly founded on *expertise in search* and *in the thematic domain under consideration* (Sections 4.8.2 and 5.1.2).

### 5.1.4.1  Basic characteristics

In terms of the basic *models of information mediation* (Figure 50) information brokers are personalized forms. A basic characterization is depicted in Figure 52.

---

[807] Cf. [Kuhlen 95, p.88-90].

[808] Cf. [Alter 96, p. 176-177].

[809] Cf. Section 2.5.5.

[810] Cf. [Kaminsky 81], [Kaminsky 83], [Kaminsky 89], [O'Leary 87], [Zelewski 87], [Klems 94], [Finke 97]. An *information broker* can be defined as 'an individual or organization who - on demand - seeks to answer questions using all sources available and who is in business for a profit,' cf. [Lunin 76] according to [Warner 95]. See [Levine 95] for a brief history of the business of information brokers.

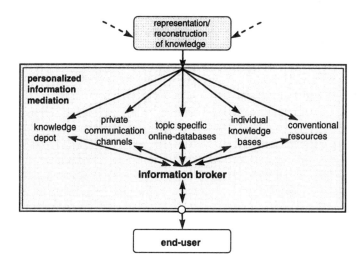

*Figure 52:*     *Personalized information mediation, adapted from [Kuhlen 95, p. 265].*

The information broker operates order-oriented, focuses a particular topic, and is not restricted to a particular source of information.[811] A major foundation of value generated by the information broker is the critical judgment and comment of the information mediated concerning it's value for the client's particular information need.[812] Hence, the information broker's business has a significant portion of intellectual information processing activities, i.e., information processing performed by human actors rather than computers.[813]

The orientation of the service to the information need of a particular client implies a low degree of reusability of the information gathered (exploitation of economies of scale). Hence, the information broker usually does not store the information systematically,[814] and the client will be charged all costs incurred for search plus a fee for the intermediary's services.[815]

### 5.1.4.2  Activities of information brokers

The basic tasks of information intermediaries have become obvious from Section 5.1.3. Hence, the activities of information brokers will be discussed in brief.[816]

---

[811]  Cf. [Zelewski 87, p. 739-741].

[812]  Cf. [Bessler 85, p. 170].

[813]  These activities can be labeled as *information refinement* [Taylor 86] or *condensation of information* [Schmidt 92, p. 40-42].

[814]  Cf. [Bessler 85, p. 171]. The search for information on behalf of a single user has also implications for the business of the information broker, see Section 4.4.4.3.

[815]  Cf. [O'Leary 87, p. 26-28]. See Section 4.4.1.3 as well.

[816]  See [Zelewski 87, p. 741] for a comprehensive treatment.

## A) Analysis of the information need

The identification of the *information need* is the starting point of all subsequent activities, it is therefore the precondition for the success of the information intermediary.[817] On the one hand, the information broker has to discover the end-user's *subjective information need* (arrow A in Figure 49). On the other hand, the information broker must aim to analyze which information is *objectively necessary* for the question the information seeker pursues to answer[818] (arrow C in Figure 49).

The information broker can apply several *interviewing techniques* to discover the client's subjective information need. In addition, *sympathetic understanding* is required and the analysis of the objective information need requires a high degree of *technical knowledge*. Therefore, the information intermediary has to be an *expert* in the special field under consideration.[819]

## B) Analysis and selection of information sources

The information broker chooses the appropriate information source depending on the results of the analysis of the information need, personal experiences, and practical knowledge about available information sources.[820] Usually more than one information source has to be accessed, and the results received from different sources have to be compared as a plausibility check.

Therefore, the second intermediary competency besides the expertise in a special field is the *knowledge about particular information sources* and the appropriate mode of access.

## C) Search and evaluation of information

From an abstract point of view, the search for information performed by the information broker is characterized by what was said about the information acquisition of information intermediaries in general (Sections 4.2 and 4.3.2). However, information brokers search for information that has multiple dimension,[821] thus, they usually have to gather multiple objects of information to be processed in later phases. The quality level offered by the broker[822] for each of the dimensions will be derived from the preceding analysis of the client's (objective) information need.

---

[817]  Cf. [Zelewski 87, p. 741] and [Kuhlen 95, p. 347-348].

[818]  Cf. [Schmidt 92, p. 36-38].

[819]  Cf. [Biglaiser 93], Section 3.2.3.2, and Section 4.8.2.

[820]  See Section 4.4.2, [Zelewski 87, p. 742-743], and [Drenth 91, p. 128-129].

[821]  The information broker's information processing is at least synthetic (Section 5.1.3.3), which implies that usually multiple information items have to be searched. In the terms of the basic model of an information intermediary this would require multiple search processes or the description of information items by a vector of attributes, cf. Section 4.2.1.

[822]  Cf. Section 4.3.2.

The knowledge about the *distribution of the quality levels*[823] of information sources is a further competency of the information broker.

Information brokers can also offer services like *periodical scanning and monitoring*[824] of different information sources with regard to a particular topic.[825]

### D) Information processing

The information is processed (Figure 51) with regard to the objective information need determined in earlier phases. Information processing is not a linear process, but has to intend *steps back to earlier phases* to refine the information need or the selection of information sources.

### E) Presentation of results

The presentation of the results is the completion of the activities and has to focus the client's individual information need as well as the client's ability to interpret and apply the information.

The basic activities of information brokers and the phases described so far can be summarized by means of a SADT diagram[826] (Figure 53). In addition to the processes depicted in the figure, the client's feedback about the quality of the result may require the refinement of search and information processing.

---

[823] In most cases no exact knowledge about the distribution of attributes will be available or even possible. In these cases the intermediary has to estimate the stopping rule for the search process from past experiences, cf. Section 4.2.1.

[824] *Monitoring* refers to the control of a set of information sources with regard to a particular information. Whereas, *Scanning* is the non-directed search for information that might be relevant for a particular topic. Cf. [Zelewski 87, p. 740].

[825] Cf. [Bessler 85, p. 172], [Knoblich 85, p. 571], [Zelewski 87, p. 740], [Kuhlen 95, p. 380]. These services are labeled as *current-awareness services*, cf. [Nink 91, p. 81] and [Rowley 92, p. 13-14].

[826] SADT stands for Structured Analysis and Design Technique, cf. [Heinrich 94, p. 107 fp.], [Stahlknecht 97, p. 295 fp.].

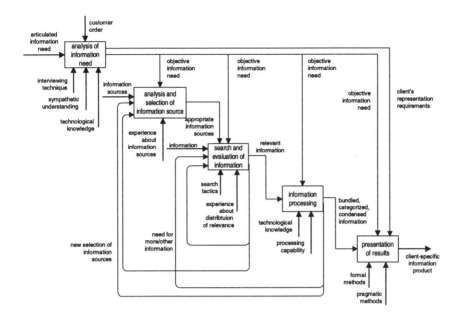

*Figure 53:     SADT diagram of the basic activities of information brokers.*

### 5.1.4.3  Critical success factors and the acceptance of information brokers

The need for information mediation or brokerage in knowledge intense domains was revealed by the comparison of the subjective demand and availability of information (Section 5.1.1). However, an actual demand for services provided by information intermediaries can only be generated if further preconditions are met.[827] The potential client has to be subjectively convinced about the benefits resulting from the services to be willing to pay the price charged. Additionally, the services have to be advantageous, either in quality of the result or in price, over other forms of information acquisition. For example, the service of an information broker has to be advantageous over personal search for information.[828] Further problems occurring in this context are caused by fundamental properties of information. One is the fact that the true value of information can only be determined if the information is completely revealed,[829] the other is the credibility of the information source.[830] For example, the information broker can be subject to uncertainty

---

[827]   Cf. [Zelewski 87, p. 744].

[828]   Cf. Section 4.3.2.3.

[829]   Cf. Section 2.1.5.

[830]   Cf. Section 2.3.

because the intermediary may have incentives to provide incomplete information or to reduce effort[831] in providing the service. Remedies for these situations, for example, the information broker's reputation, were already discussed in Section 2.3.3.

Measures to found a broad acceptance of the business of information brokers are the following:[832]

- *Personal contacts*: Especially in case of technological information interpersonal relations are preferred to other forms of contacts mediated by communication technologies.
- *Regional component*: A high valuation of personal contacts results in an advantage of regionally organized information brokers over centralized ones.[833]
- *Industry-orientation*: The information broker has to specialize in a certain topic to serve the specific needs of clients from a particular industry.[834]
- *One source of information*: Information brokers should aim to be the sole source of information for their clients. If the required information cannot be provided completely by the information broker, the broker subcontracts other information brokers to acquire the information.
- *Network of information brokers*: The information broker's specialization on a particular topic results in a rather narrow market segment for the single information broker. To provide information services for a broader range of problems, information brokers can join a network of cooperating brokers, each specialized on a particular topic.[835]

To conclude, the major *critical success factors* of (human) information brokers are competencies like sympathetic understanding and technological knowledge combined with the capability of analytic (intellectual[836]) information processing and personal relationships.[837]

### 5.1.5 Further examples of information intermediaries

Economic agents that can be conceived as information intermediaries (Definition 3) can be found in other markets as well. In general, in markets with incomplete information one would expect the emergence of intermediaries who help other

---

[831] Cf. Section 3.3.2.

[832] Some arguments are taken from [Kuhlen 95, p. 353 fp.]. See [Nink 91, p. 99 fp.] as well. The critical success factors of information intermediaries summarized in Section 4.8.2 apply to information brokers as well.

[833] Cf. [Weitzel 87] according to [Kuhlen 95, p. 354].

[834] Cf. Sections 4.4.2.3 and 4.4.3.3.

[835] Cf. [Kuhlen 95, p. 390 fp.].

[836] Cf. [Denning 94, p. 134-135].

[837] According to Nink information brokerage is a combination of the *transfer of information* and *consulting*, cf. [Nink 91, p. 7]. See [Kuhlen 95,p. 347] as well.

market participants to efficiently gather, process, and disseminate information (Section 2.5.2). Examples are labor market intermediaries, real estate brokers, and marriage brokers.[838] Other examples are brokers specialized in matching of supply and demand in financial markets[839] and organizations for testing the quality of goods and services.[840]

## 5.2 Network-based intermediaries

### 5.2.1 Basic characteristics

Electronic markets[841] based on information and communication networks,[842] i.e., the Internet[843] as well as corporate networks, have induced an increasing demand for *network-based intermediaries* as mediators between providers of products, services, and information and their clients and consumers.[844] Other designations for these network-based intermediaries can be found in literature: *Cybermediaries* [Sarkar 96], *electronic brokers* [Resnick 95], *electronic intermediaries* [Benjamin 90], [Bailey 97].

The major service of network-based intermediaries is matching of opposite parties in electronic markets[845] and the provision of further value-adding services.[846] The basic function of matching market participants from opposite market sides, labeled as the *electronic brokerage effect*, can offer consumers: (a) an increase of the number of alternatives that can be considered, (b) an increase of the quality of the alternative eventually selected, and (c) a decrease of the costs of the entire product

---

[838] Cf. [Bull 87], [Yavas 94], [Gehrig 96], [Spulber 96a].

[839] Cf. [Coym 95].

[840] In Germany this kind of institution is known as *Stiftung Warentest* (http://www. stiftung-warentest.de).

[841] *Electronic Markets* and *Electronic Commerce* are discussed in: [Malone 87a], [Malone 87c], [Bakos 91a], [Bakos 91b], [Schmid 93], [Benjamin 95], [Kuhlen 95, p. 73-80], [Kalakota 96], [Zbornik 96], [Wigand 96], [Hoffman 96], [Whinston 97].

[842] For the information technologies and concepts involved in these networks see [Picot 96, p. 115-195], [Kalakota 96], [Zbornik 96].

[843] The Internet cannot be put on a level with the WWW, however, services like Gopher [Kuhlen 95, p. 467-471] and WAIS [Kuhlen 95, p. 464-467] have lost significance with the emergence of the WWW [Kuhlen 95, p. 471-487], [Berners-Lee 92], see [Whinston 97, p. 12].

[844] Cf. [Malone 87a], [Benjamin 90].

[845] Cf. [Malone 87a, p. 488].

[846] Cf. [Resnick 95], [Sarkar 96], [Bailey 97].

selection process.[847] In particular, network-based intermediaries can reduce search costs,[848] be experts in the evaluation of product and service quality and therefore be guarantors of quality,[849] be a trusted provider of information,[850] offer personalized information products,[851] and retain privacy in transactions.[852] These functions are an image of those performed by 'traditional intermediaries' (Chapter 3). Nevertheless, the emergence of electronic networks can threaten the business of traditional intermediaries, especially those intermediaries providing services that can be easily bypassed or replaced by direct contacts[853] between consumers and producers.[854] Concluding from this, network-based intermediaries have to (a) offer services that cannot be provided by producers of products, services, and information, (b) gain competencies that cannot be replicated or imitated by potential competitors, and (c) have to focus a particular thematic domain with their service (Section 4.8.2).[855]

In electronic markets, early movers in offering a service will usually have an advantage over followers.[856] However, leadership in technology alone will only open 'a window of opportunity,' because technology can be replicated or imitated by potential competitors.[857] Moreover, the analysis of competition in the basic model of information intermediaries has shown that the leadership in providing a service can be easily threatened (Section 4.5.2.3). Therefore the critical success factors for information intermediaries, derived from the basic model of an information intermediary (Section 4.8.2), apply to a great extent to network-based intermediaries as well.

---

[847]  Cf. [Malone 87a, p. 488]. These effects were already discussed as *functional sources of transaction cost reductions through intermediation* (Section 3.2.3.2). See the basic model of information intermediaries as well (especially Sections 4.3.2.1 and 4.3.2.3).

[848]  Cf. [Resnick 95, p. 290], [Bakos 97b], and Section 3.2.3.2.

[849]  Cf. [Whinston 97, p. 158-168], and Section 3.2.3.2.

[850]  Cf. [Whinston 97, p. 152-162], [Bailey 97].

[851]  Cf. [Whinston 97, p. 168, 325-328], and Sections 4.8.2 and 5.3.1. The provision of personalized information products also addresses the problem of unauthorized reproduction and distribution of products by consumers, cf. [Whinston 97, p. 325].

[852]  Cf. [Resnick 95, p. 290].

[853]  Cf. [Ravindran 94], [Benjamin 95], [Steinfeld 96].

[854]  The change of industrial structure through electronic networks and electronic commerce is comprehensively discussed in literature. See, for example, [Benjamin 95], [Picot 96], [Sarkar 96], [Whinston 97, p. 45-46].

[855]  See, for example, survival strategies for intermediaries in the book business value chain in [Brenner 97].

[856]  Cf. [Bakos 91a, p. 307].

[857]  Cf. [Bakos 91a, p. 307].

## 5.2.2  Support of transaction phases in electronic commerce

The management and the execution of transactions is a core competency of 'traditional intermediaries' (Section 3.2). The activities involved in transactions[858] in electronic networks are to a large extent coordination tasks, i.e., these tasks require communication and the exchange of information between the transaction partners.[859] The information flow[860] involved in the processes is multidimensional, different types of information are involved, and the information flow can be assigned to different phases of the transaction (Section 3.2.2.2). Information involved in the transaction process is, for example, product information, financial information, logistical information, information about property rights, marketing information, and reverse-marketing information.[861] The potential support of the particular phases by network-based intermediaries will be examined in the following sections.

### 5.2.2.1  The information phase

A differentiated view of the information phase takes into account three successive activities, which can be passed through recursively if necessary:[862]

- Acquisition of *information about the market*: Information about the industry, market activities, goods and services offered on the market by competing sellers, and the quality level that can be expected on the market.
- *Search for transaction partners*: The aim is to match two or more opposite market participants with complementary needs (Section 2.2 and 4.1.1).[863]
- Acquisition of *information about the transaction partner* (i.e., *evaluation*, Section 4.2.3.3): Information about the products and services offered, the transaction partner's reliability, and trustworthiness (Section 2.3.2).

These activities require qualifications and competencies of network-based intermediaries already derived from the basic model of information intermediaries (Section 4.8.2). If these activities should be supported by information technologies, some requirements have to be met.

---

[858] Following the conception of external and internal transaction costs (Section 3.2.2.2), transactions can be characterized as *external transactions*, i.e., transactions in a market context, and *internal transactions*, i.e., transactions within an organizational context.

[859] According to *Nissen's integrated commerce model* Electronic Commerce is a sequence of transfers and exchanges, cf. [Nissen 96].

[860] Other flows involved in market transactions are the flows of money, goods, title flows, and promotion flows, cf. [Kotler 88, p. 531].

[861] Cf. [Zbornik 96, p. 134].

[862] Cf. [Zbornik 96, p. 138 fp.]. See [Beam 96b] and [Nissen 96] as well.

[863] For further treatment of matching activities of intermediaries see [von Ungern-Sternberg 84], [Gehrig 93], [Yavas 94], and [Yavas 96], and Section 4.1.2.

First, the products and services exchanged in the transaction have to be described by means of electronic media.[864] The description has to cover all relevant product attributes like price, geometry, physical, chemical, and functional properties, and it has to be storable in digital form. In general, the complexity of the product description is a major determinant of a product's potential for being traded in electronic markets.[865] In general, several dimensions of the product description,[866] especially with regard to transactions in electronic markets, can be distinguished:[867]

- *Description methods*: description of product attributes, references to other information sources or a description in form of a sample of the product or service.
- The *form of the description*:
  - *informal*: e.g., the individual description of the product,
  - *semiformal*: e.g., the description of products according to a predetermined set of characteristics.
  - *formal*: description by formal languages or by construction data.
- The *medium used to transfer the description*: e.g., text, hypertext, graphics, videos, virtual reality worlds.

Second, the transfer of this information between potential transaction partners has to be enabled by agreements about standard languages, protocols, and product descriptions used within the system.[868] An essential part of services provided by network-based intermediaries can therefore be the enforcement of *standardized product descriptions and product evaluation processes* to allow potential clients a comparison of different offers,[869] and the provision of *standardized communication channels* to reach potential transaction partners.[870]

A digitized product description is the precondition for support and processing of product information by network-based intermediaries. The concepts and technologies applied are very much the same as those of network-based information intermediaries, which will be discussed in Section 5.3.

---

[864] Cf. [Zbornik 96, p. 116 fp.].
[865] Cf. [Malone 87a, p. 486-487].
[866] For example, a product can be semi-formally described by a given set of product attributes and the medium can be a HTML document or an XML/EDI document ([Peat 97], http://www.xmledi.net).
[867] Cf. [Zbornik 96, p. 120].
[868] Cf. [Zbornik 96, p. 71-74], [Buxmann 96a].
[869] Cf. [Lee 96, p. 143-144].
[870] Cf. [Zbornik 96, p. 143-147].

### 5.2.2.2 The negotiation phase

In the negotiation phase the price and other terms of the exchange are determined via bargaining.[871] The terms to be negotiated are mainly the objects to be exchanged, their quality, the amount exchanged, the form and the level of the compensation, and the conditions of the contract (the terms of delivery and of payments, supplements, and credits).[872] If negotiation fails, a step back to the information phase will be necessary. During the negotiation phase multiple information transfers between the potential transaction partners are necessary until all participants agree on the terms of the contract. The negotiation phase can be supported by network-based intermediaries, for example, by:

- *Provision of standardized contracts*: Predefined contracts eliminate the need to negotiate contracts for the individual case, therefore reduce the need for extensive information transfer. The intermediary providing a standardized contract usually guarantees its accuracy and takes over some of the risks involved in the transaction.[873]
- *Negotiation on behalf of the transaction partners*: Potential transaction participants may have an incentive to delegate the negotiation to the intermediary, who can be expected to have more experience about the market, about bargaining tactics, and a better bargaining position.
- *Provision of an infrastructure that supports the negotiation*: Auctions[874] are basic examples of market systems to support the negotiation about prices for standardized products. The provision of a secure communication infrastructure, providing privacy and anonymity can be a further service of network-based intermediaries.[875]

The information transferred during the negotiation phase affects the competitiveness of the transaction partners more than information exchanged in the preceding information phase. Hence, the support of the negotiation phase faces even higher demands on the *reliability* and the *trustworthiness* of the intermediary and the secure transfer of the information.

### 5.2.2.3 The execution phase

The execution of the transaction consists of logistic flows, i.e., the transfer of the product, and financial flows as well as information flows.[876] Electronic products,

---

[871] Cf. [Kotler 88, p. 690]. For an overview of electronic negotiations see [Beam 96b], [Beam 97].
[872] Cf. [Meyer 90, p. 147 fp.], [Gebauer 96, p. 17].
[873] Contracting with two market sides is a fundamental activity of 'traditional intermediaries,' cf. Section 3.3.
[874] See [Beam 96a] for Internet-based auctions and [McAfee 87] for auctions in general.
[875] Cf. [Resnick 95, p. 290].
[876] Cf. [Zbornik 96, p. 154].

e.g., software, news, and texts, can be easily exchanged over electronic networks. Physical products are usually transferred by specialized service providers in the distribution channel. Financial transactions can be triggered over electronic networks, e.g., in form of credit card payments, or completely executed over the underlying information infrastructure, e.g., payments via electronic cash.[877] The coordination of the execution and the service providers involved in the transaction requires extensive information transfer between all participants.[878] A network-based intermediary can fulfill these coordination tasks between the individual actors, control the execution process, and give feedback about the process status to the consumer.[879]

### 5.2.2.4 Summary and discussion

The previous sections have revealed multiple opportunities for network-based intermediaries to support the information intense phases of transactions in electronic markets. Figure 56 summarizes possible functions and possible flows from an abstract point of view. In particular cases, however, network-based intermediaries might only support some of the phases or only some of the participants of the transaction.[880]

In general, several groups of services can be distinguished. Zbornik, for example, categorizes services supporting transactions in electronic markets as follows: market information services, brokerage services, security services, execution services, communication services, gateway services, and services for system management.[881]

---

[877]    CyberCash (http://www.cybercash.com) is an example of a credit-card based payment system on the Internet. The Ecash system developed by *DigiCash* (http://www.digicash.com) is an example of a coin-based electronic payment system. For an overview of electronic payment systems see [Kalakota 96, p. 295-331], [Wayner 96], [Cerqueiro 96], [Whinston 97, p. 407-462], [Brown 97].

[878]    Cf. [Alt 95], [Zbornik 96,p. 154].

[879]    Logistics services, for example, provide the opportunity and the technological infrastructure to provide feedback about the delivery status of the freight, for example, the *United Parcel Service* (http://www.ups.com) and *Federal Express* (http://www.fedex.com).

[880]    Cf. [Hünerberg 96, p. 135], [Beam 96b].

[881]    Cf. [Zbornik 96, p. 145-162].

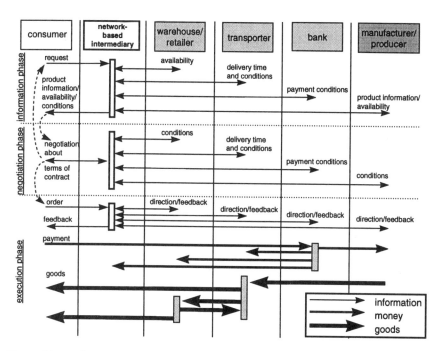

*Figure 54:*     *Summary of possible support functions of network-based intermediaries for transactions in electronic markets.*

A particular example is an *Electronic Product Catalog* (EPC)[882] operated and maintained by the intermediary. These systems support the information and negotiation phase by providing multidimensional representations of product information as well as retrieval, classification, and ordering systems. The execution phase can be supported by integration of electronic payment systems and connection to logistics services.[883] Network-based intermediaries that only support the information phase can be conceived as network-based information intermediaries, e.g., search engines, directories, and matching services (Section 5.3).

Besides functional aspects, the organization and economic operation of network-based intermediaries poses various questions. In principle, an EPC can be operated by one or more suppliers, consumers, or by independent intermediaries; a further possibility is the joint operation by agents from different stages in the value chain.[884] To ensure free competition among suppliers and/or consumers, an ideal EPC should be operated by a neutral actor, e.g., an economically and legally

---

[882]   Cf. [Segev 95], [Jiang 96], [Handschuh 97], [Schmid 97]. Other labels are *Mediating Electronic Product Catalog* [Handschuh 97] or simply *Electronic Catalog* [Segev 95].
[883]   Cf. [Zimmermann 97].
[884]   Cf. [Zbornik 96, p. 123-130].

independent intermediary.[885] However, the formation of a particular organizational design for the operation of an EPC depends on a number of opposing influences and interests. For example, consumers desire to achieve higher market transparency, in contrast to that, suppliers aim to secure their own distribution channels. In general, the opportunity of direct comparability of products in electronic markets and EPCs may promote price competition and reduce the sellers' market power.[886] In particular, suppliers of highly standardized products will usually have little incentives to achieve easy comparison of their products and services with those of other market participants.[887]

These circumstances will have influences on the arrangement of the intermediary's assortment and the services provided. However, the competition for clients between intermediaries may urge the intermediary to offer a service advantageous for clients (see Section 4.5, especially Section 4.5.2.2.1).

### 5.2.3  Example domains of network-based intermediaries

It has already become obvious that network-based intermediaries operate in various domains. Some examples are given in the following:

**A) Transactions in market environments**
EPCs stand for a broad class of network-based intermediaries. These can differ in the thematic orientation of the service and the scope of services provided (Section 5.2.2.4). Especially in the business-to-business domain a number of directories, mainly supporting the information phase of a transaction, can be found. *Trade Compass* (http://www.tradecompass.com), for example, provides an Internet-based supplier database, a 'broker service' to search for particular offers on a number of Internet sites, and further business specific information services. Another example is the *Unibex Global Business Center* (http://www.unibex.com), providing business users the opportunity to enter descriptions for their products and services, and the matching of requests from potential buyers with product descriptions registered in the database. Examples can also be found in the business-to-consumer domain, for example, the *Electronic Mall Bodensee* (http://www.emb.net) is an electronic marketplace with a regional focus to support information needs of consumers, citizens, and businesses in the region.[888] The Electronic Mall Bodensee covers services like electronic payments, and logistics services as well. Systems that are not based on monetary compensation between transaction partners, but on the

---

[885]  Cf. Definition 2 (Section 3.1.3), and [Zbornik 96, p. 124].

[886]  Cf. [Bakos 91b].

[887]  An example can be observed in Andersen Consulting's *Bargain Finder* (http://bf.cstar. ac.com/bf), an intelligent agent searching CD-stores for the cheapest offer. The system enforces price competition between suppliers, as a consequence, most CD-stores lock out the agent from their online available storefronts, cf. [Bailey 97].

[888]  Cf. [Zimmermann 97].

multilateral exchange of goods are barter networks. Examples for this type of intermediary are: *Barter.Net* (http://www.barter.net), and *Euro Barter Business* (http://www.ebb-online.com).

The preceding examples mainly focus the exchange of physical products that require traditional forms of delivery. In contrast, digital products, e.g., software, can be easily transferred via electronic networks. Hence, network-based intermediaries focusing these products are able to support all transaction phases over the electronic network. *The Java Repository* (http://java.wiwi.uni-frankfurt.de)[889] is an example of such an intermediary focusing the domain of Java[890] software components.[891] It provides software developers the opportunity to register, present, and trade their software resources via the Internet.[892] The evaluation process of the software resources is supported by ratings and comments entered by users of the software. Payments between buyers and sellers are mediated by the intermediary and completely executed over the Internet by means of an Ecash system.[893]

Another possibility to handle all transaction phases over the Internet is the provision of services over the network. An example is the provision of decision support technologies over the WWW; *DecisionNet* (http://dnet.as.nps.navy.mil/dNethome.html)[894] facilitates transactions between providers and consumers of such technologies. Other network-based intermediaries supporting transactions over the Internet are financial intermediaries offering access to trading systems over the Internet, e.g., *E\*Trade* (http://www.etrade.com), and e.Schwab (http://www.schwab.com).

## B) Coordination in an organizational context

Information technologies enable the formation of virtual organizations and network communities.[895] The management of these organizational systems poses demands like establishing trust and the design of contracts, and have a particular need for coordination, support of conflict situations as well as the design and

---

[889] The *Java Repository* focuses the support of the information phase and the execution phase. For further information see [Buxmann 96b], [Buxmann 97a], [Buxmann 97b], [Buxmann 97c].

[890] Cf. [Gosling 95] and http://java.sun.com.

[891] A comparable intermediary for C++ software components is the *REGINA Component Information System* (http://www.findcomponents.com).

[892] The aim of the Java Repository is to support the reuse of software elements over the Internet and so to increase the productivity of software development, cf. [Buxmann 97c].

[893] Cf. [Buxmann 97a, p. 1429-1432]. For Ecash see [Kalakota 96, p. 299-310], and the *DigiCash* web site http://www.digicash.com.

[894] Cf. [Bhargava 95a], [Bhargava 95b], [Bhargava 95c].

[895] Cf. [Bakos 91b], [Szyperski 93], [Rayport 96], [Nouwens 96], see Section 3.2.2.3 as well. A variety of examples is discussed in [Boddy 96].

maintenance of an information infrastructure.[896] Network-based intermediaries can support these functions. One example is the *DEVICE system* (http://www.iwi.uni-sb.de/device),[897] an intermediary to support and manage the exchange of co-operations in virtual organizations, e.g., by mediating potential partners and providing template contracts as well as customer order forms. Other intermediaries support and maintain virtual competence centers, e.g., the *kiesel system* (http://www.kiesel.de), a virtual competence center for environmental issues, and the *Competence Network Electronic Commerce* (CNEC, http://www.cnec.org), a network of experts in electronic commerce.

**C) Trusted Third Parties (TTPs)**
The importance of trust in relationships between market participants and transaction partners has already become obvious.[898] *Certification authorities*[899] or *Trusted Third Parties* (TTPs)[900] are network-based intermediaries providing services to achieve trust in relationships over electronic networks. TTPs provide services that guarantee the integrity and authenticity of messages as well as the authenticity of communication partners in electronic networks.[901]

**D) Provision of service functions**
Intermediaries providing service functions in electronic networks can be, for example, gateways, services for protocol conversion, EDI-clearing services.[902]

## 5.3 Network-based information intermediaries

### 5.3.1 Basic characteristics

The increasing amount of information produced and the easy access to numerous information sources via communication networks causes an increasing demand for *network-based information intermediaries* as mediators between information sources and their users.[903] The major advantages of information technologies

---

[896] Cf. [Szyperski 93, p. 199-201], [Introna 97].
[897] Cf. [Hirschmann 97].
[898] Cf. Section 2.3.2. See [Froomkin 96], [Reagle 97] as well.
[899] See [Lizzeri 96] for a treatment of economic aspects of *certification intermediaries*, i.e., intermediaries that search out information of privately informed parties and reveal part of it to uninformed parties.
[900] Cf. [Froomkin 96], [Cerny 97], [Nehl 97].
[901] Cf. [Cerny 97, p. 616].
[902] Cf. [Zbornik 96, p. 147], [von Westarp 97].
[903] Cf. [Malone 87b], [Goldberg 92], [Wiederhold 92].

applied for information acquisition, processing, and dissemination are clearly the higher speed, the larger amount of information that can be processed within a given time, and lower costs compared to human labor. Compared to traditional information intermediaries (Section 5.1) this opens new areas for services and applications of network-based information intermediaries.[904] However, competencies like analytic information processing, e.g., the valuation and critical judgment of information, and sympathetic understanding of the information seeker's information need (Section 5.1.4.3), that are characteristic for human information intermediaries,[905] have to be imitated by information systems, further performed by human actors or have to be delegated to the end-user. Which of these possibilities will be applied for a particular information intermediary depends on the degree of value creation by the information intermediary and the positioning of the service in the market for information. The *degree of value creation* of the information intermediary can be roughly described by the information processing activities, especially the manipulation of information (Section 5.1.3.3), performed by the information intermediary.

The essential requirements for the design and technological realization of network-based information intermediaries have already become obvious from the basic model of information intermediaries (Section 4.8.2) and from the analysis of basic concepts of information intermediaries (Section 5.1). The business of information intermediaries poses the demand for cross-sectional reuse of information and, simultaneously, for personification of the service,[906] requiring the determination of the individual information seeker's information need. Matching the clients' information needs with the information available to the information intermediary will result in the provision of customized information products.[907]

To provide the service, the network-based information intermediary has to select appropriate information sources, gather, process and disseminate the information (Section 5.1.3). The intermediary's 'expertise in search,' a major foundation of the business of information intermediaries, will be represented by the methods for information processing, and the information technology applied. This will be one determinant of the quality of the results obtained from the information intermediary.[908] The other determinant is the selection of information sources and the quality of the information offered by the selected information sources.

---

[904] Cf. [Resnick 95], [Sarkar 96].

[905] See, for example, [Alter 96, p. 28].

[906] Cf. Section 4.1.1, see [Sheth 94, p. 8], and [Whinston 97, p. 313] as well.

[907] See, for example, [Foltz 92], [Loeb 92], and [Whinston 97, p. 327].

[908] This refers to the quality of results obtained from an information retrieval or information filtering system, which can, on a technological basis, be expressed by the values of *recall* and *precision*, cf. Section 2.1.3. These measures neglect dimensions like credibility and style.

## 5.3.2  Environmental circumstances

The environmental conditions of network-based information intermediaries are determined by the properties of the particular market for information the service is operating in (Section 4.3.1). On the suppliers' market side these conditions are determined by properties of the information (Section 2.1.5), the information sources (Sections 2.2 and 2.3), and the access to the information sources. On the consumers' market side the intermediary has to focus characteristics of potential users, i.e., usage patterns, capabilities, and requirements on the information retrieved. Figure 55 summarizes the dimensions of the major environmental circumstances that characterize a particular application of a network-based information intermediary. The different dimensions can be roughly divided into two main groups: the acquisition of information and the usage of the service.

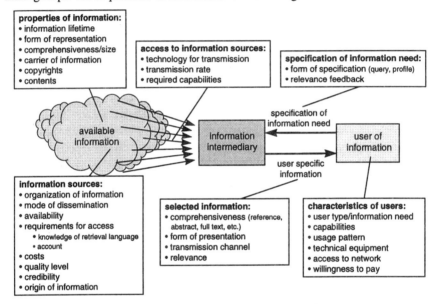

*Figure 55:*     *Environmental circumstances of network-based information intermediaries.*

### 5.3.2.1  Acquisition of information

The intermediary's acquisition of information is determined by the properties and aspects of the information that is mediated and by characteristics of the information sources:

**Properties of information:**
- The *lifetime of the information* determines the value of the information for the user. The time required by the information intermediary for information acquisition, processing, and dissemination must be considerably less than the lifetime

of the information, e.g., financial news have a very short lifetime compared to technology reports.[909]

- The information can occur in different *forms of representation*, e.g., textual (numerical data, text[910]), graphics (raster graphics, vector graphics), video, sound;[911] these are usually referred to as multimedia-information.
- The *comprehensiveness* of textual information can be, for example, full-text information, abstracts,[912] or meta-information like references. Closely connected to this is the *size* of the single information item.
- *Carriers of information* can be books, video tapes, or other electronic storage media, however, in the domain of communication networks information is usually stored and transferred electronically.
- The *copyright* owner for a particular information can be either the source of the information or a party different from the information source.[913] These have to be taken into account by the information intermediary in copying and disseminating the information.
- The *contents* of the information can be, e.g., technological information, market information (product descriptions or information about potential transaction partners (Section 5.2.2.1)), news, entertainment etc..

**Information sources:**
- Information sources, e.g., online-databases and libraries, usually have a particular *organization of the information* (Section 2.1.3).
- The *dissemination* of information from the source can be on user request, i.e., a pull for information, or pushed by the source, e.g., in form of an information feed (for news messages), or entered by suppliers (for directories). Update of the information source can be regularly, irregularly, or not at all.
- The *availability* of the source can be regularly, irregularly, only once.[914]
- The *access of the information source* may require a special account, knowledge of the particular retrieval language, and technical equipment,[915] and it may cause *costs*.
- Information sources offer a particular *quality level*[916] and have a particular *credibility* (Section 2.3.2). Further, the information offered by the source can be primary or secondary information (*origin of information*).

---

[909] Cf. [Loeb 92, p. 41].
[910] Cf. [Rowley 92, p. 15].
[911] Cf. [Grauer 97, p. 39-50].
[912] Cf. [Kuhlen 97].
[913] Cf. Section 2.5. See [Whinston 97, p. 175-212] for aspects of copyright protection for electronic products.
[914] Cf. [Knoblich 85, p. 564].
[915] Cf. Section 5.1.3.1.
[916] For quality characteristics concerning online-databases see [Kuhlen 95, p. 289-292].

### 5.3.2.2 Usage of the service

The usage of the information intermediary can be described by the way the information need is specified, the characteristics of the user, and the form of information that users receive.

**Specification of the information need:**
The *information need* can be *specified* in various forms:[917] *Queries* can be regarded as the representation of an immediate information need (short-term interest), whereas *profiles* usually represent regular information interests (long-term interests) of the information seeker. The specification of a particular information need can be refined and improved by feedback about the relevance of retrieved information (*relevance feedback*[918]). Queries as well as profiles can be expressed by keywords selected by the information seeker, which is the simplest method for the implementation.[919] Other methods have been developed to overcome problems inherent in simple keyword matching,[920] e.g., vector space models,[921] or the learning of intelligent software agents from past behavior.[922]

**Characteristics of users:**
- *User types* can range on a scale between proactive, i.e., users with a very well-defined information need that is usually formulated as a query or a profile, and casual, i.e., users having no immediate and specific information need.[923] Proactive users can be expected to actively participate in the determination of their information need, e.g., by formulating queries, defining profiles, and giving relevance feedback. In contrast, casual users, who demand information as a daily news service or for entertainment, are not likely to be willing to engage in lengthy interactions with the system in order to articulate the current information need.
- Closely connected with the type of information need is the users' *willingness to pay* for the service (see Section 4.3.2.3).
- The *capabilities* of users to formulate queries and to interpret and apply the results of the service may vary (Sections 5.1.1 and 5.1.3.5).
- *Usage pattern*: The *session duration* and the *frequency of usage* may vary, e.g., usage can be continuous, regular, irregular, or only a single session.[924] This has consequences for the method to specify the information need that can be

---

[917]   Cf. [Belkin 92, p. 30-33].
[918]   Cf. [Belkin 92, p. 31, 37].
[919]   Cf. [Foltz 92, p. 52].
[920]   Cf. [Belkin 92] for an overview.
[921]   Cf. Section 5.3.3.1 and [Salton 83], [Belkin 92, p. 32-33], [Foltz 92].
[922]   Cf. [Maes 94].
[923]   Cf. [Loeb 92, p. 41].
[924]   Cf. [Loeb 92, p. 41-42], [Belkin 92, p. 31-32].

applied, e.g., the specification of a user profile will only be useful for repeated usage of the system.

- The *technical equipment* necessary to access the service offered by the information intermediary and the connecting *network* should have a wide spreading among potential users of the information intermediary (Section 4.4.4.3).

**Selected information (user specific information):**

- The information sent to the information seeker will have a particular *comprehensiveness*, e.g., abstracts or meta-information, depending on the information processing activities of the information intermediary (Section 5.1.3.3) and the comprehensiveness of the original information.
- The *representation* of the information has to focus the client's information need, capabilities, technical equipment, and characteristics of the *transmission channel*.
- The information selected will have a certain *relevance* for the specified information need, which determines the quality of the information intermediation service. Feedback about the relevance of retrieved information can augment the quality of the result in an iterative process.

### 5.3.3  Matching of information needs and available information

Information technologies that can be applied to realize network-based information intermediaries have to focus the provision of customized information for the client. In the following, information retrieval (IR) and information filtering (IF) will be reviewed as base technologies for matching of clients' information needs with available information.

#### 5.3.3.1  Information retrieval

Information retrieval[925] systems have the aim to enable users to find documents that satisfy a particular information need while minimizing the amount of irrelevant information.[926] In IR systems exact match and best match retrieval models can be distinguished.[927] In *Boolean retrieval*, an example of *exact match retrieval models*, the query is expressed by words or phrases possibly combined with operators of Boolean logic.[928] The exact match IR system returns all documents containing the combination of words specified in the query without ranking of relevance. These systems can be refined, for example, by use of thesauri in which

---

[925]  See [Salton 83] for a comprehensive treatment of IR systems and [Kuhlen 95, p. 279-281] for basic models of information retrieval.

[926]  Cf. [Belkin 92, p. 30], [Foltz 92, p. 52].

[927]  Cf. [Belkin 92, p. 32], [Belkin 87].

[928]  Cf. [Salton 83].

relationships among terms with similar meaning are encoded.[929] *Best match IR systems* allow the ranking of results according to their relevance for the particular query.[930] These systems are based on the *vector-space model* or the wide class of *probabilistic IR models*. In the vector space model documents and queries are treated as vectors in a multidimensional space. The dimensions of the vector space are the single words occurring in the documents and in the query, the elements of the vectors are the weights of the words in the document and the query.[931] The underlying assumption is that the more similar the vector of a document is to that of a query, the more relevant is the document to the query,[932] the results can therefore be ranked according to their relevance to the query. Probabilistic IR models[933] rank all documents in an IR database in order of their probability of relevance to the query. The probabilities can be calculated from a variety of sources, e.g., the statistical distribution of terms in the whole database and in relevant and non-relevant documents.[934]

Examples for IR systems can be found in a great variety in corporate networks and on the Internet, especially the WWW.[935]

**The main characteristics of IR systems are:**
- IR systems usually address users' short-term interest that can be (more or less) satisfied by performing the retrieval,[936] the usage pattern of the IR system is thus typically a single session.
- The application of an IR system requires the user to have an idea about the result of the request and the ability to formulate queries,[937] these can be refined by relevance feedback. Hence, typical users of IR systems are proactive users (Section 5.3.2.2).

---

[929] See [Gauch 89], and [Smith 89, p. 250-252] for examples.

[930] Cf. [Belkin 92,p. 32-33].

[931] The weights of a single word $i$ can be, for example, determined by the product of the *term frequency tf(i)*, i.e., the occurrence frequency of the word in the document, and the *inverse document frequency idf(i)=Log(n_0/df(i))* (with $n_0$=number of documents in the system and *df(i)*=number of documents in the system that contain the word $i$), cf. [Sheth 94, p. 22], [Salton 83].

[932] Cf. [Belkin 92, p. 32-33], see [Deerwester 90], and [Foltz 92] for *Latent Semantic Indexing* (LSI), an extension of the basic vector model.

[933] These are based on the *Probability Ranking Principle*, cf. [Robertson 77] according to [Belkin 92, p. 33].

[934] A particular example is the *inference net model*, based on Bayesian inference networks, cf. [Belkin 92, p. 33].

[935] See [Teuteberg 97], [Jeusfeld 97], [Lynch 97], [Whinston 97, p. 269-270], [Peterson 97], [Bekavac 96].

[936] Cf. [Belkin 92, p. 32], [Foltz 92, p. 52].

[937] Cf. [Belkin 92, p. 30-31].

- IR systems are usually applied to textual data.[938] The sources of information (original information sources or meta-information) have a similar quality level and relatively low variability over time.[939]

### 5.3.3.2 Information filtering

While IR is applied to find relevant information, information filtering (IF) is usually applied to remove irrelevant information from a *stream of* (unstructured or semi-structured) *information* in order to reduce the amount of information to a manageable and understandable set.[940] Depending on the concept applied for filtering, IF systems can be classified as cognitive, economic, or social.[941] *Cognitive* (*content-based*) IF systems chose information items based on the characteristics of their contents, i.e., these apply methods from IR. Examples are positive and negative keyword-filtering techniques.[942]

*Economic* IF systems are based on various kinds of cost-benefit assessments and explicit or implicit pricing mechanisms. These systems can be designed to reduce, for example, the amount of unsolicited mail a user receives. This can be achieved by charging the sender of a mail message costs that reflect some of the costs borne by receivers.[943]

*Social* IF systems select information based on recommendations and annotations from other users or simply by the origin of the information. Social IF systems, also labeled as *collaborative filtering systems* or *recommender systems*, are based on the collaboration of multiple users.[944] Users' reactions to documents they read are recorded, and matching of different users is performed by correlating users with similar preferences to predict a particular user's opinion and valuation of an item.[945] Reactions or opinions from users in a certain community are usually

---

[938] However, recent commercial products have also addressed multimedia retrieval, cf. [Grauer 97, p. 70-82], [Croft 95].

[939] Cf. [Belkin 92].

[940] Cf. [Foltz 92, p. 53], [Belkin 92].

[941] This classification of IF systems was based on a survey of information sharing in organizations, cf. [Malone 87b].

[942] *Selective Dissemination of Information* (SDI), a method to match documents with the scientific interests of researchers, applies a user profile made up of keywords to select relevant articles, cf. [Foltz 92, p. 52]

[943] Cf. [Malone 87b, p. 399].

[944] Cf. [Resnick 95 p. 292-294], [Resnick 97 p. 56], a list of commercial collaborative filtering technologies can be found at http://sims.berkeley.edu/resources/collab/index.html.

[945] Cf. [Goldberg 92, p. 61], [Maes 94, p. 39-40], [Resnick 94], [Konstan 97].

collected in form of (explicit or implicit[946]) ratings for particular items.[947] The predictions and recommendations are derived by statistical methods.[948] Hybrid IF systems can be the combination of social information filtering methods with content-based methods.[949]

**The main characteristics of collaborative IF systems are:**
- Information needs represent long-term interests and tastes, these are expressed by profiles, e.g., keywords, ratings.[950] Hence, IF systems require repeated usage, and short-term variations in user interests cannot be taken into consideration.
- Collaborative IF is based on correlations between different users, this enables these systems to discover information, more generally items, that may be of interest for a particular user without having the user to formulate a particular query.[951]
- The recommendation obtained from collaborative IF systems can only be explained as a correlation with preferences of other users in the user cluster.
- The utilization of ratings allows the application of social IF systems to domains with items that have no simple representation, e.g., music, films,[952] and the judgment of items according to dimensions like quality, authoritativeness, or respectfulness.[953]

### 5.3.4 Abstract architecture of network based information intermediaries

The environmental conditions of the intermediary service (Section 5.3.2) are determined by the particular market chosen by the information intermediary.[954] Together with the critical success factors (Section 4.8.2) this gives a framework for the choice of a particular information technology to realize the network-based service. The review of IR and IF technologies has revealed the major characteristics and possibilities for their application (Sections 5.3.3.1 and 5.3.3.2): IF systems are predominantly applied to satisfy information seekers' long-term interests, whereas IR technologies are usually applied to satisfy short-term information needs.

---

[946] *Explicit ratings* for an item can be given in form of marks, cf. [Balabanovic 97], [Maes 94, p. 39-40], *implicit ratings* can be derived from user behavior, for example, the time a user spends reading a document, cf. [Konstan 97].
[947] Cf. [Konstan 97].
[948] Cf. [Shardanand 95], [Shardanand 94].
[949] Cf. [Balabanovic 97].
[950] Cf. [Belkin 92, p. 30].
[951] Cf. [Maes 94, p. 40], [Balabanovic 97, p. 67].
[952] Cf. [Maes 94, p. 39-40], [Shardanand 94].
[953] Cf. [Resnick 94].
[954] Cf. Section 4.3.1.

Besides the possession of efficient search and matching technologies, a further core competency of information intermediaries is knowledge acquisition about the environment. Knowledge acquisition concerns three domains: knowledge about clients' preferences, about sources of information, and about the thematic domain[955] under consideration. Knowledge about clients can only be acquired from users, either directly, i.e., by requiring potential users to enter personal data, or indirectly,[956] i.e., by observation and learning of user behavior.[957] Knowledge about the thematic domain usually has to be incorporated by the intermediary, e.g., in form of a thesaurus for an IR systems or an expert system.[958] Knowledge about information sources usually has to be treated in similar manner. However, the evaluation of the correlation between clients' acceptance and rejection of particular results that were obtained from the intermediary with the original source of the information and the particular topic under consideration can lead to knowledge about the information sources.[959]

The information offered by the intermediary has to be provided by means of technologies that have a wide spreading and acceptance among potential users.[960] Internet technologies, i.e., the TCP/IP protocol, HTML, web-browsers etc., fulfill this requirement. In general, network-based information intermediaries can be characterized as *push services*, sending the information to the client, or *pull services*, requiring the client to actively request the information from the intermediary. Push services have to broadcast their information, e.g., in form of email messages or by means of a client/server application connecting the information intermediary with potential clients.[961] Pull services can be efficiently realized on basis of WWW servers and the HTTP protocol.[962]

---

[955]  [Smith 89], and [Shute 93] label this knowledge as *subject-dependent expertise*. One effect of domain specific knowledge can be a reduction of the number of information sources to be taken into account in the search process, cf. [Jeusfeld 97, p. 498-499]. See Section 4.4.2 as well.

[956]  Cf. [Maes 94, p. 33].

[957]  Learning of user behavior by computer systems is the domain of artificial intelligence and especially applied in intelligent agent systems, cf. [Maes 94], [Mitchell 94], [Armstrong 95], [Lieberman 95], [Balabanovic 95], [Joachims 96], [Rhodes 96].

[958]  Cf. [Drenth 91].

[959]  This technique is applied by the Meta-Search Engine *SavvySearch* (http://guaraldi.cs.colostate.edu:2000/) to gather information about the Search Engines queried, cf. [Howe 97].

[960]  Cf. Section 4.4.4.3.

[961]  Examples are *PointCast* (http://www.pointcast), and *Netscape's NetCaster* (http://www.netscape.com). These client/server applications require a permanent connection and therefore have to be implemented directly on basis of the TCP/IP protocol. The HTTP protocol is not appropriate because it is *stateless*, i.e., the connection between client and server is dropped after the server has responded the client's request, cf. [December 95, p. 379], [Stevens 96].

[962]  Cf. [December 95].

The hypertext paradigm of the WWW[963] allows users to select hypertext links to related information sources and follow their individual path through the information supplied on the network. In hypertext systems different search and access strategies can be distinguished:[964] Besides *browsing, exploration*, and *navigation*, being a more or less directed and systematic search for information in the network structure of the hypertext, *queries* are important to filter and access information in database systems. Depending on the particular application, push-service intermediaries will provide access to their services via hypertext navigation and exploration, and/or access via database queries.[965]

Figure 56 shows an abstract architecture of a network-based information intermediary consisting of three logical units: the source, the intermediary, and the user equipment.[966]

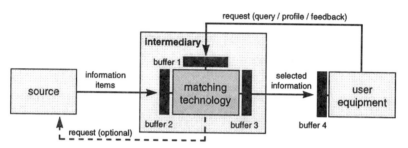

*Figure 56:*    *Abstract view on the architecture of a network-based information intermediary, extension of [Loeb 92].*

In order to cope with the time characteristics of supply and demand of information (Section 5.3.2) and to perform information processing tasks, several buffers (buffer 1-4 in Figure 56) with different properties may be appropriate:

- *Buffer 1* stores users' requests for information, user profiles, and contingent feedback for repeated use as well as for analytical purposes. The duration of the storage depends on the usage patterns (Section 5.3.2.2), the analyses performed, and the capacity of the buffer.
- *Buffer 2* stores information from information sources and/or meta-information about the information sources. Active information sources push their information to the intermediary, whereas passive sources need to be queried by the

---

[963]    Cf. [Berners-Lee 92], [Kuhlen 95, p. 427-430, 471].

[964]    Cf. [Herczeg 94, p. 135-138].

[965]    Directories, e.g., *Yahoo* (http://www.yahoo.com), are the prototype of systems providing navigational access, whereas search engines, e.g., *AltaVista* (http://www.altavista.digital. com), provide the opportunity of database queries. However, hybrid forms exist as well, e.g., *InfoSeek* (http://www.infoseek.com).

[966]    Loeb describes a comparable architecture for a generalized filtering system, cf. [Loeb 92, p. 40].

intermediary.[967] The update interval of the buffer mainly depends on the lifetime of the information. The required capacity of buffer 2 is determined by the size of the information items stored and the number of information items stored, both depending on the thematic area and the width of the focus of the service.

- *Buffer 3* allows the caching of repeatedly requested information, which reduces the workload of the intermediary's information processing systems.
- *Buffer 4* temporarily stores information received from the intermediary on the client's machine for repeated access, which allows some extra processing before the information is viewed by the user, and additionally may reduce network traffic.

### 5.3.5  Examples of network-based information intermediaries

Examples for network-based information intermediaries can be found in a variety of environments, Section 5.3.2 has already outlined the basic possibilities. Some typical forms of network-based information intermediaries, mainly characterized by the services provided and the technology applied, are reviewed in the following.

**A) Subject directories**

Subject directories[968] are based on a classification of the thematic domain under consideration (Section 2.1.3). The information intermediary arranges the information items, e.g., web sites, product offers etc., according to the classification scheme and stores some meta-information, e.g., descriptions, references. The organization and maintenance of the subject directory is usually an intellectual task, i.e., it is carried out by humans, having the advantage that information items can be rated, and the evaluation can be offered as a service to clients. The disadvantages of these systems are: The classification as well as the arrangement of information items in particular categories is usually not unequivocal, complicating search in the subject directory. A second argument is that operation and updating of the directory poses high demand for human labor, i.e., high marginal costs for an additional information item included in the subject directory compared to automatic information processing. A possibility to reduce operational costs of the directory is to delegate entry and update of information items to the information source, and only review updated entries; this is done in some commercial directories.

---

[967] Information gathering can be performed automatically by robots, cf. [Teuteberg 97, p. 374-376], [Koster 96] and http://info.webcrawler.com/mak/projects/robots/robots.html.

[968] Subject directories have to be distinguished from distributed *X.500 directory services* providing user information as well as security and other information in LANs, cf. [Radicati 94].

*Yahoo* (http://www.yahoo.com) is the most famous subject directory on the Internet,[969] it includes a great variety of thematic domains and mainly takes whole web sites as information items, however, it only covers 1-2% of the whole Internet.[970] Other examples focus a special thematic domain and try to achieve a complete coverage of all available information sources, for example, the *Gamelan directory* (http://www.gamelan.com) focusing the domain of Java applets on the Internet, or the *DoctorDirectory* (http://www.DoctorDirectory.com), a directory of physicians in the USA.

These services are usually offered free to owners of information sources and users, financing is usually done via advertising.[971] In financing via advertising two general forms have to be distinguished: If owners of the sources of information registered in the directory are allowed to advertise, a certain danger of biased evaluations by the intermediary occurs;[972] advertising for products complementary to those covered by the subject directory poses less danger.[973] The availability of secure and widely accepted online micropayment systems would open information intermediaries the opportunity to finance their services by charging a single request (*pay per use*).[974]

Some similarities between directories and EPCs (Sections 5.2.2.4, and 5.2.3) have become obvious. However, EPCs offer further support functions for the coordination of transactions that are usually not provided by directories.

**B) Search Engines**

*Robotic Internet Search Engines*[975] are information intermediaries that gather information via *web robots* traversing the web's hypertext structure,[976] and use IR technologies to allow users to retrieve the information. The main characteristics of

---

[969] The InterNIC (http://www.internic.net) operates and maintains a *directory of directories* (http://ds.internic.net/dod) providing references to other directory services.

[970] Cf. [Peterson 97].

[971] The user-specific information provided by the information intermediary offers a variety of opportunities for directed advertising. Advertisements can be related to a user's profile or to the query entered. See [Hoffman 96] for an overview.

[972] Cf. [Resnick 97, p. 58].

[973] For example, the service of the DoctorDirectory is financed via 'targeted health care specific and geographically sensitive interactive marketing,' cf. 'About Us' on http://www.DoctorDirectory.com.

[974] This was analyzed in the basic model of information intermediaries (Chapter 4), see Section 5.4.1.

[975] For a discussion of Search Engines see [Peterson 97], [Teuteberg 97], [Jeusfeld 97]. A list of Internet Search Engines can be found at: http://www.sil.org/internet/guides.html. Besides WWW sites, some Search Engines focus FTP-sites or UseNet News.

[976] Cf. [Koster 96], see http://info.webcrawler.com/mak/projects/robots/robots.html as well.

IR systems therefore apply to Search Engines.[977] Search Engines differ in their coverage of information sources, in the requirements on query formulation as well as the quality of the results. Some *Meta-Search Engines* have addressed this situation, these provide the opportunity to query existing Search Engines in parallel and return an aggregated result. Examples are *SavvySearch* (http://guaraldi.cs. colostate.edu:2000/)[978] and *MetaCrawler* (http://www.metacrawler.com). Search Engines are usually financed via advertising, however, these systems offer an opportunity for usage based payments as well as directories.

**C) Recommender Systems**

Recommender Systems are based on the concept of social IF. Examples are systems for the filtering of emails from distribution lists,[979] filtering of news messages from Usenet news,[980] and recommendation systems for various interests.[981] In practical applications social IF systems can suffer from manipulations from content owners.[982] Other possible problems are free-rider problems,[983] and start-up problems:[984] Social IF systems are based on contributions from a large number of users, each benefiting more the more users participate. Individual users, however, can increase their utility by consuming recommendations without providing new ones themselves, hence, ratings have characteristics of a public good. Monetary compensations transferred between consumers and providers of ratings, resulting in a *market for evaluations*, can be a remedy for this problem.[985] Shares of the payments received from consumers of recommendations can in principle be applied to finance the intermediary service,[986] however, advertising is applied more often.

---

[977] One main shortcoming of Internet Search Engines is the network traffic resulting from web robots; currently up to 20 % of HTTP requests alone should result therefrom, cf. [Teuteberg 97, p. 375].

[978] Cf. [Howe 97].

[979] *Tapestry*, cf. [Goldberg 92].

[980] *GroupLens* (http://www.cs.umn.edu/Research/GroupLens/), cf. [Resnick 94], [Konstan 97]. For a comparison of news filtering software see [Kilander 96].

[981] Examples are *FireFly* (http://www.firefly.net), *PHOAKS* (http://www.phoaks.com) cf. [Terveen 97], *FAB* (http://fab.stanford.edu), cf. [Balabanovic 97]. A list of publicly available on-line recommendation systems can be found at http://fab.stanford.edu /papers/table.shtml.

[982] Cf. [Resnick 97, p. 57].

[983] Cf. [Avery 96], [Avery 97], and Section 2.5.1.

[984] A major start-up problem is a low number of participants so that early users will not benefit from using the system, cf. [Maltz 95], [Avery 96].

[985] *Markets for evaluations* are comprehensively discussed in [Avery 96].

[986] Cf. [Resnick 97, p. 58].

**D) News Services**

News services make substantial use of content-based IF technologies to filter news from a number of sources, e.g., news agencies, newspapers, magazines, and other official sources mostly available over the network, and direct it to subscribers of the service. *NewsPage* (http://www.newspage.com), for example, applies content-based filtering combined with domain specific knowledge bases for filtering. The dissemination of the news can be in form of client pull or it is pushed by the intermediary. News services address long-term interests, registering of users is required for all services, and the intermediaries are financed by advertising, (e.g., *Point-Cast*: http://www.pointcast.com) or by a subscription charged from clients (e.g., *The Wall Street Journal Interactive Edition*: http.//www.wsj.com).

## 5.4 Summary: economic aspects of network-based information intermediaries

### 5.4.1 Business models for network-based information intermediaries

The operation and maintenance of network-based intermediaries is costly, usually high fixed costs and small marginal costs for an additional user arise.[987] While in transactions in electronic markets some form of monetary transfer is involved, which can be exploited to finance network-based intermediaries (Section 5.2.2.3, and Figure 54),[988] network-based information intermediaries are usually not directly involved in the transfer of payments between consumers and suppliers. This poses particular circumstances for financing network-based information intermediaries. Possible business models are summarized in Table 11.[989]

---

[987] Cf. [Lee 96, p. 137].

[988] The basic possibilities of intermediary contracts were outlined in Section 3.3. These can be applied to network-based intermediaries supporting transactions in electronic markets as well.

[989] *Business models* for information intermediaries have the aim 'to generate revenues sufficient to cover' the costs of operation, cf. [Resnick 97, p. 58]. The business models mentioned here cover intermediary services that provide assistance in the search for information, cf. Section 4.1.1.

*Table 11:*    *Business models for financing network-based information intermediaries.*

| **Charging consumers of information** | |
|---|---|
| Subscription for a time period | • adequate for repeated usage of the service<br>• requires registration of every potential user<br>• can generate data about consumers' preferences and behavior<br>• problems with the protection of users' privacy are possible |
| Pay-per-use | • adequate for single-session services<br>• requires the availability of online payment systems enabling micropayments |
| **Charging information sources** | |
| Subscription for 'being indexed' by the information intermediary | • Information sources have to pay a fee for being reviewed and indexed by the information intermediary, this does not necessarily imply the rating of the source's quality by the intermediary.<br>• Requires the intermediary's awareness and reputation on the consumers' market side. |
| Sale of 'quality certificates' to information sources | The information intermediary evaluates information sources and grants 'quality certificates.'990 This can achieve trust in information sources if a reputable information intermediary provides a valuation of the source's quality,991 e.g., by publishing the ratings for information sources. |
| **Other sources of income** | |
| Sale of advertising space:<br>• per time<br>• per exposures | • feasible for web sites with high access rates<br>• danger of biased evaluations or product descriptions992 |
| Sale of marketing information about users | • requires the registration of users<br>• disregard of users' privacy<br>• negative effects on intermediary's reputation are possible |
| Provision of the service as a showcase for particular technologies | The provider of the service aims to sell the underlying technology, e.g., IR technology of Search Engines, and uses the service as an opportunity to demonstrate the performance. |

---

990    Cf. Section 3.2.3.2, Table 6, and [Lizzeri 96].
991    Cf. Sections 2.3.3 and 3.4.1.
992    Cf. Section 5.3.5, and [Resnick 97, p. 58].

In the current state of the Internet, financing via advertising[993] is the most common form for services offered by network-based information intermediaries. However, as indicated in Table 11 advertising is less appropriate for services with lower access rates, and involves some risk of providing biased information, especially for services relying on evaluations and recommendations.[994] The risk of biased evaluations can be lowered by advertising only for complementary products. However, a rest of distrust of the information intermediary may remain among users reducing the intermediary's reputation on the market.

Another approach is financing the service via fees charged either from the supplier of information or the consumer of information. Charging the suppliers of information, and offering, for example, a directory or rating service on the Internet, requires a high awareness and reputation of the information intermediary on the consumers' market side, because only fulfilling this prerequisite the owners of information sources will be willing to pay the intermediary for being indexed or certified. Charging consumers for the service offered by the information intermediary offers two basic possibilities, both requiring a critical number of users to recover the fixed costs of providing the service.[995] First, the subscription for a certain period of time is appropriate for services addressing users' long-term interests and information needs. Second, users can be charged every single time using the service (*pay per use* or *usage-based fee*), this procedure is appropriate for services focusing short-term information needs. The *basic model of an information intermediary* has outlined the basic possibilities and circumstances of this possibility to finance an information intermediary from an abstract point of view (Chapter 4).

The application of usage-based fees to real-life situations requires the availability of payment systems that allow a secure, fast, easy, anonymous, and inexpensive transfer of payments over the electronic network.[996] The transfer of payments from consumers to the intermediary may not take considerably longer than the response time of the intermediary, and it may not cause considerable marginal costs, neither for the consumer nor the intermediary. The amounts transferable by the payment system have to be in the range of fractions of the smallest monetary unit to several monetary units. Encryption-based micropayment technologies can fulfill these requirements.[997] These technologies are currently in its development or trial phase, and before a wide spreading and acceptance of micropayment technology can be

---

[993] Cf. [Hoffman 96].

[994] See the examples in Section 5.3.5, and [Resnick 97].

[995] See Section 4.4.4.

[996] Cf. [Buxmann 97a, p. 1430-1432], [Kalakota 96, p. 269-272].

[997] See [Brown 97] for a brief review of micropayment systems. Examples for these systems are *DigiCash's Ecash* (http://www.digicash.com), *CyberCash's CyberCoin* (http://www.cybercash.com), and *Digital's Millicent* (http://www.millicent.digital. com). See [Janson 95], [Kalakota 96, p. 295-331], [Panurach 96], [Wayner 96], [Lynch 96], [Asokan 97] for electronic payment systems in general.

achieved, further questions have to be answered, for example, how to deal with multiple standards of micropayment systems currently available. So the basic model of an information intermediary discussed in this treatise is visionary in this regard. However, the model can be a starting point for future research on business models of network-based information intermediaries.

## 5.4.2 Differentiation of prices and quality

The basic model of an information intermediary revealed that an information intermediary can cover only a share of all information seekers on the market with the service offered (Result 1 in Section 4.3.2.3). The individual information seeker's decision about consulting the intermediary is based on the quality level offered and the price charged by the information intermediary.[998] As was assumed in the model and as is obvious in practical situations, information seekers vary in their valuation for a certain quality level, which can be expressed by their willingness to pay for that quality level. Therefore, offering a particular price-quality combination the information intermediary will only serve a share of the whole market, some information seekers prefer personal search or will consult information intermediaries with different price-quality combinations.[999] The introduction of quality differences[1000] for the services offered allows the information intermediary to address a much broader clientele than with a flat fee and a fixed quality level.[1001] The high degree of personification of the information provided,[1002] enables the information intermediary to discriminate[1003] between customers with different willingness to pay by offering different quality levels in parallel. For example, information seekers with a high valuation for quality will choose a service with higher quality level and can be charged a higher fee, whereas the lower quality level offered for a lower price is sufficient for information seekers with a lower valuation for quality.

---

[998] In the basic model the information seeker's decision was based on the comparison of the quality-price combination offered by the intermediary with the expected result from a personal search process (Section 4.3.2.3). In a practical situation the information seeker will only make an estimation of the result obtainable from a personal search for information, cf. Section 4.2.1.

[999] See the discussion of competition between information intermediaries, here especially Figure 44 and Section 4.5.2.2.

[1000] A different strategy for pricing digital information products is the bundling of different goods, cf. Section 2.5.4 and [Bakos 96].

[1001] See Section 2.5.4.

[1002] In ideal forms the information provided by the intermediary is focused on the information seekers' individual information need (Sections 5.1.1 and 5.3.1), and therefore is usually of little use for other information seekers.

[1003] See Section 2.5.4, and [Varian 89, p. 640].

The practical realization of quality differences can follow several dimensions that can be derived from the basic conception of network-based information intermediaries.[1004] For example, the information sources covered to produce the user specific information, or the matching technology applied can be varied by the information intermediary to introduce differences in the quality level of the information service. The association of IR and IF technologies with the considerations about quality differentiation and price discrimination stated above, is a domain that can further contribute to the theory and practical operation of network-based information intermediaries.[1005]

### 5.4.3 Competitive advantages of information intermediaries

The business of information intermediaries is subject to a number of influences from the sources of information, consumers, and competitors. The basic model of an information intermediary treated the business of information intermediaries from a theoretical point of view and derived critical success factors (Section 4.8.2). The analysis of the concepts of 'traditional' information intermediaries as well as of new forms of network-based information intermediaries completed the list of core competencies. Figure 57 summarizes the principal competitive advantages of information intermediaries within Porter's framework of industry competition.[1006]

The figure outlines what was already stated about competition for intermediaries in general (Section 3.5.1), this applies to information intermediaries as well. On the one hand, intermediaries compete with other intermediaries in their own industry as well as with new market entrants. On the other hand, information intermediaries compete with direct transactions of the market participants, e.g., personal search processes of information seekers.

The analysis of competition between indentical information intermediaries (Section 4.5) has outlined the significance of differentiation of the services provided. The focus on a particular target market, i.e., thematic domain and target audience, can be a further strategy for competition within the industry of information intermediaries.[1007] Barriers to entry for new entrants can be built up by established information intermediaries in form of domain specific knowledge, possession of efficient search tactics and technologies, and by awareness and

---

[1004] From an abstract point of view, these dimensions can be the timeliness, detail, response time of the service, cf. [Whinston 97, p. 326]. The treatment of the information intermediary within the basic model of an information intermediary as well as the characterization of the intermediary's environment (Figure 55 in Section 5.3.2) allows a more precise determination of the measures to design the different service levels.

[1005] Best match IR technologies (Section 5.3.3.1), for example, offer the opportunity to vary the quality of the result obtained in a query.

[1006] Cf. [Porter 92, p. 26], see [Bloch 96] as well.

[1007] See the analysis of the supply market side (Section 4.4.2) and the target audience (Section 4.4.3) as well.

reputation on the market. These competitive advantages can also be a protection against a tendency for disintermediation,[1008] which is given by the opportunity of direct contacts between information seekers and information sources enabled through information and communication infrastructures like the Internet.[1009] In addition, markets for information require services that pose demand for third parties, e.g., guaranteeing quality.[1010] Substitutes for established information intermediaries can be new technologies, e.g., intelligent software agents, supporting information seekers in their search for information.[1011] However, these technologies can be introduced in the services of information intermediaries as well.

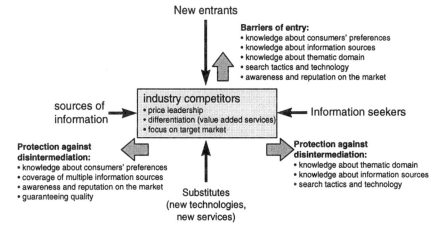

*Figure 57:*    *Competitive advantages of information intermediaries within Porter's framework of industry competition.*

---

[1008]  See [Benjamin 95] for the elimination of intermediaries (disintermediation) in the retail market.

[1009]  The *model of direct mediation of information* in Section 5.1.2 gives the framework for these direct transactions in markets for information. See Section 4.3.2.3 for the 'competition' of the information intermediary with personal search processes of information seekers in the basic model of an information intermediary.

[1010]  See Section 2.3.3, and see Section 3.2.3.2 for the functions of intermediaries.

[1011]  Cf. [Maes 94], [Mitchell 94], [Balabanovic 95], [Lieberman 95], [Rhodes 96].

# 6 Conclusion

## 6.1 Summary

The topic of the present thesis was the analysis of information intermediaries, particularly with regard to applications in open Wide Area Networks like the Internet. As a fact, information is gaining importance for today's economies, but the increasing amount of available information and the decreasing density of information relevant to a particular task incident thereto call for possibilities to efficiently match information needs with available information. Intermediaries operating in physical distribution channels or in financial markets have demonstrated that the introduction of a specialized middleman in the relationship between opposite market sides can efficiently bridge incompatibilities between supply and demand. Information intermediaries can play a similar role in markets for information, in which information can be conceived as an economic commodity.

From an abstract point of view, information intermediaries can be conceived as economic information processing systems, performing search for information on behalf of the end-users of that information as their basic function. The economic aspects of search processes can be treated by means of a microeconomic search model. The introduction of an independent, risk neutral, profit maximizing information intermediary in an optimal sequential search model is taken as the theoretical nucleus for the formal treatment of the business of information intermediaries. A central assumption of the model is that information seekers have the opportunity to decide between personal search processes and the consultation of the information intermediary. The single information seeker will buy information from the intermediary, if the quality offered and the price charged are preferable to a personal search process.

The *basic model of an information intermediary* allowed to formally treat the business of information intermediaries, study the influences of environmental conditions, and derive critical success factors. The major foundations of the business of information intermediaries are: (a) the exploitation of economies of scale in applying information once gathered, (b) the expertise in search and information processing, and (c) domain specific knowledge, i.e., knowledge about the thematic domain under consideration and about appropriate sources of information. Offering a particular quality level and charging a certain price for the services, the information intermediary can serve a particular share of all potential information seekers on the market. The intermediary's profit can be maximized by adjusting the offer to the environmental conditions. In general, the information intermediary's profit is c.p. (a) decreasing with decreasing density of relevant information on the market, (b) increasing with an increasing homogeneity of the target audience addressed by the intermediary service, and (c) increasing with growing awareness of the intermediary on the market.

Furthermore, the basic model was applied to study the effects of competition in a duopoly of similar information intermediaries as well as the welfare effects of the intermediary's presence on the market. Within the scope of the basic model competition between information intermediaries can take place in the dimensions of prices and quality. Competition either solely in prices or solely in the quality level offered can become ruinous, whereas for competition in price-quality combinations the position of the follower is preferable to that of the leader and both intermediaries are economically viable. The monopolistic information intermediary can augment social welfare through the services provided on the market, however, the magnitude of the effect is significantly dependent on the environmental conditions.

The range of information processing activities performed by real-life information intermediaries is much broader than that covered in the abstract framework of the basic model of information intermediaries. Therefore, the functions and information processing activities were treated in further detail to refine the notion of information intermediaries, and information brokers were examined as typical examples.

The potential functions of intermediaries in electronic networks cover the broad domain of support of transactions, either in electronic markets or in an organizational context, and the mediation of information. The activities involved in transactions are to a large extent coordination tasks, requiring communication and the exchange of information between potential transaction partners. Network-based intermediaries can offer various services to support the phases of transactions in electronic markets. Electronic Product Catalogs are typical examples for this kind of intermediaries.

Network-based information intermediaries are mediators between information sources and information seekers, offering services that help information seekers either to locate relevant information in the network or to reduce the amount of available information to a manageable and understandable set. The basic characteristics of these information intermediaries were described, and the basic technologies and architectures for their realization were reviewed.

The work closed with a discussion of economic aspects of network-based information intermediaries that are closely related to the basic model treated in the main part of the work. Potential business models for network-based information intermediaries were reviewed. Usage-based fees, comprehensively covered by the theoretical model, are one possibility for financing an information intermediary. However, these require the availability of online micropayment systems that are currently still in developing stage, so the present work is visionary in this regard.

The provision of personalized information products offers the opportunity for product and price differentiation. The theoretical treatment within the basic model outlined the starting point for dimensions that can be taken to achieve differentiation in the service quality offered by the information intermediary. The major competitive advantages of information intermediaries were finally summarized in Porter's framework of industry competition.

## 6.2 Outlook: the future of network-based intermediaries?

The future role of intermediaries in the world of electronic networks is not undisputed. The Internet enables direct contacts between consumers and producers, hence, the middlemen can be omitted to reduce transaction costs by the amount the intermediaries claim for their services.[1012] However, that the world is not that easy can be seen only because of the variety of intermediary services offered on the Internet (*cybermediaries*). Intermediaries do not only provide functions like the mediation of contacts, but also offer the user a bundle of further services as quality assurance, certification, coordination of transaction partners, settlement of payment services and so forth.[1013] Especially in the world of electronic networks, in which a supplier is nothing more than an IP-address, intermediaries play an important role to establish trust in the relationship between transaction partners.[1014] As Electronic Commerce is likely to gain further importance in the future, the role of Trusted Third Parties (TTPs) will therefore be a field with increasing demand for independent network-based intermediaries.

Network-based intermediaries will not be restricted to the realm of transactions in electronic markets, the coordination of relationships in virtual organizations and virtual teams[1015] can be an important domain for future middlemen as well, the coordination of virtual competence centers and networks consisting of experts in a thematic domain are the first examples to be observed today.[1016]

Besides the developments of intermediaries in the domain of electronic markets, network-based information intermediaries will further gain importance with the growth and accumulation of information available over electronic networks. Technological developments will heavily influence the appearance, the design, and

---

[1012] Cf. [Benjamin 95].

[1013] Cf. Sections 3.2 and 5.2.

[1014] Cf. [Froomkin 96], [Rebel 97], see Section 2.3.3 as well.

[1015] Cf. Section 3.2.2.3, especially Figure 6.

[1016] These network-based intermediaries require theoretic approaches going beyond the one discussed in the present work, for example, the detailed treatment of the information processing activities of the intermediary (see Section 4.7.6) or the explicit representation of the intermediary's knowledge within the model.

the particular services offered by network-based information intermediaries.[1017] For example, intelligent agent technologies will allow a further customization of the information services offered for the individual user,[1018] Java, CORBA, and other network technologies will allow to further distribute information processing tasks of an information intermediary between client and server.[1019] Micropayment technologies will open new opportunities for information intermediaries to finance the services offered,[1020] which will open the way for the provision of services that are currently withhold because of lacking possibilities for cost recovery.

Detached from the particular realization and design of the service, the business of network-based information intermediaries will be founded on some rather fundamental principles, that were already outlined earlier:[1021] the exploitation of economies of scale (reuse of information), expertise in search and in information processing, possession of domain specific knowledge, and reputation. The abstract model introduced in the present work can be a starting point for future research on business models of network-based information intermediaries.

---

[1017] For the effects of information technology on organizations in general see [Österle 95], [Picot 96], [Wigand 97].

[1018] Cf. [Maes 94], [Mitchell 94], [Etzioni 95], [Reese Hedberg 95].

[1019] See, for example, Java RMI, Java Beans (http://java.sun.com), for CORBA see [Mowbray 95], [Ben-Natan 96].

[1020] Cf. Section 5.4.1.

[1021] Cf. Section 4.8.2, see Section 5.4.3 as well.

# 7 References

[Admati 86]      Admati, A. R.; Pfleiderer, P.: A Monopolistic Market for Information; Journal of Economic Theory, Vol. 39, 1986, p. 400-438.

[Admati 90]      Admati, A. R.; Pfleiderer, P.: Direct and Indirect Sale of Information; Econometrica, Vol. 58, No.4, July 1990, p. 901-928.

[Akerlof 70]     Akerlof, G. A.: The Market for Lemons: Quality Uncertainty and the Market Mechanism; Quarterly Journal of Economics, Vol. 84, 1970, p. 488-500.

[Akman 96]       Akman, V.; Surav, M.: Steps Towards Formalizing Context; AI Magazine, 1996, Vol. 17, No. 3, Fall 1996, p. 55-72.

[Alchian 72]     Alchian, A. A.; Demsetz, H.: Production, Information Costs, and Economic Organization; American Economic Review, Vol. 62, 1972, p. 777-795.

[Allen 90]       Allen, B.: Information as an Economic Commodity; American Economic Review, Vol. 80, No. 2, May 1990, p. 268-273.

[Alt 95]         Alt, R.; Cathomen, I.; Klein, S.: CIL - Computerintegrierte Logistik; Report from the Competence Center Electronic Markets, Institute for Information Management, University St. Gallen, IM2000/CCEM/21, April 1995.

[Alter 96]       Alter, S.: Information Systems: A Management Perspective; Second Edition, Menlo Park, California, 1996.

[Amihud 80]      Amihud, Y.; Mendelson, H.: Dealership Market: Market Making with Inventory; Journal of Financial Economics, Vol. 8, 1980, p. 31-53.

[Andel 92]       Andel, N.: Finanzwissenschaft; 3. Auflage, J. C. B. Mohr (Paul Siebeck), Tübingen, 1992.

[Anderson 89]    Anderson, J. R.: Kognitive Psychologie: Eine Einführung; 2. Auflage, Spektrum der Wissenschaft Verlagsgesellschaft, Heidelberg, 1989.

[Anderson 96]    Anderson, S. P.; de Palma, A.; Thisse, J.-F.: Discrete Choice Theory of Product Differentiation; MIT Press, Cambridge, 1996.

[Antonelli 92]   Antonelli, C.: The Economic Theory of Information Networks; In: Antonelli, C. (ed.): The Economics of Information Networks, Amsterdam, 1992, p. 5-27.

[Armstrong 95]   Armstrong, R.; Freitag, D.; Joachims, T.; Mitchell, T.: WebWatcher: A Learning Apprentice for the World Wide Web; In: AAAI Spring Symposium on Information Gathering, Stanford, CA, March 1995.

[Arrow 62]       Arrow, K.: Economic Welfare and the Allocation of Resources to Invention; In: National Bureau of Economic Research: The Rate and Direction of Inventive Activity: Economic and Social Factors, Princeton, 1962, p. 609-625.

| | |
|---|---|
| [Arrow 69] | Arrow, K.: The Organization of Economic Activity, The Analysis and Evaluation of Public Expenditure: The PPB System; Joint Economic Committee, 91st Congress 1st session, 1969, p. 59-73. |
| [Arrow 85] | Arrow, K. J.: The Economics of Agency; In: [Pratt 85], p. 37-51. |
| [Asokan 97] | Asokan, N.; Janson, P.; Steiner, M.; Waidner, M.: State of the Art in Electronic Payment Systems; IEEE COMPUTER, Vol. 30, No. 9, 1997, p. 28-35. |
| [Avery 96] | Avery, C.; Resnick, P.; Zeckhauser, R.: The Market for Evaluations; Workingpaper, Harvard Kennedy School of Government, Cambridge MA, 1996. |
| [Avery 97] | Avery, C.; Zeckhauser, R.: Recommender Systems for Evaluating Computer Messages; Communications of the ACM, Vol. 40, No. 3, March 1997, p. 88-89. |
| [Bagnoli 89] | Bagnoli, M.; Lipman, B. L.: Provision of Public Goods: Fully Implementing the Core through Private Contributions; Review of Economic Studies, 1989, Vol. 56, p. 583-601. |
| [Bagwell 91] | Bagwell, K.; Riordan, M. H.: High and Declining Prices Signal Product Quality; The American Economic Review, Vol. 81, No. 3, March 1991, p. 224-239. |
| [Bagwell 93] | Bagwell, K.; Ramey, G.: Adverstising as Information: Matching Products to Buyers; Journal of Economics & Management Strategy, Vol. 2, No. 2, Summer 1993, p. 199-243. |
| [Bagwell 94] | Bagwell, K.; Ramey, G.: Coordination Economics, Advertising, and Search Behavior in Retail Markets; The American Economic Review, Vol. 84, No. 3, 1994, p. 498-517. |
| [Bailey 97] | Bailey, J. P.; Bakos, J. Y.: An Exploratory Study of the Emerging Role of Electronic Intermediaries; International Journal of Electronic Commerce, Vol. 1, No. 3, Spring 1997. |
| [Bakos 91a] | Bakos, J. Y.: A Strategic Analysis of Electronic Marketplaces; MIS Quarterly, Vol. 15, No. 3, September 1991, p. 295-310. |
| [Bakos 91b] | Bakos, J. Y.: Information Links and Electronic Marketplaces: Implications of Interorganizational Information Systems in Vertical Markets; Journal of Management Information Systems, Vol. 8, No. 2, Herbst 1991. |
| [Bakos 96] | Bakos, J. Y., Brynjolfson, E.: Bundling Information Goods: Pricing, Profits and Efficiency; Working Paper Sloan School of Management, 1996, http://www.gsm.uci.edu/~bakos/big.pdf. |
| [Bakos 97a] | Bakos, J. Y.; Brynjolfsson, E.: Aggregation and Disaggregation of Information Goods: Implications for Bundling, Site Licensing and Micropayment Systems; 1997, http://www.gsm.uci.edu/~bakos/aig.pdf. |

[Bakos 97b]        Bakos, J. Y.: Reducing Buyer Search Costs: Implications for Electronic Marketplaces; Management Science, Vol. 43, No. 12, December 1997.

[Balabanovic 95]   Balabanovic, M.; Shoham, Y.: Learning Information Retrieval Agents: Experiments with Automated Web Browsing; In: AAAI Spring Symposium on Information Gathering, Stanford CA, March 1995, http://robotics.stanford.edu/people/marko/papers/lira.ps.

[Balabanovic 97]   Balabanovic, M.; Shoham, Y.: Content-Based, Collaborative Recommendation; Communications of the ACM, Vol. 40, No. 3, March 1997, p. 66-72.

[Balderston 58]    Balderston, F. E.: Communication Networks in Intermediate Markets; Management Science, Vol. IV, January 1958, p. 154-171.

[Baligh 67]        Baligh, H. H., Richartz, L. E.: Vertical Market Structures; Allyn and Bacon, Boston, 1967.

[Bamberg 76]       Bamberg, G.; Coenenberg, A. G.; Kleine-Doepke, R.: Zur entscheidungsorientierten Bewertung von Informationen; Zeitschrift für Betriebswirtschaftliche Forschung, Vol. 28, 1976, p. 30-42.

[Banerjee 92]      Banerjee, A. V.: A Simple Model of Herd Behavior; Quarterly Journal of Economics, Vol. 107, No. 3, p. 797-817.

[Bartels 78]       Bartels, H. G.: Logistik; In: Handwörterbuch der Sozialwissenschaften, 13. Auflage, Stuttgart, 1978, p. 54-72.

[Barth 96]         Barth, K.: Betriebswirtschaftlehre des Handels; 3. Auflage, Gabler, Wiesbaden, 1996.

[Bartling 80]      Bartling, H.: Leitbilder der Wettbewerbspolitik; Verlag Franz Vahlen, München, 1980.

[Beam 96a]         Beam, C.; Segev, A.; Shanthikumar, J. G.: Electronic Negotiation through Internet-based Auctions; CITM Working Paper 96-WP-1019, Fisher Center for Information Technology and Management, University of California, Berkeley, Dec. 1996, http://haas.berkeley.edu/~citm/wp-1019-summary.html.

[Beam 96b]         Beam, C.; Segev, A.: Electronic Catalogs and Negotiations; CITM Working Paper 96-WP-1016, Fisher Center for Information Technology and Management University of California, Berkeley, Aug. 1996, http://haas.berkeley.edu/~citm/wp-1016-summary.html.

[Beam 97]          Beam, C.; Segev, A.: Automated Negotiations: A Survey of the State of the Art; Wirtschaftsinformatik, Vol. 39, No. 3, 1997, p. 263-268.

[Bekavac 96]   Bekavac, B.: WWW-Suchmaschinen und Kataloge: Der findet; IX, 7/1996, p. 102-109.

[Belkin 82]   Belkin, N. J.; Oddy, R. N.; Brooks, H. M.: ASK for Information Retrieval: Part I. Background and Theory; Journal of Documentation, Vol. 38, No. 2, 1982, p. 61-71.

[Belkin 87]   Belkin, N. J.; Croft, W. B.: Retrieval Techniques; In: Williams, M. E. (ed.): Annual Review of Information Science and Technology, Elsevier, 1987, p. 109-145.

[Belkin 92]   Belkin, N. J.; Croft, W. B.: Information Filtering and Information Retrieval: Two Sides of the Same Coin?; Communications of the ACM, Vol. 35, No. 12, December 1992, p. 29-38.

[Ben-Natan 95]   Ben-Natan, R.: CORBA - A Guide to the Common Object Request Broker Architecture; McGraw-Hill, New York, 1995.

[Benjamin 90]   Benjamin, R. I.; de Long, D. W.; Scott Morton, M. S.: Electronic Data Interchange: How Much Competitive Advantage?; Long Range Planning, Vol. 23, No. 1, 1990, p. 23-40.

[Benjamin 95]   Benjamin, R.; Wigand, R.: Electronic Markets and Virtual Value Chains on the Information Superhighway; Sloan Management Review, Winter 1995, p. 62-72.

[Berger 80]   Berger, J. O.: Statistical Decision Theory - Foundations, Concepts and Methods; Springer, New York, 1980.

[Berners-Lee 92]   Berners-Lee, T.; Cailliau, R.; Groff, J.; Pollermann, B.: World-Wide Web: The Information Universe, Electronic Networking: Research, Applications and Policy; Meckler Publications, Vol. 2, No. 1, 1992, p. 52-58.

[Bessler 85]   Bessler, H.: Die Informationsbetriebe - Typologie und Marketingpolitik; Dissertation Universität Göttingen, Fachbereich Wirtschaftswissenschaften, 1985, (Gesellschaft für Informationsmarktforschung, Bd. 1 der Schriftenreihe: „Betriebswirtschaftliche und juristische Beiträge zum Informations- und Kommunikationswesen").

[Bhargava 95a]   Bhargava, H. K.; Krishnan, R.; Müller, R.: On Sharing Decision Technologies over a Global Network; Proceedings of the International Conference on Automation, Indore (India), December 1995, http://mmm.wiwi.hu-berlin.de/~rmueller/oopsla/bhargava/OOPSLA.html.

[Bhargava 95b]   Bhargava, H. K.; Krishnan, R.: On Generalized Access to a WWW-based Network of Decision Support Services; Proceedings of the Third ISDSS Conference, Hong Kong, June 1995.

[Bhargava 95c]   Bhargava, H. K.; King, A. S.; McQuay, D.S.: DecisionNet: Modeling and Decision Support Over the World Wide Web; Proceedings of the Third ISDSS Conference, Hong Kong, June 1995.

| | |
|---|---|
| [Bhattacharya-Thakor 93] | Bhattacharya, S.; Thakor, A. V.: Contemporary Banking Theory; Journal of Financial Intermediation, Vol. 3, 1993, p. 2-50. |
| [Biglaiser 93] | Biglaiser, G.: Middlemen as Experts; RAND Journal of Economics, Vol. 24, No. 2, Summer 1993, p. 212-223. |
| [Biglaiser 94] | Biglaiser, G.: Middlemen as Guarantors of Quality; International Journal of Industrial Organization, Vol. 12, 1994, p. 509-531. |
| [Birchall 94] | Birchall, A.; Deakin, A.; Rada, R.: Knowledge Automation and the Need for Intermediaries; Journal of Librarianship and Information Science, Vol. 26, No. 4, 1994, p. 181-192. |
| [Blahut 87] | Blahut, R. E.: Principles and Practice of Information Theory; Addison-Wesley, Reading, Massachusetts, 1990. |
| [Bloch 96] | Bloch, M.; Pigneur, I.; Segev, A.: On the Road of Electronic Commerce - A Business Value Framework, Gaining Competitive Advantage and some Research Issues; Working Paper, Fisher Center for Information Technology and Management, University of California, Berkeley, 1996, http://www.stern.nyu.edu/~mbloch/docs/roadtoec/ec.html. |
| [Boddy 96] | Boddy, D.; Gunson, N.: Organizations in the Network Age; Routledge, London, 1996. |
| [Bode 93] | Bode, J.: Betriebliche Produktion von Information; Deutscher Universitätsverlag, Wiesbaden, 1993. |
| [Bode 97] | Bode, J.: Der Informationsbegriff in der Betriebswirtschaftslehre; Zeitschrift für Betriebswirtschaftliche Forschung, Vol. 49, 1997, p. 449-468. |
| [Bohr 96] | Bohr, K.: Economies of Scale und Economies of Scope; In: Kern, W.; Schröder, H. H.; Weber, J.: Handwörterbuch der Produktionswirtschaft, 2. Auflage, Stuttgart, C. E. Poeschel Verlag, 1994, p. 375-386. |
| [Bössmann 81] | Bössmann, E.: Weshalb gibt es Unternehmungen?, Der Erklärungsansatz von Ronald H. Coase; Zeitschrift für die gesamte Staatswissenschaft, Vol. 137, 1981, p. 667-674. |
| [Bray 89] | Bray, M.: Rational Expectations, Information, and Asset Markets; In: [Hahn 89], p. 243-277. |
| [Brenner 97] | Brenner, W.; Kolbe, L.; Hamm, V.: The Net: Extinction or Renaissance for Intermediaries - An Analysis of Core Competencies in the Book Business; Proceedings of the 5th European Conference on Information Systems (ECIS '97), Volume 1, 1997, p. 130-144. |
| [Bretzke 94] | Bretzke, W. R.: "Make or buy" von Logistikdienstleistungen: Erfolgskriterien für eine Fremdvergabe logistischer Dienstleistungen; In: Isermann, H. (ed.): Logistik: Beschaffung, Produktion, Distribution; Verlag Moderne Industrie, München, 1994, p. 321-330. |

[Bronstein 89]     Bronstein, I. N.; Semendjajew, K. A.: Taschenbuch der Mathe-
                   matik; 24. Auflage, Berlin, 1989.

[Brown 97]         Brown, E.: Micropayments: No Small Change. Micropayment
                   schemes promise to make the Web profitable -- one penny at
                   time; NewMedia, June 23, 1997, http://www.hyperstand.com/
                   NewMedia/97/08/fea/Micropayments_Small_Change.html.

[Brynjolfsson      Brynjolfsson, E.: Information Assets, Technology, and Organiza-
94]                tion; Management Science, Vol. 40, No. 12, December 1994, p.
                   1645-1662.

[Buder 97]         Buder, M.; Rehfeld, W.; Seeger, T.; Strauch, D. (eds.): Grundla-
                   gen der praktischen Dokumentation: Ein Handbuch zur Einführ-
                   ung in die fachliche Informationsarbeit; Bd. 1, 2, München,
                   1997.

[Bull 87]          Bull, C.; Ornati, O.; Tedeschi, P.: Search, Hiring Strategies, and
                   Labor Market Intermediaries; Journal of Labor Economics, Vol.
                   5, No. 4, 1987, p. S1-S17.

[Büschgen 91]      Büschgen, H. E.: Das kleine Börsenlexikon; 19. Auflage, Verlag
                   Wirtschaft und Finanzen GmbH, Düsseldorf, 1991.

[Butters 77]       Butters, G. R.: Equilibrium Distribution of Sales and Advertising
                   Prices; Review of Economic Studies, Vol. 44, No. 3, 1977, p.
                   465-491.

[Buxmann 96a]      Buxmann, P.: Standardisierung betrieblicher Informationssys-
                   teme; Gabler, Wiesbaden, 1996.

[Buxmann 96b]      Buxmann, P.; König, W.; Rose, F.: The Java Repository - An
                   Electronic Intermediary for Java Resources; Proceedings of the
                   7th Annual Conference of the International Information Manage-
                   ment Association (IIMA), Estes Park (Colorado), December
                   1996.

[Buxmann 97a]      Buxmann, P.; Rose, F.; König, W.: An Electronic Market for
                   Java Software Elements; Proceedings of the 5th European Con-
                   ference on Information Systems (ECIS '97), Volume 3, 1997, p.
                   1423-1435.

[Buxmann 97b]      Buxmann, P.; König, W.; Rose, F.: Aufbau eines Elektronischen
                   Handelsplatzes für Java-Applets; In: Krallmann, H. (ed.): Wirt-
                   schaftsinformatik '97, Physica-Verlag, Heidelberg, 1997, p. 35-
                   48.

[Buxmann 97c]      Buxmann, P.; König, W.; Rose, F.: Wiederverwendung von Soft-
                   ware-Elementen: Das Java Repository; Oberweis, A.; Sneed, H.
                   M. (ed.): Software Management '97, Stuttgart, 1997, p. 195-207.

[Cerny 97]         Cerny, D.; Pohl, H.: Trusted Third Parties und Sicherheitsinfra-
                   strukturen; Wirtschaftsinformatik, Vol. 39, No. 6, 1997, p. 616-
                   622.

[Cerqueiro 96]    Cerqueiro, A.; Kosuge, Y.: Electronic Payment Systems on the Internet; 1996, http://www.sloan.mit.edu/15.967/group02/pay_main.htm.

[Chan 86]    Chan, Y.; Greenbaum, S. I.; Thakor, A. V.: Information Reusability, Competition and Bank Asset Quality; Journal of Banking Finance, Vol. 10, 1986, p. 243-253.

[Chatterjee 83]    Chatterjee, K.; Samuelson, L.: Bargaining under Incomplete Information; Operations Research, Vol. 31, No. 5, September-October 1983, p. 835-851.

[Chatterjee 90]    Chatterjee, K.; Samuelson, L.: Perfect Equilibria in Simultaneous-Offer Bargaining; International Journal of Game Theory, Vol. 19, 1990, p. 237-267.

[Chemmanur 94]    Chemmanur, T. J.; Fulghieri, P.: Investment Bank Reputation, Information Production, and Financial Intermediation; The Journal of Finance, Vol. XLIX, No. 1, March 1994, p. 57-79.

[Cheung 83]    Cheung, S. N. S.: The Contractual Theory of the Firm; Journal of Law and Economics, Vol. 26, No. 1, 1983, p. 1-21.

[Clower 75]    Clower, R.; Leijonhufvud, A.: The Coordination of Economic Activities; American Economic Review, Vol. 65, 1975, p. 182-188.

[Coase 37]    Coase, R. The Nature of the Firm; Economica, Vol. 14, No. 16, 1937, p. 386-405.

[Coase 93]    Coase, R.: The Nature of the Firm: Meaning; In: Williamson, O. E.; Winter, S. G. (eds.): The Nature of the Firm - Origins, Evolution, and Development, New York, 1993, p. 48-60.

[Commons 34/90]    Commons, J. R.: Institutional Economics; New Brunswick NJ, 1990 (Originally published in 1934).

[Cooper 88]    Cooper, R.; John, A.: Coordinating Coordination Failures in Keynesian Models; Quarterly Journal of Economics, August 1988, p. 441-463.

[Corsten 90]    Corsten, H.: Betriebswirtschaftslehre der Dienstleistungsunternehmen; Oldenbourg, München, 1990.

[Cosimano 96]    Cosimano, T. F.: Intermediation; Economica, Vol. 63, 1996, p. 131-143.

[Coym 95]    Coym, P.: Broker; In: Gerke, W. (ed.): Enzyklopädie der Betriebswirtschaftslehre, Bd. 6, Handwörterbuch des Bank- und Finanzwesens, 2. Auflage, 1995, p. 727-735.

[Crawford 82]    Crawford, V. P.; Sobel, J.: Strategic Information Transmission; Econometrica, Vol. 50, No. 6, November 1982, p. 1431-1451.

[Croft 95]    Croft, W. B.: What People Want from Information Retrieval?; D-Lib Magazine, November 1995, http://www.dlib.org/dlib/november95/11croft.html.

[Csányi 92]        Csányi, V.: Nature and Origin of Biological and Social Informa-
                   tion; In: [Haefner 1992], p. 257-278.
[Darby 73]         Darby, M. R.; Karni, E.: Free Competition and the Optimal
                   Amount of Fraud; Journal of Law and Economics, Vol. 16, 1973,
                   p. 67-88.
[Dasgupta 80]      Dasgupta, P.; Stiglitz, J. E.: Industrial Structure and the Nature
                   of Innovative Activity; Economic Journal, Vol. 90, 1980, p. 266-
                   293.
[Dasgupta 89]      Dasgupta, P.: The Economics of Parallel Research; In: [Hahn
                   89], p. 129-148.
[December 95]       December, J.; Ginsburg, M.: HTML and CGI Unleashed;
                   Sams.Net Publishing, Indianapolis (IN), 1995.
[Deerwester 90]    Deerwester, S.; Dumais, S. T.; Furnas, G. W.; Landauer, T. K.;
                   Harshnan, R.: Indexing by Latent Semantic Analysis; Journal of
                   the Amercian Society for Information Science, Vol. 41, No. 6,
                   1990, p. 391-407.
[DeGroot 70]       DeGroot, M. H.: Optimal Statistical Decisions; McGraw Hill,
                   New York, 1970.
[Demsetz 68]       Demsetz, H.: The Cost of Transacting; Quarterly Journal of Eco-
                   nomics, No. 97, 1968, p. 33-53.
[Denning 94]       Denning, R.; Smith, P. J.: Interface Design Concepts in the
                   Development of ELSA, an Intelligent Electronic Library Search
                   Assistant; Information Technology and Libraries, June 1994, p.
                   133-147.
[Diamond 84]       Diamond, D. W.: Financial Intermediation and Delegated Moni-
                   toring; Review of Economic Studies, Vol. 51, 1984, p. 393-414.
[Diamond 91]       Diamond, D. W.: Monitoring and Reputation: The Choice
                   Between Bank Loans and Directly Placed Debt; Journal of
                   Political Economy, Vol. 99, 1991, p. 689-721.
[Doyle 89]         Doyle, C.: Strategy Variables and Theories of Industrial Organi-
                   zation; In: [Hahn 89], p. 149-162.
[Drenth 91]        Drenth, H.; Morris, A.; Tseng, G.: Expert Systems as Infor-
                   mation Intermediaries; Annual Review of Information Science
                   and Technology (ARIST), Vol. 26, 1991, p. 113-154.
[Eccles 85]        Eccles, R. G.: Transfer Pricing as a Problem of Agency; In:
                   [Pratt 85], p. 151-186.
[Eco 77]           Eco, U.: Einführung in die Semiotik; Fink, München, 1977.
[Edgeworth         Edgeworth, F. Y.: Mathematical Psychics. An Essay on the
1881]              Application of Mathematics to the Moral Sciences; London,
                   1881, New York, 1961.

| | |
|---|---|
| [Ehemann 83] | Ehemann, K.: Randomisierung in statistischen Entscheidungs-problemen mit linearer partieller Information; In: Beckmann, M. J.; Eichhorn, W.; Krelle, W. (eds.): Mathematische Systeme in der Ökonomie; Königstein, 1983, p. 141-149. |
| [Ehrenberg 97] | Ehrenberg, D.: Informationsgesellschaft - Information Society; In: Mertens, P. et al. (eds.): Lexikon der Wirtschaftsinformatik, Springer, Berlin, 1997, p. 203-204. |
| [Eisenführ 94] | Eisenführ, F.; Weber, M.: Rationales Entscheiden; 2. Auflage, Springer, Berlin, 1994. |
| [Engelbrecht-Wiggans 80] | Engelbrecht-Wiggans, R.: Auctions and Bidding Models: A Survey; Management Science, Vol. 26, No. 2, 1980, p. 119-142. |
| [Engelbrecht-Wiggans 83] | Engelbrecht-Wiggans, R.; Milgrom, P. R.; Weber, R. J.: Competitive Bidding and Proprietary Information; Journal of Mathematical Economics, Vol. 11, 1983, p. 161-169. |
| [Esser 77] | Esser, H.; Klenovits, K.; Zehnpfennig, H.: Wissenschaftstheorie Teil 1: Grundlagen und Analytische Wissenschaftstheorie; 1977. |
| [Etzioni 95] | Etzioni, O.; Weld, D. S.: Intelligent Agents on the Internet: Fact, Fiction, and Forecast; IEEE Expert, August 1995, p. 44-49. |
| [Falk 92] | Falk, B. R.; Wolf, J.: Handelsbetriebslehre; 11. Auflage, Verlag moderne Industrie, Landsberg/Lech, 1992. |
| [Fama 70] | Fama, E.: Efficient Capital Markets: A Review of Theory and Empirical Work; Journal of Finance, Vol. 25, May 1970, p. 383-417. |
| [Feess 97] | Feess, E.: Mikroökonomie: Eine spieltheoretisch- und anwendungsorientierte Einführung; Metropolis, Marburg, 1997. |
| [Feinberg 77] | Feinberg, R. M.; Johnson, W. R.: The Superiority of Sequential Search: A Calculation; Southern Economic Journal, Vol. 43, No. 4, April 1977, p. 1594-1598. |
| [Feller 71] | Feller, W.: An Introduction to Probability Theory and its Applications; John Wiley & Sons, New York, 1971. |
| [Ferstl 93] | Ferstl, O. K.; Sinz, E. J.: Grundlagen der Wirtschaftsinformatik; Band 1, Oldenbourg, München, 1993. |
| [Fikes 95] | Fikes, R.; Engelmore, R.; Farquhar, A.; Pratt, W.: Network-Based Information Brokers; Working Paper, Knowledge System Laboratory, Stanford University, Working Paper KSL-95-13, 1995, ftp://ftp-ksl.stanford.edu/pub/KSL_Reports/KSL-95-13.ps. |
| [Finke 97] | Finke, W. F.: Informationsbroker; In: Mertens, Peter et al. (eds.): Lexikon der Wirtschaftsinformatik, Springer, Berlin, 1997, p. 202-203. |
| [Foltz 92] | Foltz, P. W.; Dumais, S. T.: Personalized Information Delivery: An Analysis of Information Filtering Methods; Communications of the ACM, December 1992, Vol. 35, No. 12, p. 51-60. |

[Forsyth 86]     Forsyth, R.: Machine Learning; In: Yazdani, M.: Artificial Intelligence - Principles and Applications; Chapman and Hall Computing, London, 1986, p. 205-225.

[Froomkin 96]    Froomkin, M.: The Essential Role of Trusted Third Parties in Electronic Commerce; 75 Oregon L. Rev. 49, 1996, (The Law and Entrepreneurship Program: Innovation and the Information Environment, Symposium Volume), http://www.law.miami.edu/~froomkin/articles/trusted1.htm.

[Gabler WI-     Gabler Wirtschafts-Lexikon, Bd. 1: A-K, 12. Auflage, Wies-
LEX 88]         baden, 1988.

[Gallager 86]    Gallager, R. G.: Information Theory and Reliable Communication; John Wiley & Sons, New York, 1986.

[Garella 89]     Garella, P.: Adverse Selection and the Middleman; Economica, Vol. 56, 1989, p. 395-400.

[Garman 76]      Garman, M. B.: Market Microstructure; Journal of Financial Economics, Vol. 3, 1976, p. 257-275.

[Gastwirth 76]   Gastwirth, J. L.: On Probabilistic Models of Consumer Search for Information; Quarterly Journal of Economics, Vol. 90, No. 1, 1976, p. 38-50.

[Gauch 89]       Gauch, S.; Smith, J. B.: An Expert System for Searching Full Text; Information Processing and Management, Vol. 25, No. 3, 1989, p. 253-263.

[Gebauer 96]     Gebauer, J.: Informationstechnische Unterstützung von Transaktionen; Deutscher Universitätsverlag, Wiesbaden, 1996.

[Gehrig 93]      Gehrig, T.: Intermediation in Search Markets; Journal of Economics and Management Strategy, Vol. 2, Spring 1993, p. 97-120.

[Gehrig 96]      Gehrig, T.: Natural Oligopoly and Customer Networks in Intermediated Markets; International Journal of Industrial Organisation, Vol. 14, 1996, p. 101-118.

[Gerke 95]       Gerke, W.; Pfeufer, G.: Finanzintermediation; In: Gerke, W. (ed.): Enzyklopädie der Betriebswirtschaftslehre, Bd. 6 Handwörterbuch des Bank- und Finanzwesens, 2. Auflage, 1995, p. 727-735.

[Gibbons 92]     Gibbons, R.: Game Thoeory for Applied Economists; Princeton University Press, Princeton, 1992.

[Gilboa 91]      Gilboa, I.; Lehrer, E.: The Value of Information - An Axiomatic Approach; Journal of Mathematical Economics, Vol. 20, 1991, p. 443-459.

[Glosten 85]     Glosten, L. R.; Milgrom, P. R.: Bid, Ask and Transaction Prices in a Specialist Market with Heterogeneously Informed Traders; Journal of Financial Economics, Vol. 14, 1985, p. 71-100.

[Goldberg 92]     Goldberg, D.; Nichols, D.; Oki, B. M.; Terry, D.: Using Collaborative Filtering to Weave an Information Tapestry; Communications of the ACM, December 1992, Vol. 35, No. 12, p. 61-70.

[Gosling 95]      Gosling, J.; McGilton, H.: The Java Language Environment - A Whitepaper; Sun Microsystems Computer Company, 1995, http://java.sun.com.

[Gould 80]        Gould, J. P.: The Economics of Markets: A Simple Model of the Market-making Process; Journal of Business, 1980, Vol. 53, No. 3, pt. 2, p. 167-187.

[Grauer 97]       Grauer, M.; Merten, U.: Multimedia: Entwurf, Entwicklung und Einsatz in betrieblichen Informationssystemen; Springer, Berlin, 1997.

[Gravelle 92]     Gravelle, H.; Rees, R.: Microeconomics; second edition, Longman, London, 1992.

[Griebel 82]      Griebel, H.-D.: Zur Theorie des Handelsbetriebes. Ein spieltheoretischer Beitrag zur Theorie des Binnenhandels; Dissertation, Universität Frankfurt a. M., 1982.

[Grossman 80]     Grossman, S.; Stiglitz, J.: On the Impossibility of Informationally Efficient Markets; The American Economic Review, Vol. 70, 1980, p. 393-408.

[Grudowski 97]    Grudowski, S.: Marketing für die Informationsvermittlung; In: [Buder 97], Bd. 2, p. 822-845.

[Guimaraes 95]    Guimaraes, P.: A Simple Model of Informative Advertising; Economic Working Papers Archive (EconWPA), Electronic Working Papers in Economics, ewp-io/9508003, 1995, http://wueconb.wustl.edu/eprints/io/papers/9508/9508003.abs.

[Gümbel 82]       Gümbel, R.: Die Produktionsfunktionen in der "Harris-Andler-Formel" zur Bestimmung der optimalen Bestellmenge; Zeitschrift für Betriebswirtschaftliche Forschung, Vol. 34, 1982, p. 258-274.

[Gümbel 85]       Gümbel, R.: Handel, Markt und Ökonomik; Wiesbaden, Gabler, 1985

[Guntram 85]      Guntram, U.: Die Allgemeine Systemtheorie; Zeitschrift für Betriebswirtschaft, Vol. 55, No. 3, 1985, p. 296-323.

[Gurley 60]       Gurley, J. G.; Shaw, E. S.: Money in a Theory of Finance; Baltimore, 1960.

[Gutenberg 83]    Gutenberg, E.: Grundlagen der Betriebswirtschaftslehre, Erster Band: Die Produktion; 24. unveränderte Auflage, Berlin, Heidelberg, New York, 1983.

[Hackett 92]      Hackett, S. C.: A Comparative Analysis of Merchant and Broker Intermediation; Journal of Economic Behavior and Organization, Vol. 18, 1992, p. 299-315.

[Haefner 92]    Haefner, K. (ed.): Evolution of Information Processing Systems: An Interdisciplinary Approach for a New Understanding of Nature and Society; Springer, Berlin, 1992.

[Haefner 92b]   Haefner, K.: Evolution of Information Processing - Basic Concept; In: [Haefner 92], p. 2-46.

[Hahn 89]       Hahn, F. H.: The Economics of Missing Markets, Information, and Games; Clarendon Press, Oxford, 1989.

[Haken 88]      Haken, H.: Information and Self-Organization: A Macroscopic Approach to Complex Systems; Springer, Berlin, 1988.

[Haken 92]      Haken, H.: The Concept of Information Seen from the Point of View of Physics and Synergetics; In: [Haefner 92], p. 153-168.

[Hänchen 85]    Hänchen, T., v. Ungern-Sternberg, T.: Information Costs, Intermediation and Equlibrium Price; Economica, Vol. 52, 1985, p. 407-419.

[Handschuh 97]  Handschuh, S.; Schmid, B. F.; Stanoevska-Slabeva, K.: The Concept of a Mediating Electronic Product Catalog; International Journal of Electronic Markets, University of St. Gallen, Switzerland, Vol. 7, No. 3, 1997, p. 32-35.

[Hansen 76]     Hansen, U.: Absatz- und Beschaffungsmarketing des Einzelhandels; Bd. 1 u. 2., Göttingen, 1976.

[Hansson 90]    Hansson, O.; Holt, G.; Mayer, A.: Toward the Modeling, Evaluation and Optimization of Search Algorithms; In: Brown, D. E.; White, C. (eds.): Operations Research and Artificial Intelligence: The Integration of Problem-Solving Strategies, 1990.

[Harrington 96] Harrington, L.; Reed, G.: Electronic Commerce (finally) comes of age; The McKinsey Quarterly, 1996, No. 2.

[Hartung 89]    Hartung, J., Elpert, B.; Klösener, K.-H.: Statistik: Lehr- und Handbuch der angewandten Statistik; Oldenbourg, München, 1989.

[Hayashi 92]    Hayashi, K.: From Network Externalities to Interconnection: The Changing Nature of Networks and Economy; In: Antonelli, C. (ed.): The Economics of Information Networks, Amsterdam, 1992, p. 195-215.

[Hayek 45]      Hayek, F. A.: The Use of Knowledge in Society; American Economic Review, Vol. 35, September 1945, p. 519-530.

[Heinrich 94]   Heinrich, L. J.: Systemplanung: Planung und Realisierung von Informatik-Projekten; Bd. 1, Oldenbourg, München, 1994.

[Hellwig 88]    Hellwig, M.: Banking, Financial Intermediation and Corporate Finance; In: Giovanni, A.; Mayer, C. et al. (eds.): European Financial Integration, Cambridge, 1991, p. 35-63.

[Hennes 95]     Hennes, W.: Informationsbeschaffung Online, Wettberwerbsvorteile durch weltweite Kommunikation; Campus, Frankfurt, 1995.

[Herczeg 94]    Herczeg, M.: Software-Ergonomie: Grundlagen der Mensch-Computer-Kommunikation; Addison-Wesley Publishing Company, Bonn, 1994.

[Herget 97]    Herget, J.: Informationsmanagement; In: [Buder 97], Bd. 2, p. 781-794.

[Heuser 88]    Heuser, H.: Lehrbuch der Analysis (Teil 2); Teubner, Stuttgart, 1988.

[Hey 79a]    Hey, J. D.: A Simple Generalized Stopping Rule; Economics Letters 2, 1979, p. 115-120.

[Hey 79b]    Hey, J. D.: A Note on Consumer Search and Consumer Surplus; Bulletin of Economic Research, Vol. 31, 1979, p. 61-66.

[Hey 79c]    Hey, J. D.: Uncertainty in Microeconomics; Martin Robertson Oxford, 1979.

[Hey 81a]    Hey, J. D.; McKenna, C. J.: Consumer Search with Uncertain Product Quality; Journal of Political Economy, Vol. 89, No. 1, 1981, p. 54-66.

[Hey 81b]    Hey, J. D.: Economics in Disequilibrium; Martin Robertson, Oxford, 1981.

[Hinterhuber 92]  Hinterhuber, H. H.: Strategische Unternehmensführung: I Strategisches Denken - Vision, Unternehmenspolitik, Strategie; Walter de Gruyter, Berlin, 1992.

[Hirschmann 97]  Hirschmann, P.; Scheer, A.-W.: Architecture of a Co-operation Exchange for the Continuous Design of Virtual Organizations; Proceedings of the 5th European Conference on Information Systems (ECIS '97), Volume 3, 1997, p. 1191-1198.

[Hirshleifer 73]  Hirshleifer, J.: Where are we in Theory of Information?; American Economic Review, Vol. 63, 1973, p. 31-39.

[Hirshleifer 71]  Hirshleifer, J.: The Private and Social Value of Information and the Returns to Inventive Activity; American Economic Review, September 1971, No. 61, p. 561-574.

[Ho 81]    Ho, T.; Stoll, H. R.: Optimal Dealer Pricing under Transactions and Return Uncertainty; Journal of Financial Economics, Vol. 9, 1981, p. 47-73.

[Hoch 97]    Hoch, D. J.: Wettbewerbsvorteile durch Information; In: Picot, A. (ed.): Information als Wettbewerbsfaktor, Kongress-Dokumentation: 50. Deutscher Betriebswirtschafter Tag 1996, Schäffer-Poeschel, Stuttgart, 1997, p. 9-35.

[Hoffman 96]    Hoffman, D.; Novak, T.; Chatterjee, P.: Commercial Scenarios for the Web: Opportunities and Challanges; JCMC, Vol. 1, No. 3, 1996, http://shum.cc.huji.ac.il/jcmc/vol1/issue3/hoffman.html.

[Holler 93]    Holler, M. J.; Illing, G.: Einführung in die Spieltheorie; 2. Auflage, Heidelberg, 1993.

| [Hopf 83] | Hopf, M.: Informationen für Märkte und Märkte für Informationen; Dissertation Universität Frankfurt, Fachbereich Wirtschaftswissenschaften, 1983, Reihe OKIOS, Band 14, Barudio und Hess Verlag, Frankfurt. |
|---|---|
| [Höring 80] | Höring, K.: Organisation der Informationsdienstleistungsbetriebe; In: Grochla, E. (ed.): Handwörterbuch der Organisation, 2. Auflage, Stuttgart, 1980, p. 914. |
| [Howe 97] | Howe, A. E.; Dreilinger, D.: SavvySearch: A Meta-Search Engine that Learns which Search Engines to Query; Workingpaper, MIT Media Laboratory, January 1997, http://daniel.www.media.mit.edu/people/daniel/papers/ss-aimag.ps.gz. |
| [Hübl 92] | Hüble, L.: Wirtschaftskreislauf und gesamtwirtschaftliches Rechnungswesen; In: Bender, D. et al. (eds.): Vahlens Kompendium der Wirtschaftstheorie und Wirtschaftspolitik, Band 1, 5. Auflage, München, 1992, p. 49-85. |
| [Hünerberg 96] | Hünerberg, R.; Heise, G.; Mann, A.: Handbuch Online-M@rketing: Wettbewerbsvorteile durch weltweite Datennetze; Verlag Moderne Industrie, Landsberg/Lech, 1996. |
| [Hüttner 94] | Hüttner, M.; Pingel, A.; Schwarting, U.: Marketing-Management: Allgemein - Sektoral - International; Oldenbourg, München, 1994. |
| [Illing 97] | Illing, G.: Theorie der Geldpolitik: Eine spieltheoretische Einführung; Springer, Berlin, 1997. |
| [Internet 97] | The Internet Domain Survey: Host Count History 1981-1997; http://www.nw.com/zone/host-count-history. |
| [Internet 98] | NUA Internt - How Many Online, January 1998; http://www.nua.ie/surveys/how_many_online/index.html. |
| [Introna 97] | Introna, L. D.; Tiow, B. L.: Thinking about Virtual Organizations and the Future; Proceedings of the 5th European Conference on Information Systems (ECIS '97), Volume 2, 1997, p. 995-1009. |
| [Ioannides 75] | Ioannides, Y. M.: Market allocation through search: Equilibrium adjustment and price dispersion; Journal of Economic Theory, Vol. 11, 1975, p. 247-262. |
| [ITU 95] | World Telecommunication Development Report 1995, published by the International Telecommunication Union (ITU), 1995, http://www.itu.int/ti/wtdr95/index.html. |
| [ITU 96] | The 1996/97 World Telecommunication Development Report, published by the International Telecommunication Union (ITU, http://www.itu.int), February 1997, (Executive Summary, p. 3). |

226    7 References

[Janko 85]      Janko, W. H.; Taudes, A.; Frisch, W.: Simultane Alternativen-
                suche und Datenpräzisierung; Diskussionspapier zum Tätigkeits-
                feld Informationsverarbeitung und Informationswirtschaft, Nr.
                13, Wirtschaftsuniversität Wien, 1985.

[Janson 95]     Janson, P.; Waidner, M.: Electronic Payment Systems; Final
                SEMPER Activity Paper 211ZR016, December 1995 (IEEE
                COMPUTER, September 1997),
                http://www.semper.org/info/211ZR019.ps.gz.

[Jensen 76]     Jensen, M.; Meckling, W.: Theory of the Firm: Managerial
                Behavior, Agency Costs, and Capital Structure; Journal of
                Financial Economics, Vol. 1/2, 1976, p. 305-360.

[Jeusfeld 97]   Jeusfeld, M. A.; Jarke, M.: Suchhilfen für das World Wide Web:
                Funktionsweisen und Metadatenstrukturen; Wirtschaftsinfor-
                matik, Vol. 39, No. 5, 1997, p. 491-499.

[Jevons 1871]   Jevons, W. S.: The Theory of Political Economy; London, 1871.

[Jiang 96]      Jiang, J. J.; Conrath, D. W.: A Concept-Based Approach to Re-
                trieval from an Electronic Industrial Directoy; International Jour-
                nal of Electronic Commerce, Vol. 1, No. 1, Fall 1996, p. 51-72.

[Joachims 96]   Joachims, T.; Freitag, D.; Mitchell, T.: WebWatcher: A Tour
                Guide for the World Wide Web; Working Paper, School of
                Computer Science, Carnegie Mellon University, 1996,
                http://www.cs.cmu.edu/afs/cs.cmu.edu/project/theo-6/web-agent/
                www/techrep.ps.Z.

[Johnson 85]    Johnson, E. J.; Payne, J.: Effort and Accuracy in Choice; Mana-
                gement Science, Vol. 31, No. 4, April 1985, p. 395-414.

[Judd 94]       Judd, K. L.; Riordan, M. H.: Price and Quality in a new Product
                Monopoly; Review of Economic Studies, Vol. 61, 1994, p. 773-
                789.

[Jürgensen 97]  Jürgensen, H.; Konstantinides, S.: Codes; In: Rozenberg, G.;
                Salomaa, A. (eds.): Handbook of Formal Languages, Vol. 1:
                Word, Language, Grammar, Springer, Berlin, 1997, p. 511-607.

[Kaas 90]       Kaas, K.-P., Marketing als Bewältigung von Informations- und
                Unsicherheitsproblemen; Die Betriebswirtschaft, No. 4, 1990, p.
                539-548.

[Kalakota 96]   Kalakota, R.; Whinston, A.: Frontiers of Electronic Commerce;
                Addison Wesley, Reading (MA), 1996.

[Kamien 70]     Kamien, M. I.; Schwartz, N. L.: Market Structure, Elasticity of
                Demand and Incentive to Invent; Journal of Law and Economics,
                Vol. 13, 1970, p. 241-251.

[Kamien 86]     Kamien, M. I.; Tauman, Y.: Fees vs. Royalties and the Private
                Value of a Patent; Quarterly Journal of Economics, Vol. 101,
                1986, p. 471-491.

| | |
|---|---|
| [Kaminsky 77] | Kaminsky, R.: Information und Informationsverarbeitung als ökonomisches Problem; München, Verlag Dokumentation, 1977. |
| [Kaminsky 81] | Kaminsky, R.: Portrait: Der Informations-Broker; Marketing-Journal, 14. Jg., 1981, Heft 1, p. 74-75. |
| [Kaminsky 83] | Kaminsky, R.: Erfahrungen eines privaten Informationsbrokers; Nachrichten für Dokumentation, Heft 4/5, 1983, p. 196. |
| [Kaminsky 89] | Kaminsky, R.: Förderung moderner Informationsvermittlung (Promoting Modern Information Brokerage); Nachrichten für Dokumentation, Vol. 40, No. 2, 1989, p. 83-86. |
| [Kampis 92] | Kampis, G.: Information: Course and Recourse; In: [Haefner 92], p. 49-62. |
| [Katz 85] | Katz, M. L.; Shapiro, C.: Network Externalities, Competition, and Compatibility; The American Economic Review, Vol. 75, p. 424-440. |
| [Kelms 94] | Klems, M.: Informationsbroking: Mit einem Informationsbroker durch die Netze und Online-Datenbanken der Welt; International Thomson Publishing, Bonn, 1994. |
| [Kiener 90] | Kiener, S.: Die Principal-Agent-Theorie aus informationsökonomischer Sicht; Physica-Verlag, Heidelberg, 1990. |
| [Kihlstrom 74a] | Kihlstrom, R.: A General Theory of Demand for Information about Product Quality; Journal of Economic Theory, 8, 1974, p. 413-439. |
| [Kihlstrom 74b] | Kihlstrom, R.: A Bayesian Model of Demand for Information about Product Quality; International Economic Review, Vol. 15, No. 1, 1974, p. 99-118. |
| [Kilander 96] | Kilander, F.: A Brief Comparison of News Filtering Software; Internet Draft, 1996, http://www.dsv.su.se/~fk/if_Dok/Comparison.ps.Z. |
| [Knoblich 85] | Knoblich, H.; Beßler, H.: Informationsbetriebe; Die Betriebswirtschaft, Vol. 45, No. 5, 1985, p. 558-575. |
| [Knorz 97] | Knorz, G.: Indexieren, Klassieren, Extrahieren; In: [Buder 97], Bd. 1, p. 120-140. |
| [Kohn 74] | Kohn, M. J.; Shavell, S.: The Theory of Search; Journal of Economic Theory, 9, 1974, p. 93-123. |
| [Kolodner 86] | Kolodner, J. L.; Riesbeck, C. K.: Experience, Memory, and Reasoning; Lawrence Erlbaum Associates, Publishers, Hillsdale and London, 1986. |
| [Konstan 97] | Konstan, J. A.; Miller, B. N.; Maltz, D.; Herlocker, J. L.; Gordon, L. R.; Riedl, J.: GroupLens: Applying Collaborative Filtering to Usenet News; Communications of the ACM, Vol. 40, No. 3, March 1997, p. 77-87. |

[Koster 96]      Koster, M.: World Wide Web Robots, Wanderers, and Spiders; 1996, http://info.webcrawler.com/mak/projects/robots/robots.html.

[Kotler 67]      Kotler, P.: Marketing - Management; Stuttgart, 1977 (german translation of the 1st edition from 1967).

[Kotler 88]      Kotler, P.: Marketing Management: Analysis, Planning, Implementation and Control; 2nd Edition, Englewood Cliff, New Jersey, 1988.

[Kratzer 97]     Kratzer, K.: Transaktion; In: Mertens, P. et al. (eds.): Lexikon der Wirtschaftsinformatik, Springer, Berlin, 1997, p. 412-413.

[Kreibich 86]    Kreibich, R.: Die Wissenschaftsgesellschaft; Frankfurt, 1986.

[Kreps 82]       Kreps, D.; Wilson, R.: Reputation and Imperfect Information; Journal of Economic Theory, 27, 1982, p. 253-279.

[Kreps 83]       Kreps, D. M.; Schcinkman J.: Quantity pre-commitment and Bertrand competition yield Cournot outcomes; Bell Journal of Economics, Vol. 14, 1983, p. 326-337.

[Kreps 90]       Kreps, D. M.: Game Theory and Economic Modelling; Clarendon Press, Oxford, 1990.

[Kreutzer 91]    Kreutzer, W.; McKenzie, B.: Programming for Artificial Intelligence: Methods, Tools, and Applications; Addison-Wesley Publishing Company, Sydney, 1991.

[Kuhlen 94]      Kuhlen, R.: Elektronische nicht-lineare Dossiers in offenen Hypertextsystemen; In: Rauch, W.; Strohmeier, F.; Hiller, H.; Schlögl, C. (eds.): Proceedings des 4. Internationalen Symposiums für Informationswissenschaft (ISI '94), Schriften zur Informationswissenschaft, Universitätsverlag Konstanz, Konstanz, 1994, p. 303-310.

[Kuhlen 95]      Kuhlen, R.: Informationsmärkte: Chancen und Risiken der Kommerzialisierung von Wissen; Universitätsverlag Konstanz, Konstanz, 1995.

[Kuhlen 97]      Kuhlen, R.: Abstracts - Abstracting - Intellektuelle und maschinelle Verfahren; In [Buder 97], Bd. 1, p. 88-119.

[Lambert 82]     Lambert, D. M.; Stock, J. R.: Strategic Physical Distribution Management; Homewood, Illinois, 1982.

[Langhein 85]    Langhein, J.: Modellvorstellungen zur Informationsvermittlung und Informationsökonomie (Some ideas on Patterns in Information Intermediary and Information Economy); Nachrichten für Dokumentation, Vol. 36, No. 6, 1985, p. 234-242.

[Laux 87]        Laux, H.; Liermann, F.: Grundlagen der Organisation: Die Steuerung von Entscheidungen als Grundproblem der Betriebswirtschaftslehre; Springer, Berlin, 1987.

[Laux 90]        Laux, H.: Risiko, Anreiz und Kontrolle; Springer, Berlin, 1990.

| [Laux 91] | Laux, H.: Entscheidungstheorie I; 2. Auflage, Springer, Berlin, 1991. |
|---|---|
| [Lazlo 92] | Lazlo, E.: Aspects of Information; In: [Haefner 92a], p. 63-71. |
| [Lee 96] | Lee, H. G.; Clark, T. H.: Impacts of the Electronic Marketplace on Transaction Costs and Market Structure; International Journal of Electronic Commerce, Vol. 1, No. 1, Fall 1996, p. 127-149. |
| [Leiner 97] | Leiner, B. M.; Cerf, V. G.; Clark, D. D.; Kahn, R. E.; Kleinrock, L.; Lynch, D. C.; Postel, J.; Roberts, L. G.; Wolff, S.: A Brief History of the Internet, version 3.1; 20 February, 1997, http://www.isoc.org/internet-history. |
| [Leland 77] | Leland, H.; Pyle, D.: Informational Asymmetries, Financial Structure, and Financial Intermediaries; Journal of Finance, 32, 1977, p. 371-425. |
| [Leland 79] | Leland, H.: Quacks, Lemons, and Licensing: A Theory of Minimum Quality Standards; Journal of Political Economy, Vol. 87, 1979, p. 1328-1346. |
| [Levine 95] | Levine, M. M.: A Brief History of Information Brokering; Bulletin of the American Society for Information Science, Feb./Mar. 1995, Vol. 21, No. 3, http://www.asis.org/Bulletin/Feb-95/levine.html. |
| [Lieberman 95] | Lieberman, H.: Letizia: An Agent That Assists Web Browsing; Proceedings of the 14th International Joint Conference on Artificial Intelligence (IJCAI'95), Montreal, Canada, 1995, http://lieber.www.media.mit.edu/people/lieber/Lieberary/Letizia/Letizia.htm. |
| [Lindquist 78] | Lindquist, M. G.: Growth Dynamics of Information Search Services; Journal of the American Society for Information Science, March 1978, p. 67-76. |
| [Lippman 76a] | Lippman, S. A.; McCall, J. J.: The Economics of Job Search: A Survey, Part I: Optimal Job Search Policies; Economic Inquiry, Vol. 14, No. 2, 1976, p. 347-368. |
| [Lippman 76b] | Lippman, S. A.; McCall, J. J.: The Economics of Job Search: A Survey, Part II: Empirical and Policy Implications of Job Search; Economic Inquiry, Vol. 14, No. 3, 1976, p. 155-189. |
| [Lippmann 79] | Lippmann, S.; McCall, J. J.: The Economics Uncertainty: Selected Topics and Probabilistic Methods; Working Paper No. 281, Western Management Science Institute, University of California, Los Angeles, 1979. |
| [Lizzeri 96] | Lizzeri, A.: Information Revelation and Certification Intermediaries; Northwestern University, Center for Mathematical Studies in Economics and Management Science, Discussion Paper No. 1094, May 1996. |

[Loeb 92]          Loeb, S.: Architecting Personalized Delivery of Multimedia Information; In: Communications of the ACM, Vol. 35, No. 12, 1992, p. 39 - 48.

[Luger 89]         Luger, G. F.; Stubblefield, W. F.: Artificial Intelligence and the Design of Expert Systems; The Benjamin/Cumming Publishing Company, Redwood City, 1989.

[Lunin 76]         Lunin, L. F.: 'Information Broker: Who, What, Why, How'; Bulletin of the American Society for Information Science, Feb. 1976.

[Lynch 96]         Lynch, D.; Lundquist, L.: Digital Money - The New Era of Internet Commerce; John Wiley & Sons, New York, 1996.

[Lynch 97]         Lynch, C.: Weltbibliothek Internet?; Spektrum der Wissenschaft, Mai 1997, p. 90-94.

[Lyons 83]         Lyons, J.: Die Sprache; Verlag C. H. Beck, München, 1983.

[Maas 80]          Maas, R.-M.: Absatzwege - Konzeptionen und Modelle, Neue betriebswirtschaftliche Forschung; Gabler, Wiesbaden, 1980.

[Mac Randal 88] Mac Randal, D.: Semantic Networks, In: Ringland, G. A.; Duce, D. A.: Approaches to Knowledge Representation: An Introduction; John Wiley & Sons, New York, 1988, p. 45-79.

[Macdonald 92] Macdonald, S.: Information Networks and the Exchange of Information; In: Antonelli, C. (ed.): The Economics of Information Networks, Amsterdam, 1992, p. 51-69.

[Macho-Stadler  Macho-Stadler, I.; Pérez-Castrillo, J. D.: An Introduction to the
97]                Economics of Information: Incentives and Contracts; Oxford University Press, Oxford, 1997.

[MacMinn 80]       MacMinn, R. D.: Search and Market Equilibrium; Journal of Political Economy, Vol. 88, No. 2, 1980, p. 308-327.

[MacNeil 78]       MacNeil, I. R.: Contracts: Adjustment of Long-Term Economic Relations under Classical, Neoclassical, and Relational Contract Law; Northwestern University Law Review, Vol. 72, 1978, p. 854-905.

[MacQueen 64]      MacQueen, J. B.: Optimal Policies for a Class of Search and Evaluation Problems; Management Science, Vol. 10, No. 4 (July), 1964, p. 746-759.

[Maes 94]          Maes, P.: Agents That Reduce Work And Information Overload; Communications of the ACM, Vol. 37, No. 7, 1994, p. 31-40.

[Malone 87a]       Malone, T. W.; Yates, J.; Benjamin, R. I.: Electronic Markets and Electronic Hierarchies; Communications of the ACM, Vol. 30, No. 6, 1987, p. 484-497.

[Malone 87b]       Malone, T. W.; Grant, K. R.; Turbak, F. A.; Brobst, S. A.; Cohen, M. D.: Intelligent Information Sharing Systems; Communications of the ACM, May 1987, Vol. 30, No. 5, p. 390-402.

[Malone 87c]   Malone, T. W.; Yates, J.; Benjamin, R. I.: The Logic of Electronic Markets; Harvard Business Review, May-June 1989, p. 166-170.

[Malone 94]   Malone, T. W.; Crowston, K.: The Interdisciplinary Study of Coordination; ACM Computer Surveys, Vol. 26, 1994, p. 87-119.

[Maltz 95]   Maltz, D.; Ehrlich, K.: Pointing the Way: Active Collaborative Filtering; In: Proceedings of the 1995 ACM Conference on Human Factors in Computing Systems, ACM, New York, 1995, p. 202-209.

[Manecke 97a]   Manecke, H.-J.: Klassifikation; In: [Buder 97], Bd. 1, p. 141-159.

[Manecke 97b]   Manecke, H.-J.; Seeger, T.: Zur Entwicklung der Information und Dokumentation in Deutschland; In: [Buder 97] Bd. 1, p. 16-60.

[Markus 87]   Markus, M. L.: Toward a 'Critical Mass' Theory of Interactive Media: Universal Access, Interdependence and Diffusion; Communication Research, Vol. 14, No. 5, October 1987, p. 491-511.

[Markus 92]   Markus, M. L.: Critical Mass Contingencies for Telecommunications Consumers; The Economics of Information Networks, 1992, p. 431-450.

[Marschak 66]   Marschak, T. A.; Yahav, J. A.: The Sequential Selection of Approaches to a Task; Management Science, Vol. 12, No. 9, May 1966, p. 627-647.

[Marschak 75]   Marschak, J.: Ökonomische Probleme der Informationsgewinnung und -verwertung; In: Beckmann, M.; Sato, R. (eds.): Mathematische Wirtschaftstheorie, Kiepenheuer & Witsch, Köln, 1975, p. 119-152.

[Martin 89]   Martin, J.: Local Area Networks: Archiectures and Implementations; Prentice Hall, Englewood Cliffs, New Jersey, 1989.

[Marvel 84]   Marvel, H.; McCafferty, S: Resale Price Maintenance and Quality Certification; RAND Journal of Economics, Vol. 15, p. 346-359.

[McAfee 87]   McAfee, R. P.; McMillan, J.: Auctions and Bidding; Journal of Economic Literature, Vol. XXV (June), 1987, p. 699-738.

[McAfee 88]   McAfee, R. P.: Search Mechanisms; Journal of Economic Theory, Vol. 44, 1988, p. 99-123.

[McCall 65]   McCall, J. J.: The Economics of Information and Optimal Stopping Rules; Journal of Business, Vol. 38, July 1965, p. 300-317.

[McCall 70]   McCall, J. J.: Economics of Information and Job Search; Quarterly Journal of Economics, No. 84, Feb. 1970, p. 113-126.

[McKelvey 90]   McKelvey, R. D.; Page, T.: Public and Private Infromation: An Experimental Study of Information Pooling; Econometrica, Vol. 58, No. 6, November 1990, p. 1321-1339.

[Menger 68]    Menger, C.: Grundsätze der Volkswirtschaftslehre, (Original 1871), Reproduction in: Hayek, F. A. V. (ed.): Carl Menger, gesammelte Werke, Bd. I: Grundsätze der Volkswirtschaftslehre, 2. Auflage, 1968.

[Mertens 91]    Mertens, P.: Integrierte Informationsverarbeitung 1, Administrations- und Dispositionssysteme in der Industrie, 8. Auflage, Gabler, Wiesbaden, 1991.

[Merz 96]    Merz, M.: Elektronische Märkte im Internet; International Thomson Publishing GmbH, Bonn, 1996.

[Meyer 63]    Meyer, C. W.: Der Zusammenhang von Funktionen und Betriebsformen des Warenhandels und seine Bedeutung für die Handelsbetriebsführung; Der Österreichische Betriebswirt, Heft 3, 1963.

[Meyer 90]    Meyer, P. W.: Integrierte Marketingfunktionen; Stuttgart, 1990.

[Miles 86]    Miles, R. E.; Snow, C. C.: Organizations: New Concepts for New Forms; California Management Review, Vol. XXVIII, No. 3, Spring 1986, p. 62-73.

[Milgrom 82]    Milgrom, P.; Weber, R. J.: The Value of Information in a Sealed-Bid Auction; Journal of Mathematical Economics, 10, 1982, p. 105-114.

[Mitchell 94]    Mitchell, T.; Caruana, R.; Freitag, D.; McDermott, J.; Zabowski, D.: Experience with a Learning Personal Assistant; Communications of the ACM, Vol. 37, No. 7, 1994, p. 81-91.

[Morgan 83]    Morgan, P. B.: Search and Optimal Sample Sizes; Review of Economic Studies, 1983 L, p. 659-675.

[Mowbray 95]    Mowbray, T. J.; Zahavi, R.: The Essential CORBA: Systems Integration using Distributed Objects; John Wiley & Sons, New York, 1995.

[Müller 87]    Müller, W.: Zur informationstheoretischen Erweiterung der Betriebswirtschaftslehre - Ein Modell der Informationsproduktion; In: Adam, D. (ed.): Neuere Entwicklungen in der Produktions- und Investitionspolitik, Gabler, Wiesbaden, 1987, p. 119-136.

[Musgrave 73]    Musgrave, R. A.; Musgrave, P. B.: Public Finance in Theory and Practice; McGraw-Hill Book Company, New York, 1973.

[Myerson 83]    Myerson, R. B.; Satterthwaite, M. A.: Efficient Mechanisms for Bilateral Trading; Journal of Economic Theory, Vol. 29, 1983, p. 265-281.

[Myerson 91]    Myerson, R. B.: Game Theory - Analysis of Conflict; Harvard University Press, Cambridge, 1991.

[Nagel 63]    Nagel, E.: Assumptions in Economic Theory; American Economic Review Proceedings, Vol. 53, May 1963, p. 211-219.

| | |
|---|---|
| [Nehl 97] | Nehl, R.: Vertrauen durch Trust Center; Datenschutz und Datensicherheit, Vol. 21, No. 2, 1997. |
| [Nelson 70] | Nelson, P.: Information and Consumer Behavior; Journal of Political Economy, 78, 1970, p. 311-329. |
| [Nieschlag 91] | Nieschlag, R.; Dichtl, E.; Hörschgen, H.: Marketing; Berlin, 1991. |
| [Nink 91] | Nink, H.: Informationsvermittlung: Aufgaben, Möglicheiten und Probleme; Deutscher Universitäts Verlag, Wiesbaden, 1991. |
| [Nissen 96] | Nissen. M. E.: Knowledge-Based Reengineering: From Mysterious Art to Learnable Craft; CITM 96-WP-1012, Fisher Center for Information Technology and Management, University of California, Berkeley, Feb. 1996. |
| [Nouwens 96] | Nouwens, J.; Bouwman, H.: Living Apart Together in Electronic Commerce: The Use of Information and Communication Technology to Create Network Organizations; JCMC, Vol. 1, Issue 3, 1996, http://shum.huji.ac.il/jcmc/vol1/issue3/nouwens.html. |
| [Novshek 80] | Novshek, W.: Equilibrium in simple spatial (or differentiated product) models; Journal of Economic Theory, Vol. 22, 1980, p. 313-326. |
| [Oberparleitner 18] | Oberparleitner, K.: Die Funktionen des Handels; Wien, 1918. |
| [Oberparleitner 30] | Oberparleitner, K.: Funktionen und Risikenlehre des Warenhandels; 1. Auflage, Wien und Berlin, 1930. |
| [Oeser 92] | Oeser, E.: From Neural Information Processing to Knowledge Technology; In: [Haefner 92], p. 320-340. |
| [O'Leary 87] | O'Leary, M.: The Information Broker: A Modern Profile; Online, November 1987, p. 24-30. |
| [Ordelheide 93] | Ordelheide, D.: Institutionelle Theorie und Unternehmung; In: Wittmann, W. et al. (eds.): Handwörterbuch der Betriebswirtschaft, 5. Auflage, Stuttgart, 1993, p. 1838-1855. |
| [Österle 95] | Österle, H.: Business in the Information Age: Heading for New Processes; Springer, Berlin, 1995. |
| [Panurach 96] | Panurach, P.: Money in Electronic Commerce: Digital Cash, Electronic Funds Transfer, and Ecash; Communications of the ACM, Vol. 39, No. 6, 1996, p. 45-50. |
| [Patterson 96] | Patterson, D. A.; Hennessey, J. L.: Computer Arcitecture - A Quantitative Approach; second edition, Morgan Kaufmann Publishers, San Francisco, 1996. |
| [Peat 97] | Peat, B.; Webber, D.: Introducing XML/EDI...; The XML/EDI Group, August 1997, http://www.xmledi.net, http://www.geocities.com/WallStreet/Floor/5815/start.htm. |

[Peck 90]      Peck, J.: Liquidity without money: A General Equilibrium Model of Market Microstructure; Journal of Financial Intermediation, 1, 1990, p. 80-103.

[Peterson 97]  Peterson, R. E.: Eight Internet Search Engines Compared; First-monday, Peer-reviewed Journal on the Internet (http://www.firstmonday.dk), Issue 2_2, 1997, http://www.firstmonday.dk/issues/issue2_2/peterson.html.

[Pfister 98]   Pfister, D.: Imitationsverhalten und Preisentwicklung von Wertpapieren; Peter Lang, Frankfurt, 1998.

[Picot 82]     Picot, A.: Transaktionskostenansatz in der Organisationstheorie: Stand der Diskussion und Aussagewert; Die Betriebswirtschaft, 1982, p. 267-284.

[Picot 86]     Picot, A.: Transaktionskosten im Handel; Betriebs-Berater, Beilage 13 zu Heft 27, 1986, p. 1-6.

[Picot 90a]    Picot, A.; Dietl, H.: Transaktionskostentheorie; Das Wirtschaftsstudium, 19. Jg.p. 178-184.

[Picot 94a]    Picot, A.; Reichwald, R.: Auflösung der Unternehmung? Vom Einfluß der IuK-Technik auf Organisationsstrukturen und Kooperationsformen; Zeitschrift für Betriebswirtschaft, Vol. 64, No. 5, 1994, p. 547-570.

[Picot 94b]    Picot, A.; Maier, M.: Ansätze der Informationsmodellierung und ihre betriebswirtschaftliche Bedeutung; Zeitschrift für betriebswirtschaftliche Forschung, Vol. 46, No. 2, 1994, p. 107-125.

[Picot 96]     Picot, A.; Reichwald, R.; Wigand, R. T.: Die grenzenlose Unternehmung: Information, Orgaisation und Management; 2. Auflage, Gabler, Wiesbaden, 1996.

[Picot96b]     Picot, A.; Ripperger, T.; Wolff, B.: The Fading Boundaries of the Firm; Journal of Institutional and Theoretical Economics (JITE), 1996, p. 65-72

[Porter 92]    Porter, M. E.: Wettbewerbsstrategie (Competitive Strategy); 7. Auflage, Campus, Frankfurt, 1992.

[Prahalad 90]  Prahalad, C. K.; Hamel, G.: The Core Competence of the Corporation; Harvard Business Review, May-June 1990, p. 79-91.

[Pratt 85]     Pratt, J. W.; Zeckhauser, R. J. (eds.): Principals and Agents: The Structure of Business; Harvard Business School Press, Boston, Massachusetts, 1985.

[Radicati 94]  Radicati, S.: X.500 Directory Services: Technology and Development; International Thomson Computer Press, London, 1994.

[Ramser 79]    Ramser, H. J.: Eigenerstellung oder Fremdbezug von Leistungen; In: Kern, W. (ed.): Handbuch der Produktionswirtschaft, C. E. Poeshel, Stuttgart, 1979, p. 435-450.

[Rasmusen 89]    Rasmusen, E.: Games and Information: An Introduction to Game Theory; Basil Blackwell, Cambridge, 1989.

[Ravindran 94]    Ravindran, S.; Barua, A.; Lee, B, Whinston, A. B.: Strategies for Smart Shopping in Cyberspace; 5th Conference on Organizational Computing, Coordination and Collaboration: Making Money on the Internet, May 1994,
http://cism.bus.utexas.edu/suri/shopper1.html.

[Rayport 96]    Rayport, J. F., Sviolka, J. J.: Die virtuelle Wertschöpfungskette - kein fauler Zauber; Harvard Business Manager, 2/1996, p. 104-113.

[Reagle 97]    Reagle, J. M.: Trust in Electronic Markets: The Convergence of Cryptographers and Economists; Firstmonday, Peer-reviewed Journal on the Internet (http://www.firstmonday.dk), issue 2, 1997,
http://www.firstmonday.dk/issues/issue2/markets/index.html.

[Rebel 97]    Rebel, T.; König, W.: Ensuring Security and Trust in Electronic Commerce: The Example of the German Digital Sigature Act; Proceedings of the International Conference of Electronic Commerce (ICEC) '98, Seoul, Korea, April 1998, p. 326-332

[Reese Hedberg 95]    Reese Hedberg, S.: Intelligent Agent: The First Harvest of Softbots Looks Promising; IEEE Expert, August 1995, p. 6-9.

[Rehäuser 96]    Rehäuser, J.; Krcmar, H.: Wissensmanagement im Unternehmen; In: Schreyögg, G.; Conrad, P. (ed.): Wissensmanagement, Walter de Gruyter, Berlin, 1996, p. 1-40.

[Reichgelt 91]    Reichgelt, H.: Knowledge Representation: An AI Perspective; Ablex Publishing Corporation, Norwood, 1991.

[Reichwald 87]    Reichwald, R.: Ein mehrstufger Bewertungsansatz zur Wirtschaftlichkeitsbeurteilung der Bürokommunikation; In: Hoyer, R.; Kölzer, G. (ed.), Wirtschaftlichkeitsrechnungen im Bürobereich. Konzepte u. Erfahrungen, Erich Schmidt Verlag, Berlin, 1987, p. 23-33.

[Reif 85]    Reif, F.: Fundamentals of Statistical and Thermal Physics; McGraw-Hill International Editions, Auckland, 1985.

[Reimer 97]    Reimer, U.: Neue Formen der Wissensrepräsentation; In: [Buder 97], Bd. 1, p. 180-207.

[Resnick 94]    Resnick, P.; Iacovou, N.; Suchak, M.; Bergstrom, P.; Riedl, J.: GroupLens: An Open Architecture for Collaborative Filtering of Netnews; Proceedings of ACM 1994 Conference on CSCW, Chapel Hill, NC, 1994, p. 175-186,
http://ccs.mit.edu/CCSWP165.html.

[Resnick 95]      Resnick, P.; Zeckhauser, R.; Avery, C.: 'Roles for Electronic Brokers'; In: Toward a Competitive Telecommunication Industry: Selected Papers from the 1994 Telecom. Policy Research Conf., G. W. Brock, Ed. Mahwah, NJ: Lawrence Erlbaum Ass., 1995, p. 289-304.

[Resnick 97]      Resnick, P.; Varian, H. R.: Recommender Systems; Communications of the ACM, Vol. 40. No. 3, March 1997, p. 56-58.

[Rhodes 96]       Rhodes, B. J.; Starner, T.: Remembrance Agent: A continuously running automated information retrieval system; Proceedings of the 1st International Conference on The Practical Application of Intelligent Agents and Multi Agent Technology (PAAM 96), 1996, p. 487-495.

[Ricardo 1817]    Ricardo, D.: Principles of Economy and Taxation; London 1817, according to: Waenting, H. (ed.): Sammlung sozialwissenschaftlicher Meister, Vol. 5, David Ricardo: Grundsätze der Volkswirtschaft und Besteuerung, 3. Aufl. von 1821, Jena, 1921, p. 119-144.

[Rich 83]         Rich, E.: Artificial Intelligence; McGraw-Hill, Singapore, 1983.

[Robertson 77]    Robertson, S. E.: The probability ranking principle in IR; Journal of Documentation, Vol. 33, No. 4, December 1977, p. 294-304.

[Rosenfield 83]   Rosenfield, D. B.; Shapiro, R. D.; Butler, D. A.: Optimal Strategies for Selling an Asset; Management Science, Vol. 29, No. 9, September 1983, p. 1051-1061.

[Ross 73]         Ross, S.: The Economic Theory of Agency: The Principal's Problem; American Economic Review, Vol. 63, No. 2, p. 134-139.

[Rothschild 73]   Rothschild, M.: Models of Market Organization with Imperfect Information: A Survey; Journal of Political Economy, Vol. 81, 1973, p. 1283-1308.

[Rothschild 74]   Rotschild, M.: Searching or the Lowest Price When the Distribution of Prices is Unknown; Journal of Political Economy, Vol. 82, 1974, p. 689-711.

[Rowley 92]       Rowley, J. E.: Organizing Knowledge; 2nd edition, Ashgate, Aldershot, 1992.

[Roy 94]          Roy, J. R.: Trade with and without Intermediaries; The Annals of Regional Science, 28, 1994, p. 329-343.

[Rubinstein 85]   Rubinstein, A.; Wolinsky, A.: Equilibrium in a Market with Sequential Bargaining; Econometrica, Vol. 53, No. 5, September 1985, p. 1133-1150.

[Rubinstein 87]   Rubinstein, A; Wolinsky, A.: Middlemen; Quarterly Journal of Economics, 1987, p. 581-593.

[Sabourian 89]    Sabourian, H.: Repeated Games: A Survey; In: [Hahn 89], p. 62-105.

| [Saliger 93] | Saliger, E.: Betriebswirtschaftliche Entscheidungstheorie: Einführung in die Logik individueller und kollektiver Entscheidungen; Oldenbourg, München, 1993. |
| [Salop 73] | Salop, S. C.: Systematic Job Search and Unemployment; Review of Economic Studies, No. 40, Apr. 1973, p. 192-201. |
| [Salop 77] | Salop, S.; Stiglitz, J.: Bargains and Ripoffs: A Model of Monopolistically Competitive Price Dispersion; The Review of Economic Studies, Vol. 44, 1977, p. 493-510. |
| [Salop 79] | Salop, S. C.: Monopolistic Competition with Outside Goods; Bell Journal of Economics, Vol. 19, 1979, p. 141-156. |
| [Salton 83] | Salton, G.; McGill, M. J.: Introduction to Modern Information Retrieval; McGraw-Hill, New York, 1983. |
| [Sarkar 96] | Sarkar, M.; Butler, B.; Steinfeld, C.: Intermediaries and Cybermediaries: A Continuing Role for Mediating Players in the Electronic Marketplace; JCMC, Vol. 1, No. 3, 1996, http://shum.cc.huji.ac.il/jcmc/vol1/issue3/sarkar.html. |
| [Sass 84] | Sass, T. R.: The Economics of Information Intermediaries; Dissertation, University of Washington, Seattle, Washington, 1984. |
| [Schäfer 43] | Schäfer, E.: Die Aufgabe der Absatzwirtschaft; 1. Auflage, Leipzig, 1943. |
| [Scheck 90] | Scheck, F.: Mechanik: Von den Newtonschen Gesetzen zum deterministischen Chaos; Springer, Berlin, 1990. |
| [Scheer 95] | Scheer, A.-W.: Wirtschaftsinformatik: Referenzmodelle für industrielle Geschäftsprozesse; 6. Auflage, Springer, Berlin, 1995. |
| [Schmid 93] | Schmid, B.: Elektronische Märkte; Wirtschaftsinformatik, Nr. 5, 1993, p. 465-480. |
| [Schmid 97] | Schmid, B. F.: Requirements for Electronic Markets Architecture; International Journal of Electronic Markets, University of St. Gallen, Switzerland, Vol. 7, No. 1, 1997, p. 3-6. |
| [Schmidt 92] | Schmidt, R.: Modelle der Informationsvermittlung. Analyse und Bewertung eines experimentellen Programms; Physica-Verlag, Heidelberg, 1992. |
| [Schmidt 93] | Schmidt, I.: Wettbewerbspolitik und Kartellrecht; 4. Auflage, Gustav Fischer Verlag, Stuttgart, 1993. |
| [Schmidt 97] | Schmidt, R.: Funktionale Informationsdienste; In: [Buder 97]; Bd. 1, p. 438-449. |
| [Schneider 94] | Schneider, T. D.: Sequence Logos, Machine/Channel Capacity, Maxwell's Demon, and Molecular Computers: A Review of the Theory of Molecular Machines; Nanotechnology, Vol. 5, No. 1, 1994, p. 1-18. |

[Schöpe 85]      Schöpe, R. H. A.: Nichtkardinale Verhandlungstheorie - Ein Beitrag zum begrifflichen Fundament spiel- und verhandlungstheoretischer Konzepte; Dissertation der Universität des Saarlandes, Saarbrücken, 1985.

[Schotter 81]    Schotter, A.; Braunstein, Y. M.: Economic Search: An Experimental Study; Economic Inquiry, Vol. XIX, January 1981, p. 1-25.

[Schumann 92]    Schumann, J.: Grundzüge der mikroökonomischen Theorie; 6. Auflage, Springer, Berlin, 1992.

[Schwuchow 97]   Schwuchow, W.: Informationsökonomie; In: [Buder 97], Bd. 2, p. 751-779.

[Segev 95]       Segev, A.; Wan, D.; Beam, C.: Designing Electronic Catalogs for Business Value: Results of the CommerceNet Pilot; Fisher Center for Information Technology and Management, University of California, Berkeley, Oct. 1995, http://haas.berkeley.edu/~citm.

[Seng 89]        Seng, P.: Informationen und Versicherungen: Produktionstheoretische Grundlagen; Gabler, Wiesbaden, 1989.

[Seyffert 51]    Seyffert, R.: Wirtschaftslehre des Handels; 1. Auflage, Köln und Opladen, 1951.

[Shaked 83]      Shaked, A.; Sutton, J.: Natural Ologopolies; Econometrica, Vol. 51, 1983, p. 1469-1483.

[Shannon 48]     Shannon, C. E.: A mathematical theory of communication; Bell System Tech. Journal, Vol. 27, 1948, p. 379-423 (part I), p. 623-656 (part II).

[Shannon 63]     Shannon, C. E.; Weaver, W.: The mathematical theory of Communication; University of Illinois Press, Urbana and Chicago, 1963.

[Shapiro 86]     Shapiro, C.: Investment, Moral Hazard, and Occupational Licensing; Review of Economic Studies, LIII, 1986, p. 843-862.

[Shardanand 94]  Shardanand, U.: Social Information Filtering for Music Recommendation; Master of Science Thesis, EECS Department, Massachusetts Institute of Technology, 1994, http://lcs.www.media.mit.edu/people/shard/ringo.ps.

[Shardanand 95]  Shardanand, U.; Maes, P.: Social Information Filtering: Algorithms for Automating 'Word of Mouth'; In: Proceedings of the 1995 ACM Conferece on Human Factors in Computing Systems, ACM, New York, 1995, p. 210-217.

[Sheth 94]       Sheth, B. D.: A Learning Approach to Personalized Information Filtering; Master of Science Thesis, EECS Department, Massachusetts Institute of Technology, 1994, ftp://media.mit.edu/pub /agents/interface-agents/news-filter.ps.

[Shigehara 97]    Shigehara, K. (Deputy Secretary-General of the OECD): Globalisation, Technology, and Jobs, A Speech at the Japan Society, London, 4 July, 1997,
http://www.oecd.org/eco/freedoc/globalis.pdf.

[Shute 93]    Shute, S. J.; Smith, P. J.: Knowledge Based Search Tactics; Information Processing & Management, 1993, Vol. 29, No. 1, p. 29-45.

[Simon 91]    Simon, H. A.: Organizations and Markets; Journal of Economic Perspectives, Vol. 5, No. 2, Spring 1991, p. 25-44.

[Smith 89]    Smith, P. J.; Shute, S. J.; Galdes, D.; Chignell, M. H.: Knowledge-Based Search Tactics for an Intelligent Intermediary system; ACM Transactions on Information Systems, Vol. 7, No. 3, July 1989, p. 246-270.

[Sowa 90]    Sowa, J. F.: Semantic Networks; In: Shapiro, Stuart C.: Encyclopedia of Artificial Intelligence; Vol. 2, John Wiley & Sons, New York, 1990, p. 1011-1024.

[Spence 73]    Spence, M.: Job Market Signalling; Quarterly Journal of Economics, Vol. 87, 1973, p. 355-374.

[Spremann 87]    Spremann, K.: Agent und Principal; In: Spremann, K.; Bamberg, G. (eds.): Agency theory, Information and Incentives; 1987, p. 3-37.

[Spremann 88]    Spremann, K.: Reputation, Garantie, Information; Zeitschrift für Betriebswirtschaft, Jg. 58, 1988, p. 613-629.

[Spremann 90]    Spremann, K.: Asymmetrische Information; Zeitschrift für Betriebswirtschaft, Jg. 60, 1990, p. 561-586.

[Spulber 96a]    Spulber, D. F.: Market Microstructure and Intermediation; Journal of Economic Perspectives, Vol. 10, No. 3, Summer 1996, p. 135-152.

[Spulber 96b]    Spulber, D. F.: Market Making by Price Setting Firms; The Review of Economic Studies, Vol. 63, 1996, p. 559-580.

[Stahlknecht 97]    Stahlknecht, P.; Hasenkamp, U.: Einführung in die Wirtschaftsinformatik; 8. Auflage, Springer, Berlin, 1997.

[Stark 79]    Stark, R.; Rothkopf, M. H.: Competitive Bidding: A Comprehensive Bibliography; Operations Research, Vol. 27, No. 2, March-April 1979, p. 364-391.

[Staud 93]    Staud, J. L.: Fachinformation Online, Ein Überblick über Online-Datenbanken unter besonderer Berücksichtigung von Wirtschaftsinformationen; Springer, Berlin, 1993.

[Staud 97]    Staud, J. L.: Wirtschaftsinformation; In: [Buder 97], Bd. 1, p. 556-571.

[Steinfeld 96]     Steinfeld, C.; Kraut, R.; Plummer, A.: The Impact of Interorganizational Networks on Buyer-Seller Relationships; JCMC, Vol. 1, No. 3, 1996, http://shum.cc.huji.ac.il/jcmc/vol1/issue3/steinfld.html.

[Steinmüller 93]   Steinmüller, W.: Informationstechnologie und Gesellschaft: Einführung in die Angewandte Informatik; Darmstadt, 1993.

[Stevens 96]       Stevens, W. R.: TCP/IP Illustrated, Volume 3: TCP/IP for Transactions, HTTP, NNTP, and the UNIX Domain Protocols; Addison-Wesley Professional Computing Series, Reading, MA, 1996.

[Stewart 1770]     Stewart, J.: An Inquiry into the Principle of Political Economy: Being and Essay on the Science of Domestic Policy in Free Nations; 1770.

[Stigler 61]       Stigler, G. J.: The Economics of Information; Journal of Political Economy, Vol. 64, No. 3, June 1961, p. 213-225.

[Stigler 62]       Stigler, G. J.: Information in the Labor Market; Journal of Political Economy, Vol. 70, No. 5, 1962, p. 94-105.

[Stiglitz 89]      Stiglitz, J. E.: Imperfect Information in the Product Market; In: Schmalensee, R.; Willig, R. (eds.): Handbook of Industrial Organization, Vol. 1, North-Holland Press, Amsterdam, 1989, p. 769-847.

[Sydow 96]         Sydow, J.; van Well, B.: Wissensintensiv durch Netzwerkorganisation - Strukturtheoretische Analyse eines wissensintensiven Netzwerkes; In: Schreyögg, G.; Conrad, P.: Wissensmanagement, Walter de Gruyter, Berlin, 1996, p. 191-234.

[Szyperski 93]     Szyperski, N.; Klein, S.: Informationslogistik und virtuelle Organisation; Die Betriebswirtschaft, 53, 2, 1993, p. 187-208.

[Tanenbaum 96]     Tanenbaum, A. S.: Computer Networks; 3rd Edition, Englewood Cliffs, 1996.

[Taylor 86]        Taylor, R. S.: Value-added processes in information systems; Ablex: Norwood N. J., 1986.

[Tellis 88]        Tellis, G.; Fornell, C.: The Relationship between Advertising and Product Quality Over the Product Life Cycle: A Contingency Theory; Theory of Marketing Research, Vol. 25, 1988, p. 64-71.

[Telser 73]        Telser, L. G.: Searching for the Lowest Price; American Economic Review, Vol. 63, No. 2, May 1973, p. 40-51.

[Terveen 97]       Terveen, L.; Hill, W.; Amento, B.; McDonald, D.; Creter, J.: PHOAKS: A System for Sharing Recommendations; Communications of the ACM, Vol. 40, No. 3, March 1997, p. 59-62.

[Teuteberg 97]     Teuteberg, F.: Effektives Suchen im World Wide Web: Suchdienste und Suchmethoden; Wirtschaftsinformatik, Vol. 39, No. 4, p. 373-383.

[Tietzel 81]      Tietzel, M.: Die Ökonomie der Property Rights: Ein Überblick; Zeitschrift für Wirtschaftspolitik, Nr. 30, 1981, p. 207-243.

[Tirole 93]       Tirole, J.: The Theory of Industrial Organization; The MIT Press, Cambridge, 1993.

[Topsoe 74]       Topsoe, F.: Informationstheorie: Eine Einführung; Teubner, Stuttgart, 1974

[Townsend 78]     Townsend, R. M.: Intermediation with Costly Bilateral Exchange; Review of Economic Studies, Vol. 45, 1978, p. 417-425.

[Tuthill 90]      Tuthill, G. S.: Knowledge Engineering: Concepts and Practices for Knowledge-Based Systems; TAB Professional an Reference Books, Blue Ridge Summit, 1990.

[van Lint 80]     van Lint, J. H.: Introduction to Coding Theory; Springer, New York, 1980

[Varian 89]       Varian, H. R.: Price Discrimination; In: Schmalensee, R.; Willig, R. (eds.): Handbook of Industrial Organization, Vol. 1, North-Holland Press, Amsterdam, 1989, p. 597-654.

[Varian 93]       Varian, H. R.: Intermediate Microeconomics: A Modern Approach; 3rd edition, W. W. Norton & Company, New York, 1993.

[Varian 94]       Varian, H. R.: Mikroökonomie; 3. Auflage, München, 1994.

[Varian 95]       Varian, H. R.: Pricing Information Goods; Working Paper, University of California at Berkeley, Jun. 1995, In: Proceedings of the Research Libraries Group Symposium on 'Scholarship in the New Information Environment', Harvard Law School, May 2-3, 1995,
                  ftp://alfred.sims.berkeley.edu/pub/papers/price-info-goods.ps.Z.

[Varian 97a]      Varian, H. R.: Buying, Sharing and Renting Information; Working Paper, University of California at Berkeley, Dec. 1997.

[Varian 97b]      Varian, H. R.: Versioning Information Goods; Working Paper University of California, Berkely, 1997.

[Viterbi 79]      Viterbi, A. J.; Omura, J. K.: Principles of Digital Communication and Coding; McGraw-Hill, New York, 1979.

[von Ungern-      von Ungern-Sternberg, T.: Equilibrium Prices in a Model with
Sternberg 82]     Differentiated Goods and Search; Zeitschrift für die gesamte Staatswissenschaft, 138, 1982, p. 22-35.

[von Ungern-      von Ungern-Sternberg, T.: Zur Analyse von Märkten mit unvoll-
Sternberg 84]     ständiger Nachfragerinformation; Lecture Notes in Economics and Mathematical Systems, No. 225, Springer, Berlin, 1984.

[von Weizsäcker   von Weizsäcker, E. U.: Erstmaligkeit und Bestätigung als Kom-
74]               ponente der pragmatischen Information; In: von Weizsäcker, E. U. (ed.): Offene Systeme I Beiträge zur Zeitstruktur, Entropie und Evolution, Klett-Cotta, Stuttgart, 1974.

[von Weizsäcker 88]    von Weizsäcker, C. F.: Aufbau der Physik; Deutscher Taschenbuch Verlag, München, 1988.

[von Westarp 97]    von Westarp, F.; Weber, S.; Buxmann, P., König, W.: Communication Services Supplied by Intermediaries in Information Networks: The EDI Example; SFB 403 - Research Report (97-02), Frankfurt University, 1997.

[Wand 96]    Wand, Y.; Wang, R. Y.: Anchoring Data Quality Dimensions Ontological Foundations; Communications of the ACM, Vol. 39, No. 11, 1996.

[Warner 95]    Warner, A. S.: Looking Back, Looking Ahead; Bulletin of the American Society for Information Science, Feb./Mar. 1995, Vol. 21, No. 3, http://www.asis.org/Bulletin/Feb-95/warner.html.

[Wayner 96]    Wayner, P.: Digital Cash: Commerce on the Internet; Academic Press Professional, Boston, 1996.

[Wegehenkel 81]    Wegehenkel, L.: Gleichgewicht, Transaktionskosten und Evolution; Tübingen, 1981.

[Weitzel 87]    Weitzel, G.: Kooperation zwischen Wissenschaft u. mittelständischer Wirtschaft: Selbsthilfe der Unternehmen auf regionaler Basis. Kritische Bewertung bestehender Modelle; Bd. 31 Ifo-Studien zu Handels- und Dienstleistungsfragen, Berlin, 1987.

[Weitzman 79]    Weitzman, M. L.: Optimal Search for the best Alternative; Econometrica, Vol. 47, No. 3, May 1979, p. 641-654.

[Whinston 97]    Whinston, A. B.; Stahl, D. O.; Choi, S.-Y.: The Economics of Electronic Commerce; Macmillan Technical Publishing, Indianapolis, 1997.

[Wiederhold 92]    Wiederhold, G.: Mediators in the Architecture of Future Information Systems; IEEE Computer, March 1992, p. 38-49.

[Wigand 96]    Wigand, R. T.; Benjamin, R. I.: Electronic Commerce: Effects on Electronic Markets; JCMC, Vol . 1, No. 3, 1996, http://shum.cc.huji.ac.il/jcmc/vol1/issue3/wigand.html.

[Wigand 97]    Wigand, R.; Picot, A.; Reichwald, R.: Information, Organization and Management: Expanding Markets and Corporate Boundaries; John Wiley & Sons, Chichester, 1997.

[Wilde 80]    Wilde, L. L.: On the Formal Theory of Inspection and Evaluation in Product Markets; Econometrica, Vol. 48, No. 5, 1980, p. 1265-1280.

[Willamson 89]    Williamson, O. E.: Transaction Costs Economics; In: Schmalensee, R.; Willig, R. (eds.): Handbook of Industrial Organization, Vol. 1, North-Holland Press, Amsterdam, 1989, p. 135-182.

[Williamson 84]    Williamson, O. E.: The Economics of Governance: Framework and Implications; Journal of Institutional and Theoretic Economics, Vol. 140, 1984, p. 195-223.

[Williamson 85]   Williamson, O. E.: The Economic Institutions of Capitalism: Firms, Markets, Relational Contracting; New York, 1985.

[Williamson 86]   Williamson, O. E.: Economic Organization: Firms, Markets and Policy Control; Brighton, 1986.

[Williamson 91]   Williamson O. E.: Comparative Economic Organization: The Analysis of Discrete Structural Alternatives; Administrative Science Quarterly, Vol. 36, 1991, p. 269-296.

[Willke 96]   Willke, H.: Dimensionen des Wissensmanagements - Zum Zusammenhang von gesellschaftlicher und organisationaler Wissensbasierung; In: Schreyögg, G.; Conrad, P. (eds.): Wissensmanagement, Walter de Gruyter, Berlin, 1996, p. 263-304.

[Wilson 85]   Wilson, R.: Reputations in Games and Markets; In: Roth, A. E. (ed.): Game-Theoretic Models of Bargaining, Cambridge University Press, Cambridge, 1985, p. 27-62.

[Winkler 89]   Winkler, G. M.: Intermediation under Trade Restrictions; Quarterly Journal of Economics, 1989, p. 299-234.

[Witt 91]   Witt, F. J.: Deckungsbeitragsmanagement; München, Verlag Vahlen, 1991.

[Wittmann 59]   Wittmann, W.: Unternehmung und unvollkommene Information; 1959.

[Wolff 95]   Wolff, B.: Organisation durch Verträge; Wiesbaden, Gabler, 1995.

[Yanelle 89a]   Yanelle, M. O.: Two Sided Competition and Endogeneous Intermediation; Working Paper, University of Basel, WWZ-DP. 8909, 1989.

[Yanelle 89b]   Yanelle, M. O.: On the Theory of Intermediation; Dissertation, Fachbereich Wirtschafts- und Gesellschaftswissenschaften, Universität Bonn, 1989.

[Yavas 92]   Yavas, A.: Marketmakers versus Matchmakers; Journal of Financial Intermediation, 2, 1992, p. 33-58.

[Yavas 94]   Yavas, A.: Middlemen in Bilateral Search Markets; Journal of Labor Economics, Vol. 12, No. 3, p. 406-429.

[Yavas 95]   Yavas, A.: Can Brokerage Have an Equilibrium Selection Role?; Journal of Urban Economics, Vol. 37, 1995, p. 17-37.

[Yavas 96]   Yavas, A.: Search and Trading in Intermediated Markets; Journal of Economics and Management Strategy, Vol. 5, No. 2, 1996.

[Yoon 81]   Yoon, B. J.: A Model of Unemployment Duration with Variable Search Intensity; The Review of Economics and Statistics, 1981, p. 599-609.

[Zahedi 96]   Zahedi, F. M.: Information and Knowledge Industry; In: Warner, M. (ed.): International Ecyclopedia of Business and Management, Routledge, London, 1996, p. 2075-2092.

[Zakon 97]        Zakon, R. H.: Hobbes' Internet Timeline v3.1; 25 August, 1997, http://www.isoc.org/zakon/Internet/History/HIT.html.

[Zbornik 96]      Zbornik, S.: Elektronische Märkte, Elektronische Hierarchien und elektronische Netzwerke; Universitätsverlag Konstanz, Konstanz, 1996.

[Zelewski 87]     Zelewski, S.: Der Informationsbroker; Die Betriebswirtschaft, Vol. 47, No. 6, 1987, p. 737-749.

[Zimmermann 97]   Zimmermann, H.-D.: The Electronic Mall Bodensee (EMB): An Introduction to the EMB and its Architectural Concepts; International Journal of Electronic Markets, University of St. Gallen, Switzerland, Vol. 7, No. 1, 1997, p. 13-17.

# 8 Appendix

## 8.1 Appendix A: development of the number of Internet hosts

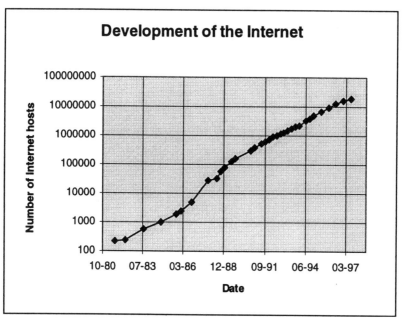

*Figure 58:*     *Development of the number of Internet hosts over time,*
              *(source: http://www.nw.com/zone/host-count-history).*

## 8.2 Appendix B: simplification of (eq. 9) using integration by parts

$$G(X_m) = [X_m \, F(X_m) + \int\limits_{X_m}^{\infty} x \, dF(x) - c] - X_m$$

$$= - X_m [1 - F(X_m)] + \int\limits_{X_m}^{\infty} x \, dF(x) - c$$

$$= x[1 - F(x)] \Big|_{X_m}^{\infty} + \int\limits_{X_m}^{\infty} x \, dF(x) - c$$

$$= \int\limits_{X_m}^{\infty} [1 - F(x)] \, dx - c$$

## 8.3 Appendix C: transformation of (eq. 12) into (eq. 13)

See [Hey 81b, p. 63] for further details.

Define: $Y = U_j(X)$.
Let $G(Y)$ be the distribution function of the random variable $Y$, then we get:

(eq. 51)    $$G(y) = P(Y \le y) = P[U_j(X) \le y] = P\big[X \le U_j^{-1}(y)\big] = F\big[U_j^{-1}(y)\big].$$

The reservation value $y^*$ for $Y$ is given by:

(eq. 52)    $$\int\limits_{y^*}^{\infty} [1 - G(y)] \, dy = c$$

Using (eq. 51) we receive:

(eq. 53)    $$\int\limits_{y^*}^{\infty} [1 - F(U_j^{-1}(y))] \, dy = c$$

substitution of $y = U_j(X)$ finally results in:

(eq. 54)    $$\int\limits_{x^*}^{\infty} [1 - F(x)] \, dU_j(x) = c.$$

qed.

## 8.4  Appendix D: proof of the indifference property

$$(eq.\ 55)^{1022} \qquad V_x = \frac{\left[-c + \int\limits_x^\infty U_j(x')\, dF(x')\right]}{[1 - F(x)]}$$

The necessary condition for an optimal reservation value $x^\bullet$ for $V_x(x)$ is a solution to:

$$(eq.\ 56) \qquad \frac{\partial V}{\partial x} = 0.$$

It follows with $f(x) = \dfrac{d\,F(x)}{d\,x}$ :

$$(eq.\ 57) \qquad \begin{aligned}
\frac{\partial V}{\partial x} &= \frac{\left[-c + \int\limits_x^\infty U_j(x')\, dF(x')\right]}{[1 - F(x)]} \cdot \frac{f(x)}{[1 - F(x)]} \ - \ U_j(x) \cdot \frac{f(x)}{[1 - F(x)]} \\
&= \frac{f(x)}{[1 - F(x)]} \cdot \left[V_x - U_j(x)\right] = 0
\end{aligned}$$

$$\Rightarrow \ \left[V_x - U_j(x)\right] = 0$$

$$\Rightarrow \ V_x = U_j(x)$$

qed.

---

1022  Cf. [Hey 81b, p. 59-60].

## 8.5 Appendix E: number of solutions of the system of equations in the broker model

The system (eq. 33) can be further simplified to:

(eq. 58)
$$\left| \begin{array}{l} \beta = \dfrac{F^I}{\left(X^I - x^*\right)} \\[2mm] \dfrac{1}{\lambda} \cdot e^{-\lambda \cdot x^*} = \dfrac{c}{\beta} \end{array} \right|$$

and combining the two equations to eliminate $\beta$:

(eq. 59)
$$\frac{1}{\lambda} \cdot e^{-\lambda \cdot x^*} = \frac{c}{F^I} \cdot \left(X^I - x^*\right).$$

Plotting the two sides of equation (eq. 59) vs. $x^*$ with different pairs of parameters $X^I$ and $F^I$ yields several cases with a different number of solutions to the system:

(1) $\dfrac{c}{F^I} \cdot X^I > \dfrac{1}{\lambda} \cdot e^{-\lambda \cdot 0} = \dfrac{1}{\lambda}$ and $-\dfrac{c}{F^I} \geq 0$    no solution

(2) $\dfrac{c}{F^I} \cdot X^I > \dfrac{1}{\lambda}$ and $-\dfrac{c}{F^I} < 0$    1 solution

(3) $\dfrac{c}{F^I} \cdot X^I < \dfrac{1}{\lambda}$ and $-\dfrac{c}{F^I} < \dfrac{\partial}{\partial x^*}\left(\dfrac{1}{\lambda} \cdot e^{-\lambda \cdot x^*}\right)\Big|_{x^*=0} = -1$    no solution

(4) $\dfrac{c}{F^I} \cdot X^I < \dfrac{1}{\lambda}$, $-\dfrac{c}{F^I} > -1$ and:

   (4a) $X^I = \dfrac{1}{\lambda} \cdot \left(1 - \ln\left(\dfrac{c}{F^I}\right)\right)$    1 solution

   (4b) $X^I > \dfrac{1}{\lambda} \cdot \left(1 - \ln\left(\dfrac{c}{F^I}\right)\right)$    2 solutions

   (4c) $X^I < \dfrac{1}{\lambda} \cdot \left(1 - \ln\left(\dfrac{c}{F^I}\right)\right)$    no solution

The value in case 4 is derived from the situation where the two sides of (eq. 59) intersect tangentially and thus have the same derivative:

$$\frac{\partial}{\partial x^{*}}\left(\frac{1}{\lambda}\cdot e^{-\lambda\cdot x^{*}}\right)=\frac{\partial}{\partial x^{*}}\left(\frac{c}{F^{I}}\cdot\left(X^{I}-x^{*}\right)\right)$$

(eq. 60)

$$\Rightarrow-\frac{\lambda}{\lambda}\cdot e^{-\lambda\cdot x^{*}}=-e^{-\lambda\cdot x^{*}}=-\frac{c}{F^{I}}$$

$$\Rightarrow x^{*}=-\frac{1}{\lambda}\cdot\ln\left(\frac{c}{F^{I}}\right)$$

Inserting $x^{*}$ back in (eq. 59) yields:

$$\frac{1}{\lambda}\cdot e^{-\lambda\cdot\left(\frac{-1}{\lambda}\ln\left(\frac{c}{F^{I}}\right)\right)}=\frac{1}{\lambda}\cdot\frac{c}{F^{I}}=\frac{c}{F^{I}}\cdot\left(X^{I}-\left(\frac{-1}{\lambda}\cdot\ln\left(\frac{c}{F^{I}}\right)\right)\right)$$

(eq. 61)

$$\Rightarrow\frac{1}{\lambda}=\left(X^{I}+\left(\frac{1}{\lambda}\cdot\ln\left(\frac{c}{F^{I}}\right)\right)\right)$$

$$\Rightarrow X^{I}=\frac{1}{\lambda}\left(1-\ln\left(\frac{c}{F^{I}}\right)\right)$$

qed.

Four of these cases are depicted in Figure 59.

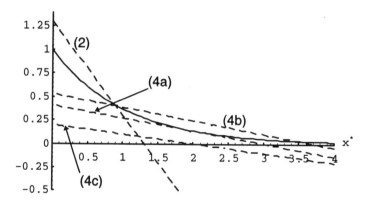

Figure 59:    Plot of the left hand side (continuous line) and the right hand side (dashed lines) of (eq. 59) for 4 different pairs of parameters $X^{I}$ and $F^{I}$ ($c=1$, $\lambda=1$).

## 8.6 Appendix F: partial derivatives of intermediary's profit

The values of $\beta_1$, $\beta_2$ and $x^*$ can be derived from the following system of equations (confer (eq. 33)):

(eq. 62)
$$\left| \begin{array}{l} x^* = \left( X' - \dfrac{F'}{\beta} \right) \\ \dfrac{1}{\lambda} \cdot e^{-\lambda \cdot x^*} \cdot \beta = c \end{array} \right|.$$

Putting the two equations together and simplifying yields:

(eq. 63)
$$\frac{1}{\lambda} \cdot e^{-\lambda \left( x' - \frac{F'}{\beta} \right)} \cdot \beta = c$$
$$\Rightarrow -\lambda \cdot \left( X' - \frac{F'}{\beta} \right) = \ln \left( \frac{c \cdot \lambda}{\beta} \right)$$

According to the theorem about differentiation of implicit functions[1023] the partial derivatives of $\beta$ can be derived as follows (the function $g(\beta, X', F')$ is auxiliary):

(eq. 64)
$$g(\beta, X', F') = \ln \left( \frac{c \cdot \lambda}{\beta} \right) + \lambda \cdot \left( X' - \frac{F'}{\beta} \right) = 0$$

(eq. 65)
$$\frac{\partial g}{\partial \beta} = -\frac{1}{\beta} + \frac{\lambda \cdot F'}{\beta^2} = \frac{\lambda \cdot F' - \beta}{\beta^2}$$
$$\frac{\partial g}{\partial X'} = \lambda$$
$$\frac{\partial g}{\partial F'} = -\frac{\lambda}{\beta}$$

(eq. 66)
$$\frac{\partial \beta}{\partial X'} = -\left( \frac{\frac{\partial g}{\partial X'}}{\frac{\partial g}{\partial \beta}} \right) = \frac{\beta^2 \cdot \lambda}{(\beta - \lambda \cdot F') \cdot}$$
$$\frac{\partial \beta}{\partial F'} = \ldots = \frac{-\beta \cdot \lambda}{(\beta - \lambda \cdot F')}$$

---

[1023] Cf. [Heuser 88, p. 295 fp.].

These implicitly derived partial derivatives of $\beta$ can be inserted in the partial derivatives of the profit $P'$:

$$\frac{\partial}{\partial X'} P'(X', F')$$

(eq. 67)

$$= \frac{\partial}{\partial X'} \left[ F' \cdot N \cdot \int_{\beta_1(X', F')}^{\beta_2(X', F')} h(\beta)\, d\beta - \frac{c}{\left[1 - F(X')\right]} \right]$$

$$= \frac{\partial}{\partial X'} \left[ F' \cdot N \cdot \int_{\beta_1(X', F')}^{\beta_2(X', F')} h(\beta)\, d\beta - c \cdot e^{\lambda \cdot X'} \right]$$

$$= F' \cdot N \cdot \left[ h(\beta_2) \cdot \frac{\partial \beta_2(X', F')}{\partial X'} - h(\beta_1) \cdot \frac{\partial \beta_1(X', F')}{\partial X'} \right] - c \cdot \lambda \cdot e^{\lambda \cdot X'}$$

$$\frac{\partial}{\partial F'} P'(X', F')$$

(eq. 68)

$$= \frac{\partial}{\partial F'} \left[ F' \cdot N \cdot \int_{\beta_1(X', F')}^{\beta_2(X', F')} h(\beta)\, d\beta - \frac{c}{\left[1 - F(X')\right]} \right]$$

$$= N \cdot \int_{\beta_1(X', F')}^{\beta_2(X', F')} h(\beta)\, d\beta - F' \cdot N \cdot \left[ h(\beta_2) \cdot \frac{\partial \beta_2(X', F')}{\partial F'} - h(\beta_1) \cdot \frac{\partial \beta_1(X', F')}{\partial F'} \right]$$

## 8.7  Appendix G: list of examples and URLs

The examples and addresses mentioned in this thesis were examined in December 1997.

| Example | URL |
|---|---|
| **Alta Vista** | http://www.altavista.digital.com |
| **Bargain Finder**: Intelligent agent searching CD-stores for the cheapest offer | http://bf.cstar.ac.com/bf |
| **Barter.Net**: Virtual barter network, multilateral trading | http://www.barter.net |
| **CNEC**: Competence Network Electronic Commerce | http://www.cnec.org |
| **CyberCash**: Provider of credit-card based payment systems, and micropayment technology (CyberCoin) for the Internet | http://www.cybercash.com |
| **DecisionNet**: Intermediary facilitating transactions between providers and consumers of decision support technologies | http://dnet.as.nps.navy.mil/dNethome.html |
| **DEVICE**: Intermediary supporting the Continuous Design of Virtual Enterprises with a Co-operation Exchange | http://www.iwi.uni-sb.de/device |
| **DigiCash's Ecash**: Coin-based electronic payment system for the Internet | http://www.digicash.com |
| **Digital's Millicent**: Micropayment system | http://www.millicent.digital.com |
| **DoctorDirectory**: Directory of physicians for the USA | http://www.DoctorDirectory.com |
| **E*Trade**: Internet-based securities broker | http://www.etrade.com |
| **e.Schwab**: Internet-based securities broker | http://www.schwab.com |
| **Electronic Mall Bodensee** | http://www.emb.net |
| **Euro Barter Business**: Virtual barter network, multilateral trading | http://www.ebb-online.com |
| **FAB**: Combination of content-based and collaborative filtering methods | http://fab.stanford.edu |
| **Federal Express**: Logistics service provider | http://www.fedex.com |
| **Firefly**: Recommendation system for music | http://www.firefly.net |

| | |
|---|---|
| **Gamelan**: Directory of Java applets on the Internet | http://www.gamelan.com |
| **GroupLens**: Collaborative filtering of Usenet news | http://www.cs.umn.edu/Research/GroupLens/ |
| Information about **Internet robots** | http://info.webcrawler.com/mak/projects/robots/robots.html |
| **Infoseek**: Search Engine providing a directory structure | http://www.infoseek.com |
| **InterNIC - Directory of Directories** | http://ds.internic.net/dod |
| **Java** | http://java.sun.com |
| **kiesel**: Virtual competence center for environmental issues | http://www.kiesel.de |
| List of commercial **collaborative filtering technologies** | http://sims.berkeley.edu/resources/collab/index.html |
| **List of Internet Directories and Searching Services** | http://www.sil.org/internet/guides.html |
| List of publicly available **recommendation services** | http://fab.stanford.edu/papers/table.shtml |
| **MetaCrawler**: Meta-Search Engine | http://www.metacrawler.com |
| **Netscape's NetCaster** (Push Service) | http://www.netscape.com |
| **NewsPage** | http://www.newspage.com |
| **PHOAKS** (People Helping One Another Know Stuff): Collaborative filtering of recommended web-pages out of Usenet News | http://www.phoaks.com |
| **PointCast** (Push News Service) | http://www.pointcast.com |
| **REGINA**: Component Information System for C++ Components | http://www.findcomponents.com |
| **SavvySearch**: Meta-Search Engine | http://guaraldi.cs.colostate.edu:2000 |
| **Stiftung Warentest** | http://www.stiftung-warentest.de |
| **The Java Repository**: Software Repository for Java software components | http://java.wiwi.uni-frankfurt.de |
| **The Wall Street Journal Interactive Edition** | http.//www.wsj.com |
| **The XML/EDI Group** | http://www.xmledi.net |

| | |
|---|---|
| **Trade Compass**: Electronic commerce services for international business customers, broker services | http://www.tradecompass.com |
| **Unibex Global Business Center**: EPC facilities for business users, opportunities for matching requests with registered offers | http://www.unibex.com |
| **United Parcel Service**: Logistics service provider | http://www.ups.com |
| **virtual-organization.net** (Institute of Information Systems, Department of Information Management, University of Bern) | http://www.virtual-organization.net |
| **Yahoo** | http://www.yahoo.com |

# List of figures

# List of tables

# List of used symbols

| | |
|---|---|
| $A_a$ | Alternative actions in the basic model of decision theory. |
| $A_{\hat{a}}$ | Optimal action in the basic model of decision theory. |
| $\alpha$ | Set of control parameters of a dynamic system. |
| $\beta_j$ | $j^{th}$ consumer's willingness-to-pay for a certain attribute value. |
| $\beta_{1;2}(X^I, F^I)$ | Willingness to pay of consumers who are indifferent between searching individually and consulting the intermediary (= boundaries of integration). |
| $\beta_{1;2}^{I_1}(X_1^I, F_1^I, X_2^I, F_2^I)$ | Boundaries of integration for intermediary 1 (2) in case of competition. |
| $c$ | Search costs for a single step in the search process. |
| $c^{Intermediary}$ | Search costs of the information intermediary achieved after investments in the efficiency of search. |
| $c^{Individual}$ | Search costs of an individual information seeker. |
| $c_E$ | Costs for the evaluation of an object's true attribute value. |
| $c_f$ | Frequency dependent costs of a transaction in the model of inventory management. |
| $c_q$ | Volume dependent costs of a transaction in the model of inventory management. |
| $C^I$ | Intermediary's expected search costs. |
| $C_1^I (C_2^I)$ | Expected search costs of intermediary 1 (2). |
| $C_C$ | Contact costs for contacts in a system of suppliers, consumers, and an intermediary in the Baligh-Richartz-effect. |
| $C_D$ | Intermediary's marginal costs for the dissemination of information. |
| $C_{total}$ | Total transaction costs in the model of inventory management. |
| $D$ | Expected return of a decision without information. |
| $D_I$ | Expected return of a decision with information. |
| $df(i)$ | Number of documents in the IR system that contain the word $i$. |
| $\vec{\nabla}$ | Gradient |
| $\vec{\nabla}_{X^I, F^I}$ | Gradient concerning the two variables $X^I$ and $F^I$. |
| $E(Y \mid X = X_i)$ | Expected return of the search process if the observed value is $X_i$. |

| | |
|---|---|
| $E[N_{clients}]$ | Expected number of clients of the information intermediary's. |
| $\varepsilon_\lambda$ | Noise introduced to achieve asymmetric information about the distribution parameter $\lambda$ in a possible extension of the basic model. |
| $\varepsilon$ | Small deviation |
| $F^I$ | Fee charged by the information intermediary to reveal the location of an object having at least the attribute value $X^I$. |
| $F^I_1, (F^I_2)$ | Fee charged by the intermediary 1 (2). |
| $F^I_{opt}$ | Optimal fee charged by the information intermediary for given environmental conditions. |
| $F^I_{min}$ | Minimum fee to be charged by two competing information intermediaries in equilibrium. |
| $F^I_{high}, F^I_{low}$ | Possible fee charged by the information intermediaries in a game with discrete strategy space. |
| $\mathcal{F}$ | Experiment in the theory of information. |
| $\boldsymbol{F}$ | Vector of fluctuating forces in a dynamic system. |
| $F$ | Frequency of a transaction in the inventory management model. |
| $F(X)$ | Cumulative distribution function of the random variable $X$. |
| $F(X, Y)$ | Bivariate distribution of the two random variables $X$ and $Y$. |
| $G(X_m)$ | Expected additional net reward from one further observation in the simple search model. |
| $g(\beta, X^I, F^I)$ | Auxiliary function used to derive partial derivatives of $\beta(X^I, F^I)$. |
| $\gamma(\lambda)$ | Cost reduction for a single step in the search process of the information intermediary to compensate an increase of $\lambda$. |
| $h(\beta)$ | Probability density function for the distribution of consumers' willingness to pay for a certain quality level. |
| $H(\beta)$ | Cumulative distribution function for the distribution of consumers' willingness to pay for a certain quality level. |
| $H(\mathcal{F})$ | Entropy in the theory of information. |
| $IN, OUT$ | Set of components of an input-output-system in systems theory. |
| $i$ | Particular word in an IR system. |
| $idf(i)$ | Inverse document frequency. |
| $I$ | Index set for the set of components of a system in systems theory. |
| $I_i$ | Result of the acquisition of information. |

| | |
|---|---|
| $IsUser(j)$ | Auxiliary function to determine whether the $j^{th}$ consumer consults the information intermediary. |
| $\lambda$ | Parameter of the exponential distribution for objects' quality. |
| $\lambda_{client}$ | Noisy distribution parameter known to the intermediary's potential client. |
| $m$ | Number of suppliers in the Baligh-Richartz-effect. |
| $\underset{X^l, F^l}{Max}\ R^l$ | Maximize $R^l$ as a function of the variables $X^l$ and $F^l$. |
| $m_t$ | Mean of a normal distribution at time $t$. |
| $n$ | Number of consumers in the Baligh-Richartz-effect. |
| $n_0$ | Number of documents in an IR system. |
| $N$ | Number of potential users of the intermediary. |
| $N_0$ | Total number of users in the market. |
| $N_{clients}$ | Number of intermediary's clients. |
| $N[\mu,\sigma]$ | Normal distribution with mean $\mu$ and standard deviation $\sigma$. |
| $N$ | Vector of deterministic part of forces in a dynamic system. |
| $\eta$ | Projection from the set of environmental states $Z$ to the set of signals $\Omega$ in the formal description of information processing systems in information economics. |
| $\omega \in \Omega$ | Signal $\omega$ from a set of signals $\Omega$ in the formal description of information processing systems in information economics. |
| $p_t$ | Precision of a normal distribution at time $t$. |
| $p = (p_1, ..., p_n)$ | Distribution of an experiment in the theory of information. |
| $P^l$ | Intermediary's expected profit. |
| $P^l_1 (P^l_2)$ | Expected profit of intermediary 1 (2). |
| $P^l_{opt}$ | Intermediary's expected profit following an optimal strategy. |
| $(p, x), (p^l, x^l), (p^h, x^h)$ | Price-quality combinations. |
| $Q$ | Total volume of a transaction in the model of inventory management. |
| $q$ | Lot size in a transaction in the model of inventory management. |
| $q(t)= (q_1(t), q_2(t), ..., q_n(t))$ | State vector of a dynamic system. |
| $q_0$ | Initial state of a dynamic system at $t = t_0$. |
| $R^U_A (X)$ | Arrow-Pratt index of absolute risk aversion. |
| $R^l$ | Intermediary's expected revenue. |

| | |
|---|---|
| $R^I{}_I (R^I{}_2)$ | Expected revenue of intermediary 1 (2). |
| $S^G$ | General system in systems theory. |
| $S^{IO}$ | Input-output-system in systems theory. |
| $S_s$ | Possible states of the environment in the basic model of decision theory. |
| $tf(i)$ | Term frequency of word $i$ in a document. |
| $U(X)$ | Utility function. |
| $U'(X), U''(X)$ | First and second derivative of the utility function. |
| $U^{Intermediary}$ | Consumers' reward from consulting the intermediary. |
| $U_j(X_i)$ | Searcher $j^{th}$'s valuation of the attribute value $X_i$. |
| $u$ | Percentage of users fulfilling characteristics to access the services offered by the information intermediary. |
| $V_I$ | Value of information. |
| $V_i \in V$ | Set to describe the components of a general system in systems theory. |
| $V_x.$ | Expected net reward following an optimal search strategy. |
| $W$ | Social welfare without an information intermediary. |
| $W^{search}$ | Social welfare of those information seekers in the market preferring personal search processes. |
| $W^{Intermediary}$ | Social welfare of those information seekers in the market consulting the information intermediary. |
| $\Delta W$ | Increase in social welfare obtained through the information intermediary. |
| $w(S_s)$ | Probability for the state $S_s$ of the environment in the basic model of decision theory. |
| $w(S_s \vert I_i)$ | Conditional probability that the environmental state $S_s$ will be realized if the result of the acquisition of information is $I_i$. |
| $w(I_i)$ | Probability that the result of the acquisition of information is $I_i$. |
| $w(\omega \vert z)$ | Conditional probability for receiving the signal $\omega$ if $z$ is the true state of the environment in the formal description of information processing systems in information economics. |
| $X$ | Random variable of the product attribute. |
| $X_i$ | Single observation of the random variable $X$. |
| $X^I$ | Quality level offered by the information intermediary. |
| $X^I{}_I, (X^I{}_2)$ | Quality level offered by intermediary 1 (2). |
| $X^I{}_{opt}$ | Optimal quality level offered by the information intermediary that maximizes the intermediary's profit. |

| | |
|---|---|
| $X^I_{max}$ | Maximum quality level offered by two competing information intermediaries in equilibrium. |
| $X^I_{high}$, $X^I_{low}$ | Possible quality levels offered by the information intermediaries in a game with discrete strategy space. |
| $x^*$ | Reservation value of the optimal search strategy. |
| $x^*_j$ | Reservation value of the $j^{th}$ searcher (information seeker). |
| $x^*(\beta)$ | Reservation value for a particular value of the willingness to pay $\beta$ in an optimal search strategy. |
| $x^*_t$ | Time dependent reservation value in a finite horizon search model. |
| $X_m$ | Maximum value of the random variable $X$ observed at some stage in the search process. |
| $Y$ | True value of an object's attribute in a two stage search process. |
| $Z$ | Set of states of the environment in the formal description of information processing systems in information economics. |
| $a \rightarrow b$ | $a$ approaches $b$ |
| $a \Rightarrow b$ | $b$ follows from $a$ |

# List of abbreviations

| | |
|---|---|
| ASK | Anomalous State of Knowledge |
| ACM | The Association for Computing |
| BSP | basic search paradigm |
| CDF | cumulative distribution function |
| CNEC | Competence Network Electronic Commerce |
| CORBA | Common Object Request Broker Architecture |
| cf. | confer |
| const. | constant |
| c.p. | ceteris paribus |
| EDI | Electronic Data Interchange |
| ed./eds. | Editor/Editors |
| e.g. | for example (exempli gratia) |
| EM | Electronic Market |
| eq. | Equation |
| EPC | Electronic Product Catalog |
| etc. | et cetera |
| fp. | following pages |
| FTP | File Transfer Protocol |
| GII | Global Information Infrastructure |
| HTML | Hypertext Markup Language |
| HTTP | Hypertext Transfer Protocol |
| i.e. | that is to say (id est) |
| IF | Information Filtering |
| IP | Internet Protocol |
| IR | Information Retrieval |
| ITU | International Telecommunication Union |
| JCMC | Journal of Computer Mediated Communication |
| LAN | Local Area Network |
| LSI | Latent Semantic Indexing |
| NYSE | New York Stock Exchange |
| p. | page |
| PDF | probability density function |
| QAT | Qualitative asset transformation |
| qed. | quod erat demonstrandum |
| R&D | Research and development |

| | |
|---|---|
| RMI | Remote Method Invocation |
| SADT | Structured Analysis and Design Technique |
| SDI | Selective Dissemination of Information |
| TCP/IP | Transmission Control Protocol/Internet Protocol |
| TTP | Trusted Third Party |
| URL | Uniform Resource Locator |
| VO | Virtual organization |
| vs. | versus |
| WAIS | Wide Area Information Servers |
| WAN | Wide Area Network |
| WWW | World Wide Web |
| XML | Extensible Markup Language |

Printing: Weihert-Druck GmbH, Darmstadt
Binding: Buchbinderei Schäffer, Grünstadt